Contemporary Issues in Teaching and Learning

Contemporary Issues in Teaching and Learning

The other published volume in this series is:

Diversity and Change: Education, Policy and Selection
edited by John Ahier, Ben Cosin and Margaret Hales.
A third volume is in preparation.

This reader is one of three, and has been prepared as part of The Open University course *Exploring Educational Issues*, a broadly based multidisciplinary course which can be studied as part of BA or BSc degrees.

This reader is part of an integrated teaching system; the selection is therefore related to other material available to students. Opinions expressed are not necessarily those of the course team or of the University.

If you would like to study this course or find our more about The Open University, please write to the Central Enquiry Service, PO Box 200, The Open University, Walton Hall, Milton Keynes, MK7 6YZ, or telephone 01908 653231. A copy of *Studying with the Open University* is available from the same address.

Contemporary Issues in Teaching and Learning

Edited by Peter Woods
at The Open University

London and New York
in association with
The Open University

First published 1996
by Routledge
11 New Fetter Lane, London EC4P 4EE

Simultaneously published in the USA and Canada
by Routledge
29 West 35th Street, New York, NY 10001

Selection and editorial matter © 1996 The Open University

Typeset in Garamond by Florencetype Ltd, Stoodleigh, Devon
Printed and bound in Great Britain by
Biddles Ltd, Guildford and King's Lynn

British Library Cataloguing in Publication Data
A catalogue record for this book is available from the British
Library

Library of Congress Cataloguing in Publication Data
A catalogue record for this book has been requested

ISBN 0–415–13719–5

Contents

Acknowlegements

Chapter 1 Abridged from White, J. and O'Hear, P. (1993) 'Aims and Values in the National Curriculum' in *Assessing the National Curriculum*, London: Paul Chapman Publishing Ltd. Reprinted with permission.

Chapter 2 Abridged from Bourne, J. and Cameron, D. (1995) 'Disciplining English: the construction of a national subject' in Murphy, P., Selinger, M., Bourne, J. and Briggs, M. (eds) *Subject Learning in the Primary Curriculum: Issues in English, Science and Mathematics*, London: Routledge. Reprinted with permission.

Chapter 3 Original commissioned chapter.

Chapter 4 Original commissioned chapter.

Chapter 5 Revised version of Chapter 11 of Alexander, R. (1992) *Policy and Practice in Primary Education*. London: Routledge. Reprinted with permission.

Chapter 6 Original commissioned chapter.

Chapter 7 Chapter 12 of Gray, J. and Wilcox, B. (1995) *Good School, Bad School: Evaluating Performance and Encouraging Improvement*, Buckingham: Open University Press. Reprinted with permission.

Chapter 8 Abridged version of Howe, C. (1993) 'Piagetian theory and primary school physics', *Early Child Development and Care* 95: 23–39. Reprinted with permission.

Chapter 9 Abridged from chapter in Kuhn, D. (ed.) (1990) *Perspectives on Teaching and Learning Thinking Skills*, vol. 2, pp. 108–26, Basel: Karger. Reprinted with permission.

Chapter 10 From *International Studies in Sociology of Education* (1994) 4 (2): 123–46. Reprinted with permission.

Chapter 11 Abridged from Chapter 2 of Mac an Ghaill, M. (1994) *From the Making of Men: Masculinities Sexualities and Schooling*, Buckingham: Open University Press. Reprinted with permission.

Chapter 12 Original commissioned chapter. Figures 12.1 and 12.6 are reprinted with permission of HMSO. Figure 12.2 is reprinted with permission of Leeds University. Figures 12.3 and 12.5 are reproduced by permission of the Open University Press. Figure 12.4 is reprinted by permission of Taylor and Francis.

Chapter 13 Abridged from Chapter 1 of Drummond, M.J. (1993) *Assessing Children's Learning*, London: David Fulton Publishers. Reprinted with permission.

Chapter 14 Professor Patricia Broadfoot's Inaugural Lecture, University of Bristol, 1993. Reprinted with permission of the author.

Introduction

EDUCATION IN CRISIS

Education always seems to be 'in crisis'. It is easy to see why this should be the case. In a general sense, what kind of educational system and processes we have embody the kind of nation we are. At an individual level, life-chances, to a great extent depend on the education we receive. But if it is a common feature of education to be 'in crisis', the last ten years have been positively cataclysmic. There has been educational change on a grand scale. A prescribed National Curriculum with standardized assessment procedures has been set in place. The control and organization of schooling has been overhauled. Teachers are developing new roles, new career structures, new cultures in adapting to the changes (D. Hargreaves 1994). Other developments, such as globalization, technological advance, and social and economic change, add to the press for the restructuring of schools and teachers' work. Educational crisis is not going to go away, but rather intensify, in the post-industrial, postmodern age (A. Hargreaves 1994).

However, if all are agreed that we need to raise educational standards, improve the quality of teaching and learning, and produce people with the knowledge and skills necessary for the new age, there are serious differences of opinion as to how it should be done, and indeed what those aims actually mean. Different sets of values, different political convictions point in different directions, leading to heated and heartfelt debate – another aspect of the sense of crisis. The fact that education is inextricably embroiled with politics complicates the issue, for there are no solutions that will satisfy all, and positions and policies have to be fought for. Hence the sense of 'struggle', and the view, at times, of education as a battlefield.

That is certainly how it has been seen by many teachers in recent years. In the schools the matter is not just a political one, but one of coping. Teacher morale has been low since they lost a major dispute over pay and conditions of service in the mid-1980s (Pollard 1992; Campbell 1993). They have been required to implement an unworkable, overloaded National Curriculum and employ time-absorbing assessment strategies to which many object on principle (Campbell

1993). They have been asked to do this while suffering cuts in resources, result-ing in losses of staff and an increase in class size. An assault has even been made on what many regard as their professional preserve of pedagogy (Alexander, Rose and Woodhead 1992). Stress and burnout among teachers has increased dramatically since 1987 – the year before the Education Reform Act which instituted the National Curriculum (MacLeod and Meikle 1994).

In a sense, education might be seen as journeying through a status passage (Glaser and Strauss 1971), whereby the educational system is passing from one state to another. Van Gennep (1960) conceived of three main stages of status passages – separation, transition and reincorporation. The legislation of the later 1980s and early 1990s sought to 'separate' the system from that of the 1944 Education Act and the hugely influential Plowden Report of 1967, replacing the liberal notions of that era with the 'market' philosophy of the Thatcher administrations (Ball 1993). Ever since, we have been going through 'transition', a stage typically marked by a sense of rapid change, much confusion, looking both forwards and backwards, experimentation, conflict and emotional upheaval.

However, there are signs that we may be coming through the transition, and moving a step nearer to the comparatively more settled state of 'reincorporation'. Some gains have certainly been made. Teachers generally have welcomed the principle of a National Curriculum, and parts of the one they have been required to teach (Campbell *et al.* 1991; Pollard *et al.* 1994). They have found ways of implementation that have met both legisla-tive needs and those of their own beliefs and values (Ball and Bowe 1992; Vulliamy and Webb 1993; Woods 1995; Woods and Jeffrey 1996). Teachers won a famous victory in 1993 when for a rare moment in history, all their unions combined to refuse to co-operate with the government's prescribed assessment programme. This led to a review of procedures, which resulted in modifications to the curriculum and assessment requirements (Dearing 1994). Also, undoubtedly, some new thinking has been required about issues like pedagogy (Alexander 1992) and how children learn (Wood 1988), and these are being fed into teacher training and development.

The articles in this book are concerned with key issues in teaching and learning. Together with the companion volume on policy, structure and control in education (Ahier, Cosin and Hales 1996), they point some ways toward reincorporation. Some of the views expressed are, inevitably, contro-versial. There is no one, clear and certain resolution of these issues. Educational crises will not be resolved by short-term, simplistic solutions, but by reasoned discussion soundly based in theory and research. The articles here are a contribution to the ongoing debate. Prominent themes running through the book are the quest for quality within a social context; the application of theory and research to practice; and the positive roles played by teachers and students in adapting to the radical changes that have been occurring in our schools.

The articles have been selected with a view to being accessible to a wide audience. The book will be of interest to teachers, student teachers, students of education at both undergraduate and postgraduate levels, and to all those with a general interest in education, such as parents and governors.

STRUCTURE OF THE BOOK

Though this book is entitled 'contemporary issues', the basic issues are really perennial. They are part of the ongoing crisis. This book concentrates on their manifestations at the end of the twentieth century. There are two broad connected issues, to do with a) teaching and b) learning. Within teaching, the issues addressed are:

What should we teach? (Chapters 1 and 2)
How should we teach it? (Chapters 3, 4 and 5), and
In what context? (Chapters 6 and 7)

With regard to 'learning', the issues are:

How and what do pupils learn? (Chapters 8, 9, 10 and 11), and
How is learning assessed? (Chapters 12, 13 and 14)

CONTENT OF THE BOOK

Teaching

What should we teach?

There has been general consensus about the need for a National Curriculum, but little agreement about what kind. White and O'Hear propose one alternative. They specify six criteria which should apply to any such curriculum. It must, for example, have clear aims, be coherent, and related to both individual and society's needs. They feel that the 1988 National Curriculum fails to meet these. They recognize that some valuable work has been done, especially in helping teachers to structure learning in their classrooms and between phases. But there is no set of clear aims. The 1988 National Curriculum is too prescriptive, narrow and incoherent. They go on to propose a new National Curriculum, guided by the values of liberal democracy as they see them. It is not just a matter of economic growth, but also 'self-determination' and concern for others. They recommend that prescription should apply only to the broad framework, leaving teachers and others with more room for local adaptation than they currently enjoy. The authors then specify the aims of a National Curriculum which embodies these principles. It should start with the conception of students as whole persons and involve personal qualities of personal and social concern, and critical awareness. They derive specific aims from those involved with the areas of learning of knowledge and understanding, experience of the arts, and practical competences, all in an interconnected, logical package. These aims would be realized through a broader canvas than applies currently, through, for example, school ethos and democratic management style, and through a new assessment system built around records of achievement. There would be more emphasis on personal qualities and basic literacy at Key Stages 1 and 2, and less on subject teaching, which they see as more appropriate at secondary level. They go on to consider the structural and resource implications, and finally propose a five-year plan for implementation of the model.

In the meantime, teachers have to work the National Curriculum they have been given. The 'struggle', consequently, has moved to sites within it – namely the subjects – with different groups vying over what they should contain and how they should be taught. Nowhere have the arguments been more contentious and heated than over English – as the national language, the keystone of the curriculum. Bourne and Cameron take the Kingman Report of 1988 as a case study of this kind of activity. The brief of this committee was to recommend a model of the English language that would underpin the English subject curriculum and programme of teacher training. Their recommendations on such thorny issues as 'grammar' and 'Standard English' were generally regarded as moderate, and accepted by many English teachers as reasonable, but Bourne and Cameron take a different view. They argue that these issues are not just about language, but, on the one hand, the social values of authority and tradition, involving certain attitudes and rules of conduct and, on the other, the identity of the nation as a uniform whole. Taking this into account, they feel that minority languages and non-standard forms were implicitly downgraded in the Kingman Report. Such differences, they argue, were seen as historical or geographical. They draw a parallel with the Welsh language, which was eventually recognized, not because of minority rights, but because the Welsh had occupied a territory over a long period. Minority groups in England, therefore, with no historical territory rights, are seen as alien in such an approach. Social class, too, was ignored, though it is usually particular social classes within regions who speak non-standard forms. The authors feel that the Report passes off Standard English as 'normal', but does not consider how its conception of normality favours a particular group, and disadvantages others. Kingman is seen as in line with thought that perceives English as a vital instrument in national identity and social cohesion. Their view is that such an approach is guided by nostalgia for a Britain of a past age.

How should we teach?

Following the institution of a prescribed curriculum in 1988, it soon became clear to the government that control over the curriculum without pedagogic direction might restrict the government's programme of changes. At the same time there was an educational thrust for reform of teaching approach deriving from Robin Alexander's 'Leeds Report' of 1991 (discussed in Alexander 1992). Alexander was critical of the fixation with progressive ideology and the way it was embedded within the culture of LEAs and Colleges of Education, operating more as a constraint than a facilitator of pupil learning. He recommended practice based less on progressive ideology and more on a mixture of methods guided by the particular aim in view. These educational considerations became mixed up with political considerations as the government seized the opportunity to mount an initiative to attack progressivism and urge a return to more traditional methods (Woods and Wenham 1995). The media joined in, creating a 'discourse of derision' about progressivism and teachers who practised it, who were held responsible for supposed low educational standards (see Wallace 1993). The Secretary of State of the day, Kenneth Clarke, urged a return to 'common sense', as if good teaching were a simple matter of one revealed truth to minds uncluttered by theory. It is, however, a little more complicated, as the articles in this section make clear.

Geoff Troman discusses what might be termed 'official' models of the 'good teacher' as contained over the years in official documents. A number of seminal papers emerged from the DES in the 1980s with titles like *Better Schools* (DES 1985a), *Education Observed 3 – Good Teachers* (DES 1985b) and *Teaching Quality* (1983). From these, Broadhead (1987) extrapolated a model of presumed good practice in which the personal qualities of teachers were the principle factor. In other words, any inadequacy was deemed to arise from within the teacher. The policy implications are on selection, and, where teachers cannot be brought up to the mark, dismissal. Such a definition, however, has to be seen within the context of growing central control of the educational system. Criteria are centrally determined, teachers themselves are less and less consulted, and rating systems are set up against which teachers can be measured.

Following the 1988 Educational Reform Act, good teaching in official documents came to be defined by the needs of the implementation of the Act. Thus, in the 1990s, a series of further papers developed the model in particular ways. The skills of 'match', subject expertise, co-ordination, collaboration, management and supervision figure prominently in a tightly specified list of teacher competences. This in turn facilitates the official inspection of teacher quality. Previously, HMI were more flexible, less specific; now, how teachers have satisfactorily restructured their work in line with official specification is the subject of close and regular monitoring by OFSTED. Management and administrative roles, competences and technical skills, rather than personal qualities, are to the fore, not unlike the situation in the late nineteenth century under the Revised Code. Troman claims that such criteria for good teaching are attached to specific historical moments, and are socially and politically constructed.

Teachers do, themselves, have views about what constitutes good teaching, but their views are not represented in the 'official' model. There are, of course, many points of detail in the latter with which most teachers would agree. But in some of the leading themes, many differ quite radically. This is evident from the Woods and Jeffrey article. They describe some teachers who are resisting the imposition of the official model, and who are in the process of constructing a new professional discourse. This particular group of teachers is working to a model which the authors describe as 'creative teaching', involving teacher and pupil ownership of knowledge, control of teaching and learning processes, and opportunities to be innovative. There is a sense of struggle and loss arising from the changes, but also a certain amount of creative adaptation. The authors discuss teacher reactions in the key areas of teaching approach, the use of time and accountability. 'Creative teaching' is depicted in contrast to the official model – one of managerialism – being a process rather than a product model, defending their time and space in the face of threatened colonization, redefining accountability to a more professional responsibility in their own terms, and having considerable emotional involvement. The latter, while crucial to their brand of pedagogy, puts them at high levels of risk with regard to stress and guilt, but there is also a sustained commitment and resolve.

Here we have two opposing models of teaching. The differences can be traced to fundamentally different sets of values. There are other versions of 'good teaching' that could be described, based on other values. These values are rarely acknowledged, groups tending to argue their causes as truths to the enlightened. Is there any way, therefore, that we can analyse teaching that takes account of such considerations? In a revised version of a chapter from his book *Policy and Practice in Primary Education*, Robin Alexander tackles this issue. Considering teacher and official views, he notes that the values invariably remain hidden. He goes on to unpack the notion of 'good practice', finding elements of value, pragmatism, empiricism and politics in different ways in which 'good' is used, and vastly different agendas with regard to 'practice' – as in the previous two articles. Most statements of 'good practice', he concludes, are incomplete in some way or other. He goes on to suggest a framework for conceptualizing practice with two main dimensions – of practice on the one hand, and ideas, values and beliefs on the other – and seven main components of content, context, pedagogy and management (relating to the practice dimension), and children, society and knowledge (relating to the ideas etc. dimension). Using this as a template, Alexander shows the partiality, in different ways, of the Plowden Report on the one hand, and HMI Reports from 1978 onwards on the other. He concludes that, conceptually – and that is where we must start, clarifying the question before seeking the answer – good primary teaching practice lies at the intersection of value, pragmatic, empirical, political and conceptual considerations. In his view, ethical and empirical questions are pre-eminent, though both depend on initial conceptualization.

In what context should we teach?

There are ways in which the school as an institution affects achievement and quality. This has long been recognized, but has become even more of an issue in recent years with the weakening in power of the LEAs, the increasing focus on the school as a unit, and new forms of accountability effected through league tables, based on national testing results. Parental choice, guided by these results, could bring about the closure of a school. There is an urgent need, therefore, to identify the factors that make a school effective, and that can turn a failing school into a successful one. There have been many studies on these issues in recent years, but most miss the complexities of schooling wherein, one suspects, most of the answers lie. They also tend to impose their constructions of meanings upon schools, instead of finding out what the teachers within them think. The two articles here take a different approach.

Brown, Riddell and Duffield offer a comparative account of how four Scottish secondary schools have responded to external pressures for change. Two of the schools serve high socio-economic status areas, and two low. One in each category is seen as showing high effectiveness, one low effectiveness. So far they have been able to find only two commonalities among the highly effective schools, and even they are manifested in different ways in the two schools. One is their history and tradition as senior secondary (or 'grammar') schools. The other is the way pupils and teachers are incorporated into the running of the school, involving a sense of common ownership. The small degree of commonality is, perhaps, the more remarkable finding. More marked are the contrasts between the high and the low socio-economic area schools, implying that strategies for improvement are likely to be highly dependent on social class. Prominent differences here are the achievement profiles, where the high socio-economic schools can concentrate more exclusively on academic work, and give good support to their comparatively small numbers of children with learning difficulties, while the other schools have other goals as well with their particular intakes, involving many more children with learning difficulties, among whom support is more thinly spread; and the motivation of both pupils and staff. It is in some of these areas that the keys to improvement lie. There is no evidence that management innovations, or the publication of results, even with value-added measures, would have any effect. The authors enter a plea for researchers to explore the issue of social class more closely and to engage with teachers' constructions of reality and their implicit theories. This, it is thought, will help bridge the gap between school effectiveness and school improvement.

Gray and Wilcox are particularly concerned in their article about 'failing' schools and how they can be improved. This has received rather less attention than school effectiveness in general. The whole notion of 'failing' is problematic, but it has become a reality that schools deemed 'ineffective' or 'failing' by inspectors face the possibility of closure. Gray and Wilcox, therefore, set out to review a number of case studies to see if any common conclusions can be drawn. These studies range over matters like charismatic leadership, and the setting up of minimal standards of 'goodness', to the deep structure of ineffective schools and the way teachers cling on to defence strategies they have constructed over the years, which reveal the extent of the problem and warn against naive optimism. Teachers' enthusiasm and commitment to change certainly has to be generated and sustained. The authors warn against taking as a yardstick reports of schools which seem to have made rapid improvement in a comparatively short space of time, since many of the contributory elements may already have been in place. In other words, a sense of realism is needed with regard to the speed and the degree to which a failing school can be 'turned round'. Similarly, one needs to recognize the complexity of the change process, and guard against any tendency to lump discrete factors together into one magic all-embracing elixir, or indeed simply to list key factors without considering their operation. Examining the literature, the authors do identify a few common elements for turning round failing schools. These include a medium- to long-term time-scale, common ownership among staff, prioritizing, and 'getting moving'. If these do not work, the closure of the school increasingly becomes an option, and the authors consider the factors most likely to make its re-opening a success. The article concludes by reviewing some recent school improvement projects in Britain, and by suggesting some ways of testing for success.

Learning

We turn, next, from teaching to learning. Intensification may threaten to deskill teachers, removing creativity from the agenda and making learners merely recipients and trainees. But all the articles here are concerned with a vastly different requirement. They are guided largely by constructivist learning theory.

How, and what, do pupils learn?

The reading by Howe addresses group work in primary schools. This has been a key issue in debates on primary pedagogy in recent years (Galton and Williamson 1992; Alexander, Rose and Woodhead 1992). So, too, has the teaching of science to a range of children of different abilities since this was introduced as a core subject in the National Curriculum. Howe brings Piagetian theory to bear on these problems, and argues that it has much to offer primary school teachers in their teaching of physics, especially through the change process of 'equilibration', involving the resolution of conflicting conceptions – though not so conflicting as to be unassimilable. The ideal forum for this would appear to be the varied group, as long as the children are set appropriate tasks. Howe summarizes three studies directed toward investigating whether this is in fact the case. From them, she concludes that there is little evidence of group work where initial conceptions differ among children having an immediate impact, though there is evidence of a longer-term impact. Questions about the best group design, however, were left unresolved. These findings led to further enquiry as to whether the dialogues – the main source of the benefits – that went on in groups could be shaped to be even more productive. Howe concludes that this could be a highly productive area for primary teachers.

Brown and Campione argue the need for critical, independent thinkers, especially in the new technological and globalized age with its rapidly changing information base. Rote learning, ever a prominent feature in our classrooms, will not do. We need to encourage critical thinking from the start, developing what the authors call 'intellectual novices', helping them acquire metacognitive skills of reading, that is, understanding and evaluating the means by which knowledge is acquired. Drawing on their research among academically marginal students in elementary classrooms organized as 'communities of learning', they consider ways of leading students towards this aim. They discuss their successful methods of 'reciprocal reading' and of a negotiated curriculum, wherein teachers and students both acted as leaders and experts, students established a sense of ownership of knowledge and formed a 'culture of learning'. Students showed expertise in particular fields, and helped each other in their own particular strengths. The authors argue that these young students were learning far more than the curriculum subject in question. They were acquiring critical learning strategies of more general application. This would appear to be a good example of teacher and student 'scaffolding' (Edwards and Mercer 1987; Maybin et al., 1992).

In the terms of Woods' paper on 'Critical students', Brown and Campione's students would be considered 'empowered'. They have ownership of knowledge, control of their own learning processes and are involved in activities relevant to their needs. Woods is basically concerned with the same issue as Brown and Campione. But whereas they set up teaching structures to try to secure such an outcome, Woods looked for examples already existing, largely in his own previous research on related issues. He worked inductively from there, seeking to identify different kinds of empowerment and the conditions that attended them. Examples include moments or periods of profound insight; the cultivation of marginality; positive trauma; communitas; and social outrage. These are all potentially states when extraordinary educational advance can be made. Woods also brings, in contrast to the developmental psychology of the previous paper, sociological theory and concepts to bear. Prominent also is attention to the aesthetic and emotional aspects of learning. Again like Brown and Campione, Woods notes the educational potential of children for each other.

The official curriculum is not all that is learnt at school. There is much else beside, generally included within the notion of the 'hidden curriculum'. One prominent line of development is in the area of gender identities – boys and girls finding out what it means for them to be male and female. Until fairly recently, thinking in this area was much influenced by sex-role socialization theory, the central point of which is that boys and girls are socialized to some degree or other into well-defined pre-existing roles which are continually being reinforced and confirmed by society in a multitude of ways. It has become clear, however, that the situation is much more complex than this; that there are a number of different influences that operate on people in different ways; that the influences themselves change; that personal agency counts for more than socialization theories allow; and that, in short, there are a number of different masculinities and femininities. In these edited extracts from Máirtín Mac an Ghaill's book *The Making of Men*, he discusses different types of masculinities that he observed in one comprehensive school (for femininities, see, for example, Mirza 1992). He shows how masculinities are not just counterparts to femininities, but are developed in particular institutional contexts, and in relation to each other. Certain groups of boys showed very different attitudes and behaviours. Some were seen as an anti-school male sub-culture, displaying all the 'macho' elements traditionally associated with masculinity. Another group was more academically positive and upwardly mobile. They became interested in the traditionally 'feminine' arts subjects, attracting ridicule from other male students and from some male teachers. Another group negotiated a new form of masculinity through the new vocational career route. Yet another group, of middle-class background, saw themselves as possessing high-status cultural capital, and gave high value to personal autonomy and to communication strategies which they used to negotiate with teachers to good effect. Mac an Ghaill goes on to discuss some of the principal influences external to the school operating on new forms of gender identity, notably changes in the labour market, in family life and structure, and in ethnicity, racism and sexuality. The article illustrates the barrenness of approaches such as those claiming sex-role socialization in any simplistic sense. It puts the case that gender identities are multiple, not singular, that they are not necessarily fixed, or even consistent, and that they are subject to a range of powerful influences.

How is learning assessed?

To test what has been learned and to guide further teaching is the ostensible business of assessment, though it does appear to serve other, less educative uses, such as accountability and selection. The readings in this section survey this field. Patricia Murphy considers the close relationship between assessment and learning, drawing on constructivist and sociocultural approaches, and challenging much current assessment practice. These approaches reveal some of the complexity of the issue. It is not a simple matter of pupils sitting down and taking a test, but involves a 'complex web of potential interactions', just as in teaching. The approach suggests that knowledge is constructed by pupils, that the meanings they generate have social and cultural bases, and that they relate strongly to the context in which they are generated. Assessment thus can help show how pupils interpret situations, knowledge vital to teachers to guide them in their teaching. Drawing on evidence from the Assessment of Performance Unit's (APU) science programme, Murphy shows the relevance of these ideas. She claims that the evidence does reveal a patterned response among and within particular groups of pupils. This applies to *content* effects, where pupils' experiences of the content guide their response but may not be taken into account by the assessor. Gender differences are prominent here, the APU science results showing differences in performance between boys and girls, mirrored by their different prior experiences. This is not just a matter of cognition, but involves affective matters like confidence and alienation – metacognitive elements that the teacher needs to know about to be effective. The author then discusses *context* effects. Since knowledge is situated, pupils will seek to contextualize tests within some reality. Many tests are artificial, but they cannot be divorced from real situations. Pupils will import their own realities in making sense of the test. Again, it would appear essential for teachers to find out what these are if they are to understand pupil responses properly. This means making context integral to assessment. Murphy goes on to consider the role of cues in assessment, arguing that helping pupils and developing ways of supporting them in assessment is not only a valid, but educationally productive action. She concludes that there is great potential in assessment for facilitating learning, and that teaching and assessment should go hand in hand. We are, however, a long way from this as yet.

The case study of one 7-year-old boy's mathematics test from Mary Jane Drummond's book illustrates some of these points. It points to the inadequacy of formal group testing that leaves content and context out of account as a way of assessing individual children's learning. The boy has learned a great deal, apparently, since starting school, notably on 'how to be a pupil' – but not much mathematics. However, Drummond is not satisfied with simply marking his answers 'wrong'. She wants to understand the *reasons* for his answers. She shows that there is a logic in this, and that there are not many mistakes in this logic. His mathematics is not much use to him, so he searches for other clues, making sense of the test in his own terms and bringing off a 'remarkable achievement, and a tribute to Jason's persistence, to his longing for meaning'. Drummond argues that this case illustrates the restricted and restrictive nature of some forms of assessment; the willing disposition of the child to learn; the extent of things already learnt by the child; the enormous potential in the reasoning, sense-making powers of the child, which are being pressed here into the service of meeting the teacher's demands rather than advancing his own learning. This one small example is repeated many times over throughout the educational system, and no doubt will be throughout Jason's career.

One might claim that, in Jason's experience above, learning is a myth, since his efforts are devoted to satisfying the teacher and working the system. It arises in this instance from what Patricia Broadfoot calls the 'myth of measurement'. In the final article in this section, and in the book, Broadfoot ranges over the history, extent and pervasiveness of the 'myth', but also suggests ways of breaking out of it and achieving some of that promotion of learning that Murphy indicates. She argues that measurement is a prominent feature of the 'credential society' and a primary symptom of the 'diploma disease', wherein certification gets out of control and breeds more and more qualifications of less and less educational worth. Measurement has failed individuals, she continues, depriving them of spontaneous enthusiasm for learning; but it has also failed to meet the economic and social needs of society. How, therefore, has it come to figure so prominently in assessment? Broadfoot explores the origins of the myth, noting especially its political aspects, for who controls the measuring has enormous power. She finds that it is the same for Chinese school admissions in the twelfth century as for the Western liberal tradition of the nineteenth century. Despite examinations coming to be based on merit, privilege still prevailed. She warns that despite, too, the exhibited defects of psychometry and 'I.Q.ism', and the demonstration that performance in examinations is strongly linked to social conditions, the diploma disease continues to spread, pointing to the curtailment of GCSE in 1990 as an indication of this.

Why is the myth so entrenched? Broadfoot is of the view that it is because it is locked into another myth – the post-Enlightenment faith in technology, science and rationality which has reinforced the belief that achievement and ability can be measured. Science thus becomes privileged over art. Indeed the latter, inasmuch as evidenced in the education of the 1960s and 1970s, has come under strong criticism from a government instituting reforms in a strongly technical-rationalist spirit. With a growing emphasis, too, the argument runs, on measurement throughout the system, it comes increasingly to define the organization of education, classroom teaching, and student learning behaviour. Broadfoot enters a strong plea for new forms of assessment that can be used positively and creatively to *promote* learning. In particular, she feels we need to address the metacognitive skills of the students, and explore ways of giving them more control over their own learning. Only by breaking out of the 'myth of measurement' can we engender the new kinds of capacities over a wide range needed in a rapidly changing society.

REFERENCES

Ahier, J., Cosin, B., and Hales, M. (1996) *Diversity and Change: Education Policy and Selection*, London: Routledge.

Alexander, R. J. (1992) *Policy and Practice in Primary Education*, London: Routledge.

Alexander, R. J., Rose, J. and Woodhead, C. (1992) *Curriculum Organisation and Classroom Practice in Primary Schools: A Discussion Paper*, London: Department of Education and Science, HMSO.

Ball, S. J. (1993) 'Education markets, choice and social class: the market as a class strategy in the UK and the USA', *British Journal of Sociology of Education* 14(1): 3–19.

Ball, S. J. and Bowe, R. (1992) 'Subject departments and the "implementation" of National Curriculum policy: an overview of the issues', *Journal of Curriculum Studies* 24(2): 97–115.

Broadhead, P. (1987) 'A blueprint for the good teacher? The HMI/DES model of good primary practice', *British Journal of Educational Studies* 25(1): 57–72.

Campbell, R. J. (1993) 'The National Curriculum in primary schools: a dream at conception, a nightmare at delivery', in C. Chitty and B. Simon, *Education Answers Back: Critical Responses to Government Policy*, London: Lawrence and Wishart.

Campbell, R. J., Evans, L., St. J. Neill, S. R. and Packwood, A. (1991) 'The use and management of infant teachers' time – some policy issues', paper presented at Policy Analysis Unit Seminar, Warwick, November.

Dearing, R. (1994) *Review of the National Curriculum: Final Report*, London: School Curriculum and Assessment Authority (SCAA) Publications.

Department of Education and Science (1983) *Teaching Quality*, London: HMSO.

Department of Education and Science (1985a) *Better Schools*, Cmnd 9469, London: HMSO.

Department of Education and Science (1985b) *Education Observed 3 – Good Teachers*, London: HMSO.

Edwards, D. and Mercer, N. (1987) *Common Knowledge: The Development of Understanding in the Classroom*, London: Methuen.

Galton, M. and Williamson, J. (1992) *Group Work in the Primary Classroom*, London: Routledge.

Glaser, B. G. and Strauss, A. L. (1971) *Status Passage*, Chicago: Aldine.

Hargreaves, A. (1994) *Changing Teachers, Changing Times – Teacher's Work and Culture in the Postmodern Age*, London: Cassell.

Hargreaves, D. H. (1994) 'The new professionalism: the synthesis of professional and institutional development', *Teaching and Teacher Education* 10(4): 423–38.

MacLeod, D. and Meikle, J. (1994) 'Education changes making heads quit', *Guardian*, 1 September: 6.

Maybin, J., Mercer, N. and Stierer, B. (1992) 'Scaffolding learning in the classroom', in K. Norman (ed.) *Thinking Voices: The Work of the National Oracy Project*, London: Hodder and Stoughton.

Mirza, H. (1992) *Young, Female and Black*, London: Routledge.

Pollard, A. (1992) 'Teachers' responses to the reshaping of primary education', in M. Arnot and L. Barton (eds) *Voicing Concerns*, London: Triangle Books.

Pollard, A., Broadfoot, P., Croll, P., Osborn, M. and Abbott, D. (1994) *Changing English Primary Schools? The Impact of the Education Reform Act at Key Stage One*, London: Cassell.

Van Gennep, A. (1960) *The Rites of Passage*, London: Routledge and Kegan Paul.

Vulliamy, G. and Webb, R. (1993) 'Progressive education and the National Curriculum: findings from a global education research project', *Educational Review* 45(1): 21–41.

Wallace, M. (1993) 'Discourse of derision: the role of the mass media within the education policy process', *Journal of Education Policy* 8(4): 321–37.

Wood, D. (1988) *How Children Think and Learn*, Oxford: Basil Blackwell.

Woods, P. (1995) *Creative Teachers in Primary Schools*, Buckingham: The Open University Press.

Woods, P. and Jeffrey, R. (1996) *Teachable Moments: The Art of Teaching in Primary School*, Buckingham: Open University Press.

Woods, P. and Wenham, P. (1995) 'Politics and pedagogy: a case study in appropriation', *Journal of Education Policy* 10(2): 119–41.

Chapter 1

Aims and values in the National Curriculum[1]

John White and Philip O'Hear

The structural weakness of the 1988 Curriculum is plain. Its basis is the 10 foundation subjects. What these are all supposed to be *for* has never been made clear, beyond the virtually uninformative prescription in the ERA [the Education Reform Act] that they are to promote the 'spiritual, moral, cultural, mental and physical development of pupils' and prepare them for adult life. A more sensible way of working out a national curriculum would have been to begin with a well-worked-out set of aims and only then ask what would be the best vehicles to realize them – *without* assuming that the only vehicles would be those found in the timetabled curriculum, and *without* assuming that the first and main thing to go for would be the traditional school subjects, rather than other ways of organizing learning. . . .

In our 1991 paper *A National Curriculum for All*, Philip O'Hear and I set out an alternative structure which avoided these weaknesses.

There is no particular virtue in a national curriculum as such: everything depends on what *kind* it is. A national curriculum can be used as a means of repression or indoctrination, as happened under Hitler and Stalin. . . . Philip and I begin from the central aim of preparing students to become citizens of a liberal democratic society. We do not interpret this narrowly, as learning about voting and other such political matters. These come into the picture, but more basic than them is the aim of passing on the core values of our kind of polity. Central among these is the value of self-determination. We all rightly take it as read that individuals should be freed, as far as practicable, from constraints of poverty, drudgery, ignorance, domination and fear which might hold them back from choosing a worthwhile life of their own. Balancing this, since we are not in the business of producing a nation of autonomous egoists, is an array of values to do with what binds us to other people – from more intimate values like friendship, through shared activities and attachments to local and national groupings, to more impersonal demands of benevolence, justice, respect for others' rights, and a concern for humanity in general. . . .

The 1988 Curriculum lays great emphasis on the acquisition of knowledge and understanding, but without making it clear why this is important.

For us, too, it is a major objective, but only because it is required by an induction in democratic values and the personal qualities that this fosters. The self-determined life requires a broad understanding of the options, vocational and other, which are open to one, of the obstacles in the way of success, and of the society within which one is making one's choices. Most of the foundation subjects – and more besides – can have a role in providing this understanding. Similarly, to take another personal quality based on a democratic value, a concern to promote the material and non-material well-being of others in one's national community requires some understanding of what this national community *is*, geographically, historically, socially and economically. Understanding its economic structure requires a grasp of technology, science and mathematics. And so on. I perhaps do not need to labour further the dependence of knowledge objectives on underlying ethical values. The main point is that any viable national curriculum should rest on a solid basis of ethical values, and in the interests of overall coherence show how these generate intellectual and other objectives, both large-scale and specific.

Structurally, as I have said, the National Curriculum is weak. It may *look* strong, with its rigid subject structure and detailed statutory demands. But this could be the illusory strength of a blind Cyclops which cannot see which way it is going. Something will have to be done to make the National Curriculum more coherent. More work needs to be done on spelling out underlying aims and working out how these are to be realized in subjects and in themes. A stronger structure is often a more flexible one. It would be good to see less attention paid to prescriptions at the periphery – the detailed statutory requirements of programmes of study and statements of attainment – and more paid to central aims and values. . . .

But what does this entail? We cannot go on for much longer trying to milk an underlying philosophy from the one line in the ERA about promoting spiritual, moral and other forms of development. A fuller account of underlying aims and values is called for.

Unfortunately, it is just at this point that David Pascall [Chairman of the National Curriculum Council] opts out. He goes on to say: 'I should also emphasise that it is not for the NCC to advocate an evangelical crusade or to publish glossy brochures about core values. All of these issues are for decision and implementation at local level.' [(Pascall 1992)]

He does not say *why* decisions about values should not be made centrally. These need not involve anything so heady as an 'evangelical crusade', only a further spelling out of what ends the foundation subjects and themes are there to serve. This is essential if the National Curriculum is not to become ossified in the way its equivalents have been in some other countries and if it is to mesh with students' personal, social and civil needs.

In any case, David Pascall is wrong in his implication that the NCC leaves value issues to localities and has nothing to do with recommendations from the centre. If we look at its published material, we see that the Working Party reports for the different subjects all have broad statements of aims for their particular area and all of these incorporate values. A few examples from reports in history, English and art are imaginativeness, aesthetic sensibility, critical thinking, pleasurable activity, independence, confidence, self-knowledge, tolerance and respect for cultural variety, objectivity. . . . There are many further examples. These values are far more determinate than the generalities of the ERA aims. As such, they are more useful in helping to shape more specific objectives.

The National Curriculum is, indeed, redolent with values. A major defect in it is that no one has tried to get them into any kind of order. In the absence of any intelligible structure to bind them together, they tend to be overlooked in favour of knowledge objectives where such a bonding is more evident. The next major task for the NCC is to engage in this task of value-ordering. It needs to establish priorities, to work out what the central values of the National Curriculum should be and how these are related to subordinate values. . . . However it goes about it, the NCC could – and should – come up with a new and detailed account of the aims and values that should be demanded of schools.

It could pave the way to this by removing some of the inconsistencies among the values embodied in the National Curriculum. The most telling example of this I know has to do with citizenship. Education for citizenship is one of the cross-curricular themes. Students are to do work on communities, a pluralist society, civic rights and responsibilities, the family, the political and legal systems, work and leisure, the public services. All this involves a lot of understanding of their own society. Among the foundation subjects a notable absentee is social studies – a subject obviously well suited for this purpose. In its absence, history is one of the more helpful vehicles to promote an understanding of society. Yet, apart from a one-term module on the causes of the Second World War, students can leave school knowing nothing of the history of the 20th century. So there are conflicting messages: on the one hand, understanding your own society is important to you as a citizen; on the other, social studies and the recent history of your own society – as distinct from, say, medieval England – are not important and neglectable. . . .

We may not now be able to rebuild the National Curriculum from scratch, but we might be able to improve it bit by bit, like a ship rebuilt at sea – provided we have a better ethical design by which to do so. . . .

Drawing on the detailed proposals presented by John White and me in O'Hear and White (1991), I will outline the structure we propose and develop a critique of the present situation. An adequate and successful national curriculum would set curriculum planning at a national and school level in the context of coherent and clear aims and values. Central to our society and its well-being is the idea of liberal democracy. Drawing on this ideal and its prime values of self-determination and the recognition of our independence on each other, we can articulate the personal qualities needed for a self-determined and socially aware life. These personal qualities are the preconditions of citizenship in a liberal democracy and thus part of the entitlement and obligation of each citizen. We classify them into three broad areas:

personal concerns (managing one's own needs, pursuing personal projects, developing qualities of character);

social involvement and concern for others (working for shared goals, enjoying friends, family, developing more general social responsibility, refraining from harming others, being impartial);

critical and reflective awareness (self-knowledge, including openness, reflectiveness about priorities among one's values, critical awareness and so on).

All these personal qualities have an educational dimension in that their development requires the systematic acquisition of knowledge, understanding, attitudes and competencies. Since possession of them is a fundamental requirement for self-determining and socially responsible participation in a liberal democratic society, it is quite proper that these values should inform our education planning, both nationally and in schools. Moreover, we can draw up a framework for the curriculum, derived from the personal qualities, that includes the *content* of the curriculum, *the wider curriculum* within the life of an effective school, a *structure for progression and choice*, and the *system for assessment and recording*.

Because this framework is at a higher conceptual level than any of the specific details of the operational curriculum, it provides a focused and coherent set of reference points against which to make the decisions of selection, structure and emphasis involved in operational planning. The lack of such a conceptual framework in the present National Curriculum lays it open to the arbitrary backtrackings and pressure group hijackings that have characterized the first five years of its implementation. The case for reform is increasingly urgent as the effects of the destructive and politicized imposition of crude and narrowing assessment instruments become apparent. It is significant that . . . two of the chief architects of the present National Curriculum, Eric Bolton and Paul Black, express grave concern that their achievements are being undermined by the crude assessment system now being imposed. What is missing from their critique, I would argue, is a recognition that the 10-subject starting point of the present National Curriculum . . . is fundamentally inadequate. Without a more satisfactory conceptual base than a simple list of subjects, any curriculum is going to be open to inconsistent change and excessive prescription as different views of learning and national need are fought out in the detail rather than in the original design. The framework developed in our paper is an attempt to show that such a task is both possible and helpful.

In terms of *the content of the curriculum*, we identify the knowledge, understanding, experience of the arts and practical competencies required for possession of the personal qualities. Often the content we describe is familiar, which is hardly surprising since there is very broad consensus about the main elements of compulsory content. Our framework, however, shows the relevance of content to educational and social values and indicates how the selection of content can be based on this relevance and not simply on assertion and whim. For example, full participation in the political process for our society is dependent on some proper knowledge and understanding of the recent history of this society and the world around it, and of the scientific and technological issues and decisions facing it. Modern world history, a grounding in science and in the basis of technology are all therefore essential areas of knowledge. Other knowledge is required for more personal reasons, such as knowledge of options open to one in work and leisure and, at least, access to the specific knowledge required for chosen fields of activity. From arguments of this kind, we develop a framework for content that gives a rational, coherent and focused basis for selecting aspects of subjects and in deciding whether and how to group them and what to make optional and compulsory. We describe the content using the following structure:

Three areas of knowledge and understanding

Personal;
Social;
Scientific and technological.

Here most, but not all, of the current subject content would be remapped, with a slimmer nationally required core to be covered, with considerable scope for local and school choice in addition. The focus and aims for each part of the compulsory content will be clear so we will be free of the arbitrariness of much of the current content.

Experience of the arts

Here all the arts would be included, and the appreciation of the built environment and natural beauty. In our view, the arts are not a different kind of knowledge but a qualitatively different area of experience. A coherent programme for arts education will develop important aesthetic, moral and human awareness alongside induction into major strands of our culture and of the pleasures of life.

Four areas of practical competencies

Communication and numeracy;
Physical movement and health and safety;
Social interaction;
Planning and organization.

Of course, these areas will principally be taught through other things, but we believe that the profile of these aspects of practical learning should be raised. We need to move away from a narrow, and often decontextualized, 'skills' approach to see that the development of competencies is the acquisition of significant skills alongside attitudes and knowledge. We cannot manage, let alone enjoy, our lives without these competencies and the proper use of them is fundamental to the social dimensions of a self-determining life. Thus the competencies take their place as the third element of the content of the curriculum.

Content is only part of the framework, since the institutional life of the school is also part of the whole curriculum, along with the structure for progression and the system for assessment. Some commentators applaud the fact that the present National Curriculum leaves schools free to decide their own ethos and values, although the NCC now has suggested that schools should be required to show what their core values are. . . . I want to examine more closely the reasons why *the wider curriculum of the effective school* should be included in the framework of an adequate national curriculum. We argue, from our essentially democratic position, that schools and individual teachers should have significant freedom of planning and curriculum decision returned to them. It is obviously vital that schools develop their own sense of community in partnership with their neighbourhoods, parents and students, not least because it is at the level of school and local community that conflicting values in a pluralist and socially and ethnically diverse society can be weighed and prioritized. However, the current 'freedom' for schools to develop the 'whole curriculum' beyond the National Curriculum leaves a vacuum in place of a real entitlement. This will extend to values and attitudes as well as to (apparently but falsely value-free) content. Certain principles and practices must pervade the whole curriculum of the school if access to the development of the personal qualities is to be guaranteed for all.

The second part of our framework, therefore, is a proposed requirement that all schools should draw up and publish policies for the following areas of school life which show how they aim to contribute to national and school aims:

the whole curriculum plan;
the code of conduct;
the structure for partnership with students and families;

the involvement of the whole school community in decision making;

the relationship with the local community;

the development of a social life and an extra-curricular programme;

the structures for promoting equal access to learning;

the establishment of interactive styles of teaching and learning and opportunities for independent learning.

What we are raising here, particularly in the last two areas, is that a national curriculum concerned with values and coherence needs to address issues of pedagogy as well as content. There is, of course, a strong link between the description of content in our framework and this second element because the practical competencies and, indeed, the relatedness of the areas of knowledge, understanding and the arts cannot be achieved without the support of an effective wider curriculum embedded in the life of the school.

A wider national curriculum does not have to be a more prescriptive one. The third element of our framework is a *structure for progression and choice*. Each key stage should have a clear focus appropriate to the age and development of the students. At Key Stage 1, for example, this would focus on literacy and numeracy and the foundation of positive learning and social experience, and be free from the present clutter of content that seems currently to be weakening literacy levels still further. By contrast, at Key Stage 4, we envisage a largely modular structure involving vocational and academic learning and linked to a comprehensive post-16 structure. I want to emphasize that a nationally set core programme of study should be just that: a core profile of work for each key stage with space for the school to add to it, to decide the structure for delivery and the context in which to see it. This would return to teachers the important role of detailed planning and contextualizing the national agenda in the light of the needs and interests of their student. This is desirable both philosophically (on the basis of self-determination for teachers and the recognition of their professionalism) but also practically. The teacher is, if properly guided, supported and monitored, in the best position to know how to get the best from the students.

Choice should not, however, extend only to those planning and delivering the curriculum. There is no intrinsic conflict between an entitlement curriculum and guaranteed access to the major areas of learning, and real choice for students in their learning. On the contrary, the development of young people for a democratic society requires that they gain experience of making guided but significant choices. We identify four levels of possible student choice within the curriculum:

within a given sequence of work, i.e. choice over the order;

between options in a sequence of work, e.g. a compulsory core task, then choice between extension tasks;

between options, where one of a variety of possibilities is required;

between voluntary activities.

All key stages should include student choice at the first two and the fourth levels, which are, of course, extremely important as motivators and supports for active learning as well as providing experience of choice. We would want to extend the principle radically, supported by a modular structure of curriculum organization, and argue that 15% of the timetable at Key Stage 3 and 30% at Key Stage 4 should be reserved for options. . . .

[In the original article, O'Hear next summarizes the fourth and final part of the White/O'Hear framework: *the system for assessing and recording*. Their detailed proposals are omitted here, but it should be noted that O'Hear considers assessment the 'ultimately crucial' part of the present National Curriculum. Because 'the basis of the present structure is the . . . 10 subjects without any prior set of values or organizing principles,' he argues, 'whoever controls the focus and nature of the Tests can, in fact, control the whole curriculum.']

I have now described all the elements of the alternative framework for an adequate national curriculum proposed by John White and myself. I have also rehearsed and updated our critique of the present National Curriculum and argued . . . the case for root and branch reform and not simply adjustment. . . .

Arguing for radical change in the National Curriculum is not . . . simply a matter of defending our position as educationists. More importantly, it is setting out the kind of structure that is needed for personal and national success. The individual citizens of our nation need a broad and high level of education, preparing them for work in a highly developed and technological economy and for life in a complex and open society. Present policies, involving failure and selection and retaining a strongly enforced divide between the academic and the practical, will not serve this need at all. There is a potentially huge consensus across industry, politicians, parents and students for an adequate national education policy. This will have to include coherence and continuity in the curriculum, the right balance of the practical and the student-centred with the theoretical and the teacher-led, a proper validation of the achievements of the whole student and a clear structure of progression through and beyond compulsory schooling. As educationists concerned with individual as well as national needs and success, we need to be ready to provide the detailed case for change that this consensus will demand when the political climate changes. Engaging in debate now . . . will allow us both to clarify and update ideas and begin to build a consensus for change. . . .

In this chapter, I have set out in some detail an alternative model which, I believe, offers real coherence and a better prospect for national and individual success. . . .

NOTE

1   This chapter is an edited version of chapters 1 and 2 (by J. White and P. O'Hear respectively) of P. O'Hear and J. White (eds) *Assessing the National Curriculum*, London: Paul Chapman.

REFERENCES

O'Hear, P. and White, J. (1991) *A National Curriculum for All: Laying the Foundations for Success*, London: IPPR
Pascall, D. (1992) *The Times Educational Supplement*, 29 May.

Chapter 2

Disciplining English: the construction of a national subject[1]

Jill Bourne and Deborah Cameron

In 1987, a Committee of Inquiry into the Teaching of the English Language [chaired by a mathematician, John Kingman] was announced by the Secretary of State for Education, Kenneth Baker. It was commissioned as part of a wider government initiative to construct a national curriculum for schools. . . .

The Kingman brief was to recommend a model of the English language, knowledge of which would form one element of the English subject curriculum whilst also informing programmes of teacher training. . . .

In this chapter, we propose to examine the . . . Kingman Report (DES 1988a), not for its practical application to English teaching, but as a historical event, as a battlefield around which ideological assumptions have been paraded and contested. Our reading of Kingman is intended to provide perspectives from which the meanings of . . . later proposals, and the responses to them, as they emerge, might also become clearer. We will focus on Kingman as a key ideological text about the state of the language and its relation to the state of the nation.

The domain of Kingman is marked out in the phrase 'English grammar', and both these words are significant if we seek to understand the meaning and context of the report. We will deal, accordingly, with the question of 'grammar' and the question of 'English'.

KINGMAN AND THE QUESTION OF GRAMMAR

Right from the start, the setting up of the Kingman Committee was perceived as contentious. The Committee put back on the agenda something – 'knowledge about language' or, less coyly, grammar – which, it was thought, had been largely abandoned in educational practice, with some theoretical support from modern linguistics as well as educational theory, under pressure from the 'liberal' ideas of the 1960s and 1970s.

The move away from grammar had never gone unopposed, however. When Kingman publicly reopened the question the rumble of discontent from traditionalist quarters turned into a roar; and their progressive opponents were equally vocal in deploring the return of grammar. What was crucial, though, was that the context for this familiar debate had changed dramatically since the 1970s.

It is, of course, a commonplace observation that people do feel strongly about language and correctness in language: perceptions of 'falling standards' and 'sloppiness' are pervasive (and have been for around 300 years). But this fact in itself does not explain why the teaching of *grammar* is so often seen as a panacea – nor indeed why grammar is so vehemently opposed by many people (linguists and teachers, for instance) who by no means deny the importance of clarity and elegance in the use of language.

To understand the peculiarly violent responses that grammar inspires we need to examine its social significance in our culture. Arguably, grammar is an innocuous concept in itself, but has become inextricably linked with less innocuous concepts such as authority, hierarchy, tradition, order and rules. Attitudes to grammar are connected with attitudes to authority; anxieties about grammar are at some deeper level anxieties about the breakdown of order and tradition, not just in language but in society at large. This point, on the face of it quite startling, is spelt out in an article written for the *Observer* newspaper in 1982 by independent school headmaster John Rae under the heading 'The decline and fall of English grammar'. At the time Rae expressed a dissenting view since the 'liberal' perspective was still in the ascendant; in the light of Kingman, though, his remarks now appear oddly prophetic.

Rae begins by making it explicit that you teach children grammar not just in order to improve their own linguistic performance (in passing, it should be said that we know of no evidence that grammar teaching has any such effect) but to make it clear to them that there are rules of conduct; people may not simply do as they please, either in language or in any other kind of social interaction. Rejecting grammar is one mark of a society which rejects rules, and the result is anarchy. As Rae comments:

> Grammar was a predictable victim of the self-indulgent sixties. It was associated with authority, tradition and elitism. Grammatical rules, like so many other rules at the time, were regarded as an intolerable infringement of personal freedom.

This argument is, of course, an absolute deformation of the critique of traditional prescriptive grammar put forward for instance by linguistics. For a linguist, it is axiomatic that every speaker has a grammar, and there is little 'personal freedom' involved, at least in Rae's sense of breaking the rules at will. The anti-prescriptivists had no desire to abolish grammar *per se* (one might as well try to abolish gravity); they wanted only to break the connection between grammar and 'authority, tradition and elitism'.

If the connection has in fact survived, it is because for our culture 'authority, tradition and elitism' form the central meaning of grammar. It is only secondarily about language at all.

Rae oblingly makes this point crystal clear towards the end of his article, where he draws an explicit parallel between grammatical and other kinds of correctness.

> There is a further claim that can be made for the restoration of the teaching of correct English. Attention to the rules of grammar and care in the choice of words encourages punctiliousness in other matters. That is not just an intellectual conceit. The overthrow of grammar coincided with the acceptance of the equivalent of creative writing in social behaviour. As nice points of grammar were mockingly dismissed as pedantic and irrelevant, so was punctiliousness in such matters as honesty, responsibility, property, gratitude, apology and so on.

It appears here that grammar is to bear an immense symbolic weight, being associated with the values of hierarchy, order and rule-government in general. That is why it is both passionately advocated and passionately opposed. A return to traditional grammar marks a return to the associated social values.

It must, however, be said that the Kingman view of grammar is *not* un-equivocally traditionalist. It is obviously significant that the report insists throughout on the euphemism 'knowledge about language' which distances it from traditional prescriptive models and placates those for whom 'grammar' would be anathema.

Because Kingman takes a moderate line on grammar – the rallying point for both traditionalists and progressives – it may well seem that the whole tenor of the report is moderate. But if we turn to the matter of what Kingman makes of 'English' we shall see that this impression is misleading.

KINGMAN AND THE QUESTION OF ENGLISH

We alluded above to the historical connection often made between the perceived state of the language and the identity of the nation. This connection is familiar in many contexts all over the world (language riots in Belgium and India; the systematic oppression of Catalan speakers under Franco; or conversely, the irredentist ambitions of Hitler in the Sudentenland). An authoritarian state frequently uses 'the national language' as a point of unity and social cohesion, and analogously, finds linguistic diversity threatening, a force to be contained or even eliminated.

The National Curriculum represents a move towards uniformity. Previously it was up to Local Education Authorities (LEAs) to determine their curricula, and in doing this they took account of local needs (e.g. the ethnic and socio-economic profile of their schools). As is well known, Britain is linguistically highly diverse, both in terms of languages spoken and of divergent varieties of English (related to region and to social class). A national curriculum must inevitably address this diversity on a greater scale than any one LEA was obliged to cope with. The tendency of Kingman was to take an authoritarian position by advocating cohesion around one variety of one language (Standard English, hereafter SE) while at the same time seeking to contain diversity by downgrading minority languages and non-standard varieties.

It is worthwhile discussing the manner in which Kingman has chosen to describe the linguistic diversity of this country. It eschews – and one imagines by conscious choice – any mention whatever of social divisions such as 'race' and class. All linguistic variation is described as either 'historical' (i.e. the English language changes through time) or 'geographical' (i.e. different accents/dialects are used in different regions of the country). Such a model of variation is actually false. It omits both class and ethnic group variation. Each variety is seen as changing within itself over time and located in its own space, without contact with other varieties or languages (except for sometimes sharing a standard written form which can cross regional boundaries). Contact and shift (which in the view of many linguists are the fundamental sources of much language change) have no place in this account.

Synchronic diversity for Kingman is a matter of regional varieties with clear boundaries. Such dialects are acceptable and to be valued as long as they are easily 'comprehensible' (to whom is not specified) and so long as they remain within spheres where their use is 'appropriate'. For as the Kingman Report (ch. 2. para. 5) remarks,

> The dialect usages of family and immediate circle are sufficient to their purposes; but membership of the smaller group entails membership of the larger, and for the wider community – that of the nation and the world – the standard language will be indispensable.

The indispensabilty of SE has apparently nothing to do with its social prestige (since the fact that it is a *class* dialect, spoken by the elite in every region, cannot be stated within the Kingman framework of 'history' and 'geography') but merely relates to its communicational appropriateness as something that belongs to 'the nation' (not to mention the world) rather than to a region, a class or an ethnic group. We shall go on to explore how Kingman fits into a tradition that makes SE the symbol of nationhood and the mark of citizenship or 'belonging'.

CITIZENSHIP AND NATIONHOOD (1): ENGLISH AND MINORITY LANGUAGES

The report has little to say directly about the position of those school pupils (in some localities up to 41 per cent, and in certain schools an overall majority of children) who are bilingual in English and another language. But Kingman's historical/geographical model of language variation has serious implications for the status of minority languages and their speakers. The covert function of the model is to strengthen and protect English at the expense of other languages; and this becomes overt in the Secretary of State's notes of 'Supplementary Guidance' (DES, 1988b) to the National Curriculum Working Group on English which took over where Kingman left off. . . . The notes enjoin readers to bear in mind 'the cardinal point that English should be the first language and medium of instruction for all pupils in England' (para. 13).

The use of the term *England* (not *Britain*) here is significant, since there is of course one minority language whose claims are respected by the government and in the national curriculum: Welsh in Wales. It is instructive to examine the case of Welsh in more detail, since contrasting attitudes to Welsh and, say, Greek or Gujerati help to clarify what assumptions are being made about language and nationhood.

Welsh was granted legal status in Wales by the Welsh Language Act of 1967 – interestingly enough, at the very time when the English language was becoming an educational issue in England following a period of immigration from the old Empire (now the 'new Commonwealth'). In England, the response to linguistic diversity was to set up structures for English language teaching, both for children and for adults. Documents of the time express the fear that the presence of pupils in English schools speaking languages other than English would be detrimental to the indigenous school population and lead to falling standards (cf. DES Circular 7/65 (DES, 1965); Commonwealth Advisory Committee, 1964).

The perceived need to 'protect' English speakers from the dangers of contact with other languages was also seen in the Welsh legislation. Welsh was granted 'equal validity' as a language alongside English in Wales. This was done to 'raise the status of Welsh' but it crucially did not threaten the position of English monolinguals in Wales either socially or economically, by requiring them to learn Welsh. Provision for bilinguals in both England and Wales was premised, in other words, on the need to affect the monolingual majority as little as possible.

The difference between the bilingual provision made possible in Wales and the compensatory English programmes favoured in England is nevertheless a significant one, and one that can be analysed precisely in terms of *territory*. The use of territorial criteria to define language provision and minority language rights is not peculiar to Kingman – indeed, it is not even acknowledged as such in Kingman – but it is crucial to our understanding of Kingman as an ideological text.

In 1967 Welsh gained equal validity only within the borders of Wales. Welsh speakers outside Wales had no claim for equal treatment. In other words, the whole discourse of language rights in the Welsh case is focused on territorial considerations, to wit, the existence of a region (historically, a nation) to which the Welsh language 'belongs'. It is a discourse of national boundaries rather than one of minority rights (as we can see very clearly from the fact that individuals travelling beyond the Welsh borders could not take their language rights with them).

The nationalistic 'land and language' argument articulates very comfortably with the right-wing ideas on the subject of English and the English literary heritage in England (e.g. Marenbon, 1987; Hillgate Group, 1987). If one allows that Welsh is the 'natural' language of Wales, it follows that English is the 'natural' tongue of England. But what is the effect of this stance on languages *without* a historic territory inside the British state? Clearly, the effect is to render such languages *alien*. If languages belong to geographical areas with unbroken continuity of use in those areas, then each has its own proper place within which speakers may have 'rights'. Punjabi in Birmingham becomes a historical accident and a territorial aberration, a temporary occupation of someone else's space. At best we can teach children to respect the languages their classmates bring to school, but the territorial model makes it clear that those languages do not 'belong' here in England. Within that model, it seems that resident bilingual communities must choose either to share in 'our' linguistic heritage or to remain 'alien' with their allegiances elsewhere.

So while multicultural education of an approved type may encourage children to show tolerance towards cultural and linguistic diversity, in the territorial model such diversity will remain exotic, transplanted rather than inherent, and will need to be contained as a possible threat to the strong ethnocentric values which inform most of the national curriculum. [It is important in this context to note that the SCAA (1994) proposals for English did not contain even one reference to the existence of bilingual children, other than Welsh-speaking bilinguals within Wales.]

If ethnocentrism was strong in Kingman, so was elitism. The presence of sizeable linguistic minorities in England is a relatively new phenomenon for the British education system, but the existence of socially conditioned variation in English itself has been a perennial issue. We can therefore examine Kingman's treatment of it by comparison with earlier pronouncements by educationalists and commissions of enquiry. Such a comparison will reveal once again that Kingman does represent a shift to an authoritarian 'national unity' perspective which recalls the late nineteenth and early twentieth centuries but goes against the more recent post-war 'liberal consensus'.

CITIZENSHIP AND NATIONHOOD (2): STANDARD ENGLISH

As we have noted already, the concept of 'Standard English' is very important in Kingman's vision of the English curriculum. We will therefore begin by looking at this concept and the problems it raises.

Standard is something of a weasel word. It has two related but rather different meanings. One of these is 'uniform', as in the idea of a standard measurement. It means ordinary, common to all, invariant, normal. But the second sense of the word is 'something to aspire to', as in the idea of 'high standards'. This means not ordinary but excellent, the best there is, not normal but *normative*.

Discussions of Standard English often exhibit a slippage between these two senses of 'standard'. Thus the normative is passed off as the merely normal; or in this specifically linguistic case, the language of a class is passed off as the common tongue of a whole people (in Kingman's terms, which exclude the concept of class, SE is the language of the nation rather than that of the family and immediate circle). On the one hand, discussions about the desirability of 'standard' trade on the associations of the term with excellence – 'the best that has been said and written in our language'. But if one asks *'whose* language exactly?', if one raises the question of social inequality and the arbitrary nature of the purported excellence, the same discussions can easily retreat into the notion of 'standard English' as a uniform practice which all English speakers have in common. . . .

Kingman assumes that SE is a 'national heritage' to which citizens have a right (and crucially also, an obligation). Like the territorial perspective discussed in the last section this is nothing new. The history of English teaching has always been about giving to the many what the few could take for granted. We should recall here that the elite who attended public schools and universities had until relatively recently little or no formal education in their own language and literature, because it was assumed to be something they already possessed by virtue of their rank: instead they followed a classics-based curriculum. To get English accepted as a teaching subject took a prolonged struggle. 'Knowledge about language' had its place in that debate too; it was used to beef up the academic credentials of English as a subject, making it more like classics and thus acceptable to the elite.

On the other hand, though, some of the strongest arguments for teaching English language and literature referred explicitly to the need to educate a wider social constituency – groups who could not be expected to cope with Greek and Latin, such as middle-class recruits to the imperial bureaucracy, women and, eventually, the working classes who were to benefit from mass education.

KINGMAN, ENGLISH AND EDUCATION

English was crucial in mass education, not only because it was easier than classics or because of the need for a literate work-force, though doubtless these were factors, but for overtly ideological reasons to do with national identity and social cohesion. This emerges clearly from a reading of relevant documents of the nineteenth and early twentieth centuries, the forerunners of Kingman. Educational policy-makers saw in English the potential for containing social conflict caused by endemic class division. . . .

In the nineteenth century . . . the ideas of commentators on the language became infused with European romanticism, which held that a language expressed the genius of a people (*'Volksgeist'*). The success of England as an imperial nation, a world leader economically and politically, combined with romantic ideas about language to produce an overtly patriotic and triumphalist attitude to English. . . .

Given the prevalence and influence of [these] ideas about language and nation, . . . it seemed obvious that a solid training in English would be an excellent foundation for a national culture. This was most vigorously advocated in politically explicit terms by the Newbolt Report of 1921 (see Crowley, 1989) and also in a polemical essay by one of the Newbolt Commissioners, George Sampson, published in the same year under the title *English for the English* (see Sampson, 1921).

Sampson, like many other people at the time, was deeply worried about the possibility of class warfare escalating as it recently had in Russia. He was clear about the role of education and culture in breaking down dangerous class divisions, and he also had a good understanding of the relation between class and language. 'In this country', he wrote, 'classes are sundered by difference in language – difference of speech is a symbol of class antagonism' (quoted in Crowley, 1989). The Newbolt Report wanted action to change that state of affairs. 'If the teaching of the language were properly provided for', it said, 'the difference between educated and uneducated speech, which at present causes so much prejudice and difficulty on both sides, would gradually disappear' (ibid.). . . .

Newbolt recommended exactly this 'common basis of education' on precisely the ground that it would bring unity between classes sharing one native language. Sampson was deeply committed to the total eradication of nonstandard varieties which he called 'language in a state of disease'. SE is the key to culture and value, and it is something all classes can be taught to share. The alternative, which Sampson conjures up in apocalyptic terms, is a society where people's primary loyalties are not to the nation but to their class, and where the lower classes have no culture of any kind. In *English for the English* Sampson warns where this will lead: 'Deny to working class children any common share in the immaterial, and presently they will grow into the men who demand with menaces a communism of the material.'

THE COMMON CULTURE

We should not, of course, deny the obvious differences between Newbolt and Kingman – the accommodation of Kingman to educational and linguistic theories unknown in 1921 is clear enough. Nevertheless there are parallels between the two documents. In both cases 'English' is advocated as the cornerstone of a national curriculum whose objective is to produce a 'common culture' in the nation's children.

The late 1980s, like the 1920s was a time when there was renewed concern with social polarization. Many people in Britain today are still dusting off the old 'two nations' rhetoric, and some are worried, as Sampson was in his time, about the potential for serious unrest among the dispossessed of the Thatcher era. In its underlying attitudes of nationalism, ethnocentrism, an authoritarian impulse to unity in culture, Kingman is far more like Newbolt than it is like the more recent Bullock and Swann reports (DES, 1975, 1985) where the model of culture was being reworked towards diversity and pluralism. As an answer to social conflict it offers a radically different solution, an 'English culture' in which all, if they are to be 'English', or at least 'British', are to take part.

But the context for Kingman is a wholly different Britain from the Britain of 1921; the rhetoric of that bygone age is singularly inappropriate even if the nation's social problems appear to be similar. The economic self-confidence, imperial majesty and political status of the nineteenth century are gone: present day conservatives are struggling to put something in its place (as a recent election slogan had it, 'Making Britain Great Again'). And this is also part of the meaning of Kingman: nostalgia.

Raymond Williams (in Osmond, 1985) has discussed what he calls the 'visible weakening of England' as a nation state, and the increasing uncertainty over whether there is any definable 'English way of life'. . . . Kingman may be about authoritarian control in a polarized nation-state, but it also contains another, less evident strand, which is a feeling of nostalgia and loss for a changed nation.

What this strand signals is a point of transition for the idea of 'Englishness' as a national identity. Because of the close connection between language and nationhood, grammar and tradition, policy documents on English are bound to reflect that transition. For the children in our schools, however, it is important that we should not look to the past, but to the future, face up to present realities, and conceptualize language (which is not the same thing as English) in the context of Britain's future.

NOTE

1. This chapter is adapted from a paper entitled 'No common ground: Kingman, grammar and the nation' in *Language and Education* 2(3). It was previously published in the present shortened form in P. Murphy, M. Selinger, J. Bourne and M. Briggs (eds) (1995) *Subject Learning in the Primary Curriculum: Issues in English, Science and Mathematics*, London: Routledge.

REFERENCES

Commonwealth Advisory Committee (1964) *Second Report*, London: HMSO.
Crowley, T. (1989) *The Politics of Discourse 1840–1987*, London: Macmillan.
Department of Education and Science (DES) (1965) Circular 7/65, London: DES
—— (1975) *A Language for Life* (the Bullock Report), London: HMSO.
—— (1985) *Education for All* (the Swann Report), London: HMSO.

—— (1988a) *Report of the Committee of Inquiry into the Teaching of the English Language* (the Kingman Report), London: HMSO.

—— (1988b) *National Curriculum English Working Group: Terms of Reference and Notes of Supplementary Guidance*. London: DES.

Hillgate Group (1987) *The Reform of British Education*, London: Claridge.

Marenbon, J. (1987) *English Our English*, London: Centre for Policy Studies.

Osmond, J. (ed.) (1985) *The National Question Again: Welsh Political Identity in the 1980s*, Llandysul: Gomer.

Rae, J. (1982) 'The decline and fall of English grammar', *Observer*, 7 February 1982.

Sampson, G. (1921) *English for the English*, London: English Association.

Schools Curriculum and Assessment Authority (SCAA) (1994) *English in the National Curriculum: Draft Proposals*, London: SCAA.

Chapter 3

Models of the 'good' teacher: defining and redefining teacher quality

Geoff Troman

INTRODUCTION

Over the past decade there has been a rapid and substantial restructuring of teachers' work in the primary school (Lawn 1988; Pollard *et al.* 1994; Woods 1995). This has received especial impetus since 1988 through central government initiatives which have introduced a mandated curriculum and assessment while also radically changing the funding and governance of schools. Being a teacher in the mid-1990s increasingly involves work which lies beyond the classroom (Campbell *et al.* 1992). It takes the forms of planning, administration, and supervision of colleagues' work, and of involvement in the external relations of marketing and work in and with the community. As workloads increase, intensification is experienced by teachers and the pressures of work erode time for reflection and leisure (Apple 1987; Hargreaves 1994). With this have come new conceptions of what 'good teaching' constitutes.

I shall trace developments in official policy on the primary school and in constructions of the 'good' teacher (Grace 1985; Lawn 1991; Woods 1996) from the 1978 Primary Survey, through policies of the early and mid-1980s, to policies of the early 1990s. I will suggest that during these three phases of policy development there has been continuity in the main policy themes relating to the personal and pedagogic attributes of the official version of the 'good' teacher. Changes, however, are evidenced in the greatly increased emphasis which is being placed upon the technical competences that facilitate the administrative and management aspects of the primary teacher's work. This changing emphasis constitutes a redefinition of the primary teacher's role in order to act as the main agent in the implementation of the restructured work of the National Curriculum, assessment and testing arrangements. I begin with the influential 1978 Primary Survey.

'GOOD TEACHING' IN 1978

The impact which the document *Primary Education in England* (HMI 1978) had on education policy and official constructions of teacher quality and the 'good' teacher was considerable. Lee and Fitz (1994) have argued that it was (together with the Secondary Survey of 1979) the policy progenitor of a National Curriculum. From a survey of 542 schools in England, Her Majesty's Inspectorate (HMI) noted that there were inconsistencies in curriculum coverage and an unacceptable variation in the 'quality' of teaching and the 'standards' which were being achieved by the schools (Richards 1987). Of all the factors HMI found to be associated with high standards they viewed three as being particularly significant – high levels of matching, good differentiation and the subject expertise of the teacher. Match is defined by HMI as the 'relationship between the standard of work children in the group were doing and that which they were considered by HMI to be capable of doing in each subject' (p. 80, para. 6.2). The closely related concept of differentiation is not defined by HMI, but seems to refer to teachers meeting the needs of the full ability range by 'providing children with learning experiences which take due account of their varying characteristics and yet which are guided by a common set of principles' (Richards 1987: 191). Teacher's subject expertise refers to their knowledge, qualifications and teaching experience in a curriculum subject and the quality of their teaching of that subject. HMI claimed these three factors interrelated in the production of high levels of match and superior pupil achievement in some areas of the primary curriculum (HMI 1978: 96, para. 7.34).

These findings led HMI to advocate posts of special responsibility for subjects. Educational standards in the primary school were to be raised through improving match through subject teaching, raising teachers' subject knowledge and making individual subject specialist knowledge available to colleagues. The teachers with special curricular responsibilites were to work with heads and be responsible for curriculum coverage in the school; producing programmes of work in terms of subjects; and being able to use appropriate pedagogic strategies to help children learn the subjects (HMI 1978: 36, para. 4.1).

In stressing the importance of the teachers with special curricular responsibility, HMI were not merely endorsing the views expressed in the Plowden Report (CACE 1967) and Bullock Report (DES 1975) or anticipating a main finding of the Cockroft Report (DES 1982). They seemed to be going beyond them (see Webb 1994). This is evident in their stance towards the generalist class teacher system, for while seeing its benefits (pp. 117–18) HMI favoured an organization in which subject specialists teach their specialism and pass on their expertise to colleagues (p. 118). This system is necessary, they claim owing to the demands of a broad subject-based curriculum. They also see it involving the whole staff:

> where the staff is eight or more strong, it may be possible to provide the
> necessary range and level of specialisation from within the staff, especially

if this requirement is taken into account when teaching appointments are made.

(HMI 1978: 119, para. 8.48)

The posts of special responsibility quite often did not involve increased salaries, status or even the allocation of non-contact time in which to complete the non-teaching managerial and administrative aspects of the role. HMI, while not problematizing the financing of primary education and its traditionally poor funding by comparison with secondary schools, advocated schools being flexible in experimenting in ways (including curriculum-led staffing policies) that would release post holders from their classes to work with colleagues.

The authors of the Primary Survey, in suggesting that all teachers could and should have some curriculum responsibility, created an image of the 'good' teacher which conforms closely to their description of the subject specialist post holder (see Campbell 1990: 122). The model of the 'good' teacher which emerges is one which possesses the personal characteristics which will facilitate the teacher not only in engaging in a more precise pedagogy involving concepts and procedures such as 'match', 'differentiation' and knowledge of children's learning but in writing programmes of study, sharing subject expertise with colleagues, working co-operatively with them and taking some responsibility for their training and supervision.

THE DEVELOPMENT OF THE 'GOOD' TEACHER IN THE 1980s

In the aftermath of the Primary Survey further policy prescriptions constructed further images of the 'good' teacher, each strongly influenced by ideas of teacher quality and 'good' practice which seem derived from the 1978 Survey report. What views, then, did the policy documents present? I shall concentrate on two of the more important.

'Teaching Quality'

Teaching Quality (DES 1983), a White Paper on teacher training, continued with the promotion of the view of the 'good' teacher which originated in the 1978 Survey. It focused strongly on issues surrounding match, subject specialism and teacher quality. *Teaching Quality* took HMI's claims about the positive relationship between subject specialism, match and higher pupil achievement in order to mount an argument that standards could be increased by matching the training of intending teachers to the work they would do (DES 1983: 8–12). This meant that, in the official view, the 'good' primary teacher would be a subject specialist who had a sound preparation in that subject either as an undergraduate or in initial teacher training. This recommendation was later incorporated in criteria for teacher education which stipulated which degree subjects were relevant to the primary curriculum and expanded the time allocation devoted to subject study in PGCE and B.Ed. courses (DES 1984). *Teaching Quality* quoted HMI's *The New Teacher in School* (HMI 1982) to state that they 'found that the personal qualities of the teachers were in many cases the decisive factor in their effectiveness'.

However, they returned to and reinforced their message on match, both in the sense of match between teachers' subject knowledge with subject taught and with the match of task to the child. In inspections HMI had found that in 'a quarter of primary school lessons seen teachers showed signs of insecurity in the subject being taught' and consequently this had an adverse effect on childrens' learning (DES 1983: 8, para. 27). In *Teaching Quality* the 'good' teacher is constructed as follows:

> Good teachers need to have a mastery of the subject knowledge they teach and the professional skills needed to teach it to children of different ages, abilities, aptitudes and backgrounds. But they also need those skills which are necessary for the effective performance of their role outside the classroom in the social and corporate life of the school, and in relationship to parents and the community.
>
> (DES 1983: 8, para. 23)

The White Paper recognized the complexity of the primary teacher's role and, like the 1978 Survey, recommended the expansion of the subject specialist consultant role as a solution to the implementation of a broad curriculum:

> The Government believe that all primary teachers should be equipped to take a particular responsibility for one aspect of the curriculum (such as science, mathematics or music), to act as a consultant to their colleagues on that aspect and, where appropriate, to teach it to classes other than their own.
>
> (DES 1983: 10, para. 33)

These recommendations, of course, referred to the academic and professional preparation of intending teachers. The authors did recognize, however, that there would be teachers already employed in schools who may be incapable (owing to their personal qualities or initial training) of adapting to new demands and a rapidly changing scene of restructured work. The employers who were charged with the introduction of the radical changes were alerted to the importance of recruitment and the 'need to inject new blood' (p. 24, para. 78) into the system. The 'good' teachers were to have the traditional skills and qualities of the primary teacher but also subject specialist and management potential to act as curriculum leaders in 'specialised roles'.

However, it was recommended that, where, despite in-service training arrangements, teachers failed to maintain a satisfactory level of performance, employers must, in the interest of the pupils, 'use procedures for dismissal'

(DES 1983: 25, para, 81). Here we have the policy implications of a model placing the emphasis on personal qualities, as opposed, for example, to competing explanations of variance in educational standards, such as the physical, economic and social context of teachers' work. Whereas the latter may have resource implications, the guarantor of 'good teaching' in the former becomes selection, training, and, where those measures have not worked, dismissal – a convenient strategy in a period of rapid changing work practices and falling rolls (see Hargreaves 1989; Woods 1990).

'Better Schools'

The White Paper *Better Schools* (DES 1985) was concerned with improving the quality of education, raising standards and getting the most from the resources which were put into schools. It sought to bring clarity to curriculum objectives (expressed as subjects), improve the effectiveness of assessment (to improve match), improve the effectiveness of teachers and the management of the teaching force, and to reform the governance of schools by increasing the involvement of parents and governors (DES 1985). Evidence was provided to indicate that three-quarters of primary and middle schools were weak in planning and implementation, that many schools did not have school policies, and, where they did, they did not influence the daily work of teachers. Further, schools were teaching a narrow curriculum which, although concentrating on basic subjects, did not teach them effectively enough (Thomas 1990: 97). The White Paper's solutions lay in the tighter management of the teacher workforce through increasing the management strategies of evaluation, appraisal and strategic planning. It saw the subject consultant's role as vital in these processes and again stressed that more use should be made of subject consultants. It was regretted that even when they were appointed:

> it is unusual for them to be given time, the status and encouragement to enable them to prepare and offer support to their colleagues and to exert the necessary influence on the whole curriculum of the school.
>
> (cited in Thomas 1990: 98)

In the continuous quest to increase educational standards, these documents advocated a wide subject-based curriculum with subject teaching and high levels of match. The teachers needed to implement this in the primary schools were seen to require not only the personal qualities of the traditional primary school generalist class teacher, but also subject expertise. This would not only enhance their own teaching, by improving match, but, through collaborative work, support and develop the subject teaching of colleagues in the school. Herein, arguably, lie the origins of the construction of the official 'good' teacher as a teacher-manager. In this view educational improvement would involve redeployment of the teaching force in a school and new measures to ensure the increased effectiveness of its management. Thus, there was increasing faith in new modes of managing teachers' work as a means of introducing reform. This was to have greater significance following the Education Reform Act of 1988.

THE 'GOOD' TEACHER IN THE AGE OF THE 1988 EDUCATION REFORM ACT

The introduction of a legislated subject-based curriculum raised many acute issues in the primary school concerning its implementation (Alexander 1994). The policies of the early 1990s were largely concerned with attempts to provide solutions to these problems. In these, the reconstructed model of the 'good teacher' took further shape. Its character and significance can be discerned in three key documents.

1.   Curriculum Organisation and Classroom Practice in Primary Schools: A Discussion Paper (DES 1992)

In 1992, Robin Alexander (Professor of Primary Education, University of Leeds), Jim Rose (Chief Inspector, HMI) and Chris Woodhead (Chief Executive, National Curriculum Council) were commissioned by the Secretary of State for Education 'to review available evidence about the delivery of education in primary schools' and 'to make recommendations about curriculum organisation, teaching methods and classroom practice appropriate for the successful implementation of the National Curriculum, particularly at Key Stage 2' (DES 1992: 5, para. 1). Though the ostensible status of the resulting document was that of a 'discussion paper', many saw it as a more hard-edged report. It certainly made a dramatic impact (see Woods and Wenham 1995).

The authors acknowledged that many primary teachers were experiencing difficulties in implementing the National Curriculum, particularly in Key Stage 2 with the prodigious content of the nine-subject curriculum. In places, they suggested that the disruption and restructuring caused by the reforms may be contributing to the teachers' difficulties (p. 11 paras. 27 and 28); or that it was the Orders themselves (p. 36, para. 129), or the low level of funding in primary by comparison with secondary schools that was the source of the problem (p. 5, para. 4). More space, however, was devoted to issues surrounding teacher competences, staff deployment and management of the teacher workforce. Primary teachers were seen to profess a dogma (i.e progressivism) which, in the opinion of the authors, was directly associated with mediocre practice (p. 9, para. 20) and an impediment to introducing 'the new procedures' (p. 15, para. 43). The authors used the concepts of the 1978 Survey such as match (p. 32) and teacher subject expertise (renamed as curricular expertise on p. 25). They also noted, as HMI (1978) had done, what they saw as a positive relationship between the variables of match, teachers' subject expertise and teaching quality:

> Our own view is that subject knowledge is a critical factor at every point in the teaching process: in planning, assessing, and diagnosing, task setting, questioning, explaining and giving feedback. . . . The introduction of the National Curriculum with its statutory demands has brought the question sharply into focus, but HMI reports since the seventies point to the close relationship which exists between the knowledge which the teacher possesses and the quality of his/her teaching.
>
> (DES 1992: 25, paras. 77 and 78)

The role of the subject specialist (now referred to as curriculum co-ordinator in the discussion paper), in implementing a subject-based curriculum which was increasingly proving to be unmanageable, was also recognized:

> The idea of the curriculum co-ordinator was developed to try to ensure that a school could make maximum use of the collective subject strength of its staff. The idea was subsequently built into initial training courses through the Secretary of State's 1984 and 1989 accreditation criteria.[1]
>
> (p. 25, para. 78)

Prescriptions were provided by the authors in the form of alternative models of staff deployment and the curriculum co-ordinator (pp. 42–5); also in listings of teacher knowledge, skills and competences necessary for raising educational standards (pp. 47–8, para.159). They include those skills to enable high levels of matching and efficient subject teaching (pp. 37–41).

The model of the 'good' teacher which emerges from this document is one not only having the qualities to facilitate work in classrooms but also having managerial competences. Here, the discussion document goes beyond the largely classroom focus of the 1978 survey and reconstructs the 'good' teacher as teacher-manager. Given the subject basis of the National Curriculum, and the traditional curriculum organization and staff deployment in the primary school (Alexander, 1984), the ideal successful implementation requires that all generalist teachers not only have specialist knowledge of nine subjects but can also teach them. The managerial task for all primary schools, therefore, is to attempt to get all teachers to the stage where they can do this. Alternatives like secondary school subject specialist teaching involving the rotation of children or teachers is administratively difficult, only works in large schools and is relatively uncommon in the primary school. The authors of the discussion document suggested that much greater flexibility was needed in how teaching roles were conceived and suggested 'four broad teaching roles':

> The *Generalist* who teaches most or all of the curriculum, probably specialising in age-range rather than subject, and does not profess specialist subject knowledge for consultancy.

The *Generalist/Consultant* who combines a generalist role in part of the curriculum with cross-school coordination, advice and support in one or more subjects.

The *Semi-Specialist* who teaches his/her subject, but who also has a generalist and or consultancy role.

The *Specialist* who teaches his/her subject full-time (as in the case of music in some primary schools).

(DES 1992: 43, para. 146)

As the first of these roles had been associated with the difficulties the authors were investigating, and the last had been largely ruled out (owing to the reasons given above), the discussion paper seemed to be promoting the flexibility of the Generalist/Consultant and Semi-Specialist roles as being most suitable for implementing the subject-based curriculum. However, the authors give only partial acknowledgement (pp. 47–8, para. 159) to the idea that supporting subject expertise for generalist teachers, can involve the subject co-ordinator in the management tasks of joint school policy formulation with colleagues; collaborative planning and decision making with colleagues; interpretation of national policy; in-service training of colleagues; organization of resources; observation of colleagues' teaching; having colleagues observe the subject co-ordinator; being responsible for teacher appraisal; supervising the work of other colleagues; providing consultancy; being responsible for standards of achievement in their subject throughout the school; keeping up to date with developments in their subject; undertaking curriculum review and monitoring; communicating aims and means to governors, parents and the community; liaising with other schools, e.g. cluster schools and secondary schools; participating in school-based schemes of initial teacher training; and assuming responsibility for the ordering, allocation and maintenance of stock and equipment for the subject. Given that in large schools each teacher will probably have a curriculum subject responsibility (not necessarily with an allowance) and in small schools may have two or three, then most teachers in the educational system will have this kind of curriculum management responsibility in addition to their role as a classroom generalist teacher.

In this discussion paper, official views coincided with those of some of the educational establishment. Alexander, for example, had from the mid-1980s been advocating modes of practice, organization and staff deployment congruent with those promoted in the discussion paper, and had been signalling the dramatic changes in the primary teacher's role (Alexander 1984; 1992). The paper, though strongly critiqued by some (see Woods and Wenham, 1995), was warmly received by some prominent members of the academic research community who had done extensive work in primary schools (Bennett 1992; Campbell 1992; Simon 1992). The view of the 'good' teacher as the extended and collaborative professional also resonates with certain features of the 'good' teacher presented by some researchers in the teacher development tradition (for example, Nias *et al.* 1992).

The 1992 discussion paper represents an official and tightly specified re-definition of the competences possessed by the 'good' primary teacher. Gone are references to the vague and largely undefined teacher qualities that HMI referred to in its discussions of teacher effectiveness in its documents of the 1980s (Hargreaves 1989; Lee and Fitz 1994; Woods 1996). The extent to which this redefined model of teacher competence has impacted on the prac-tice of primary teachers will now be considered.

2.   Primary Matters: A discussion on teaching and learning in primary schools (OFSTED 1994)

Those members of HMI who remain within the Office for Standards in Education (OFSTED) continue with some of the traditional work of HMI, including providing reports to inform the policy formulation process. As part of this work HMI still carries out research (in the form of data gathering exercises) and the compilation of school inspection reports to produce national surveys of subjects or phases. This is a greatly reduced activity as there are much fewer inspectors to carry out this role. Nevertheless, HMI surveyed 49 primary schools in its 1994 *Primary Matters* investigation of curriculum orga-nization and classroom practice. Its focus was, as the 1992 discussion paper had been, the implementation of the National Curriculum in the primary school. The model it used to assess this quality was derived from the discus-sion paper (DES 1992). Indeed, *Primary Matters* is best understood as a continuation of that report (OFSTED 1994: 1, paras. 1–7). HMI, in collecting data for its assessment of teaching quality, utilizes the view of the 'good' teacher found in the 1992 report, and operationalizes the prescriptive model of what 'good' teaching and the 'good' teacher is. Throughout its research, HMI seeks to compare the reality of schooling (as it observes it in its inspections and surveys) with the criteria which emerge from the discus-sion paper.

Like the 1993 OFSTED report on the implementation of the National Curriculum, the authors of *Primary Matters* found some 'benefits accruing from the introduction of the National Curriculum in primary schools', but also 'highlighted some serious weaknesses stemming from a mismatch between the National Curriculum, its assessment and the capabilities of primary schools and teachers (OFSTED 1994: 1). Again the existing level of teacher compe-tences had proved inadequate to implement the National Curriculum. The reasons identified for this, the exact nature of teacher inadequacy, seemed very similar to those which were identified in the 1992 discussion document, despite other research evidence concerning the sheer unmanageability of the nine-subject curriculum (Campbell *et al.* 1992; Alexander 1994). In this respect HMI seemed to be utilizing pre-specifications of teacher quality derived from that document.

A leading area of improvement noted by HMI was the use of subject co-ordinators. However, some of the principal areas of teacher weakness identified amongst a significant minority of teachers included match (p. 3, para. 13); differentiation (p. 3, para. 12); subject knowledge and subject teaching expertise (p. 3, para. 17, p. 4, paras. 18, 19); inflexibility in the balance between topic work and subject teaching (p. 5, para. 26); teacher reluctance to engage in monitoring and evaluating the work of colleagues (p. 6, para. 30); and the management and supervision of teachers' work (p. 6, para. 29). It was these teachers, we must assume, who were seen to be responsible for the slow implementation of the National Curriculum and the persisting variation of educational standards within the system.

The authors of *Primary Matters* spend a large proportion of the report in rehearsing solutions to the failure to implement the National Curriculum more fully. If one cause of the problems had been poor curriculum management, then what they recommended was more and better management of teachers' work. The key to this was seen to be, as in the previous reports, to promote the importance of the management aspects of the role of the curriculum co-ordinators. These were renamed 'subject managers' because 'co-ordinators [was] too limited a description' (p. 9, para. 37), as it certainly was if all of the likely elements of the co-ordinator's role which emerged in the 1992 discussion paper were included in it. More management by head-teachers and subject managers was seen to be the way of achieving quality teaching, subject specialism, match and rising educational standards. The authors recommend that:

> Primary schools need to carry out an audit of the subject expertise of their teaching staff and create a climate in which teachers are able to develop and share their subject expertise, irrespective of whether they hold any formal responsibilites for the management of a subject. The headteacher's subject knowledge should be included in any appraisal of the expertise available and steps should be taken over time to match more closely subject responsibilities with the subject expertise available on the staff. Gaps in expertise should be remedied partly by the appointment of new staff, including newly qualified teachers, with specifically required subject knowledge, and partly building expertise from the existing complement of staff.
> (OFSTED 1994: 9 and 10, para. 41)

More effective curriculum management is recommended by the tight specification of the headteacher's curriculum management role. The 1992 discussion paper dismissed the idea that there was a tension between financial management and curriculum management and suggested to heads that their main job was managing the curriculum (DES 1992: 46, para. 152). *Primary Matters*, too, overlooks the head's likely exacting role in financial management. HMI specifies the areas of Co-ordination, Monitoring, Evaluation (including teacher appraisal), using the OFSTED Framework for Inspection, in order for heads to become the 'resident inspector'. In this respect the headteacher's role is specifically related to particular criteria, for example: 'evaluating the whole curriculum using the criteria of breadth, balance, continuity, progression, coherence and compliance with National Curriculum requirements' (OFSTED 1994: 8). Review, monitoring, evaluation, appraisal and curriculum audit are activities that HMI felt that the subject managers should be more involved in. However, it noted that many subject managers did not have non-contact time in which they could carry out these tasks, and also found reluctance on the part of some subject managers to assume responsibility for the review and monitoring of their colleagues' work (OFSTED 1994: 6, para. 31).

We thus have in *Primary Matters* a strengthening of the redefinition of teacher quality which was begun in the 1992 discussion paper. Being a 'good' teacher now means possessing pedagogic skills, but also being a 'good' subject manager, being able to introduce reform through co-operative working and being able to engage in the supervision, review and monitoring of colleagues' subject specialist work (Lawn 1988). This clear official definition of the 'good' teacher and the 'apparently technical production criteria of the codes' for their assessment makes possible the 'efficient' judgement of teacher quality through inspection (Grace 1985).

3.   The Handbook for the Inspection of Schools (OFSTED 1993)

Nowhere are definitions of teacher quality and the 'good' teacher more clearly and closely prescribed than in *The Handbook for the Inspection of Schools*. This document was produced by HMI initially in order to train the new inspectors of the privatized inspectorate and subsequently to be used as criteria with which to judge the quality of teachers and schools in the inspection process. As it is used for the inspection of schools at all stages, from the nursery school to the sixth form college, we must regard the definition of the 'good' teacher, which arises in this document, to be applicable to all phases.

Before the privatization of the inspectorate and the formation of OFSTED, HMI did not publish the criteria it used when inspecting schools. There was, then, some uncertainty about how exactly it judged schools and teachers (Abbot 1990). By contrast, OFSTED inspectors now use predetermined criteria, which are in the public domain, and take measures, for example, monitoring by HMI, to try and ensure both standardized inspection procedures are followed and judgements made. Since September 1994, every primary school in the state educational system is to be inspected every four years by the privatized inspectorate, using the OFSTED criteria contained within the Framework for Inspection.[2] In addition to inspecting the quality and standards of pupils' learning, personal development and behaviour, inspectors will also collect data, evaluate and report on much wider aspects of school life and organization, for example the subject specialist and generalist work of teachers not only in classrooms but in the 'wider' work of management and administration, the management of resources and in collaborative work (e.g. whole-school planning, co-ordination meetings, consultancy, INSET) with colleagues. All these are key elements of the restructured work of teachers. The inspection system, therefore, represents a direct mechanism for the monitoring of the work of teacher-managers in the reordered system.

Throughout the 'Framework' the words 'standards' and 'quality' occur frequently, and teaching and learning are to be judged in terms of them. Management is evaluated according to its 'efficiency' and 'effectiveness'. The 'Framework', too, shows consistency with previous policy documents in its prescriptions concerning subject specialism and aspects of pedagogy and organization concerned with match and differentiation. Evidence concerning teachers' subject specialist knowledge and teaching expertise is to be gathered by the inspectors, prior to inspection, in the form of teachers' professional biographies (including qualifications, training and previous experience). From this data, it is possible for the inspectors to calculate the degree of 'match' between teachers' subject qualifications and the actual subjects they teach and co-ordinate. Additionally, the inspectors compile data on this aspect of teachers' work through lesson observation and attendance at meetings where subject co-ordinators work with colleagues.

For 'Quality of Teaching' the criteria are the extent to which:

- teachers have clear objectives for their lessons;
- pupils are aware of these objectives;
- teachers have a secure command of the subject;
- lessons have suitable content;
- activities are well chosen to promote the learning of that content;
- activities are presented in ways that will engage and motivate and challenge all pupils, enabling them to make progress at a suitable pace.

(OFSTED 1993, Framework: 27)

Inspectors are instructed, when compiling the report, which is derived from the implementation of the above criteria that, amongst other things, they must comment on and provide an evaluation of:

the quality of teaching provided and its effects on the quality of learning and standards of pupils' achievements;

the range of teaching techniques used and their fitness of purpose;

teachers' knowledge of subjects;

the degree to which work is matched to pupils' attainments and abilities;

(OFSTED 1993: 27 and 28)

In making a judgement based on the evaluation criteria the inspectors are instructed to make:

> a judgement on the quality of teaching, including an assessment of the suitability of the methods chosen, the teacher's confidence and competence in handling the lesson, the extent to which work is suitably differentiated for the pupils in the class or group, and the effectiveness of classroom management.
>
> (OFSTED 1993, Guidance; Inspection Organisation: 14)

Detailed specification of quality in teaching is provided for each of the National Curriculum subjects in the 'Guidance: Inspection Schedule' in the form of pen sketches of typical teacher and pupil behaviours and activities in 'satisfactory' and 'unsatisfactory' lessons. The stated purpose of this section is to assist inspectors to reach judgements on standards and quality in teaching.

One section of the 'Framework' is devoted to criteria with which to judge the 'efficiency' and 'effectiveness' of financial, curriculum and personnel management. The criteria refer to the headteacher and senior management. In primary schools, senior managers are generally class teachers. Co-ordinators, too, are judged using management criteria, and, as argued earlier, most class teachers will probably be co-ordinators too. The inspectors evaluate teacher performance in the management aspects of their co-ordination role, for example how effectively they pass on their subject expertise to others. Judgements are made with respect to teacher performance in the whole-school work of planning, curriculum audit, review, monitoring, appraisal and evaluation.

Thus teacher quality is now defined in terms of technical competences as opposed to personal qualities. Indeed, the attributes that previously teachers may or may not have had, for example co-operativeness, are now, in official discourse, obligatory technical requirements of the job (Lawn 1988).

It is in the OFSTED criteria for inspection that earlier definitions of teacher quality assume their full significance. In a discussion about teachers' work in the late nineteenth century, Gerald Grace (1985) draws a striking comparison between the context and methods of the judgement of teachers in Victorian England and contemporary developments in the evaluation of teacher quality:

> There is a cutback of educational expenditure for State provided schooling. There is a growing emphasis upon tighter accountability; a required core curriculum and a concentration upon basics. The role and strength of the inspectorate is being reappraised and changes can be expected in the ideology of inspection at all levels. Both teacher training and the work of teachers in schools are to be subject to more surveillance and to the application of more specific criteria for the assessment and evaluation of competence. Perhaps most significant of all these are suggestions that

teacher deficiencies and the deficiencies of teacher education are at the heart of the 'education problem' today. Constructs of teacher competence are again high on the agenda as are principles and procedures for determining such competence.

(Grace 1985: 13)

CONCLUSION

Definitions of teacher quality and the 'good' teacher are social constructions and subject to change at different historical moments. I have suggested that this process can be seen in an analysis of official policy on teacher quality since the 1978 Primary Survey, and that the same themes in constructions of the 'good' teacher have been underpinned and strengthened in policy developments since the Education Reform Act 1988 as teachers' work becomes dominated by the implementation needs of measures such as the subject-based National Curriculum and the changed value context of schooling (Ball 1994). While some consistency was seen between policy themes in the 1978 Primary Survey and more recent policy, there has, I have argued, been an increasingly marked emphasis on teacher competences, technical skills and managerial attributes in official constructions of the 'good' teacher. This is evident in policy on the primary school and in the official criteria used to judge teacher quality. This increased 'codification' of teacher quality has led some (for example Grace 1985) to draw parallels with the last system of the strongest controls of the definition of the teacher and teachers' work, namely the Revised Code of the nineteenth century.

Official definitions of the 'good' teacher, however, are not uncontested. Those discussed here have been the subject of widespread critical attention (Sharples 1980; Cunningham 1988; Hargreaves 1989; Brehony 1990; Hammersley and Scarth 1993; Lee and Fitz 1994). Some, in particular, stress the absence of social and resource factors in official accounts which condition 'opportunities to teach' (Hargreaves 1989; Woods 1990). Brehony (1990) argues that it was the Committee for the Accreditation of Teacher Education (CATE) criteria (DES 1984; 1989) which ensured that courses would be approved only if they provided training for subject specialism and subject co-ordination roles that produced 'a model which corresponded more to that of a secondary teacher rather than to the previously existing one of the generalist primary school teacher' (p. 115). The OFSTED criteria of standards and quality in teaching which apply to pre-school, primary and secondary phases lend support to this view. Brehony suggests that for this and other reasons the idea of the primary school as a separate and special self-contained phase which was established in the Hadow Report (CCBE/1931) has been destroyed and the notion of the 'good' teacher that its recommendations entailed is under attack. Woods (1995) finds teachers whom he describes as 'creative teachers'. An element of their creativity is their commitment to constructivist theory and practice. In this view, teaching takes precedence over managerial tasks, and the learning of the pupils begins primarily with the constructed knowledge of the child as opposed to the established knowledge of the subject disciplines. Indeed the increased knowledge of teaching and learning, which would be involved in an empirical assessment of such concepts as match and differentiation (Richards 1987), may require conceptions of 'good' teaching which are closer to the ideas of 'reflective teaching' (Pollard and Tann 1987) or the 'teacher as researcher' (Stenhouse 1975).

The implementation of official models of 'good teaching' in schools and classrooms is by no means total. In fact, there appears to be a certain degree of negotiability for teachers in schools (Ball and Bowe 1992; Vulliamy and Webb 1993), though this, of course, may change as the work of OFSTED gathers pace. Pollard *et al.* (1994) found that the majority of teachers in their national study viewed the increased managerial aspects of their role negatively. Hayes (1994) found some teachers, in his study of a primary school, to be reluctant to accept managerial responsibility because they viewed it as an extra burden which would reduce their effectiveness with their classes. Woods and Jeffrey (this volume) analyse the dilemmas that arise from the tension between the teachers' pedagogic and management roles and the human cost of this. Troman (1995) notes the development, in curriculum co-ordinators, of what appear to be multiple occupational identities. These are revealed in the perspectives of curriculum co-ordinators who are attempting to adapt to intensified work and the multiple and rapidly changing roles involved in management and teaching. Inevitably there will be spaces within schooling where contestation can occur. The teachers' successful national boycott of government testing in the early 1990s was an example of the reassertion of a mode of professionalism, involving models of the 'good' teacher and teacher quality which were at odds with those to be found in official policy.

Official versions of the 'good' teacher have been incorporated into initial teacher education. The criteria produced by CATE (DES 1984; 1989), considered to be a National Curriculum for teacher education, embody, Furlong (1992) argues, a technicist view of the teacher. Lee and Fitz (1994) claim that it has been derived from the recommendations of the 1978 Survey. New moves are now underway to further redefine the teacher and teacher quality as initial training moves to schools (Barton *et al.* 1994) and is to be controlled by the newly created Teacher Training Agency. The TTA will specify the school-based processes of training and the exit competences of the newly qualified teacher, while OFSTED monitors their implementation. It is in this context that we await future official definitions of the 'good' teacher.

NOTES

1 The requirement that all intending teachers complete a compulsory preparation for the role of curriculum co-ordinator during their training is an indication of how incorporated the image of the co-ordinator has become in official views of the 'good' teacher.
2 'The Framework for the Inspection of Schools' is one section of the *Handbook for the Inspection of Schools* (OFSTED 1993).

REFERENCES

Abbott, D. M. (1990) 'What do HMI look for?', *Education 3–13* 18(1).

Alexander, R. J. (1984) *Primary Teaching*, Eastbourne: Holt, Rinehart & Winston.

Alexander, R. J. (1992) *Policy and Practice in Primary Education*, London: Routledge.

Alexander, R. J. (1994) 'What primary curriculum? Dearing and beyond', *Education 3–13* 22(1): 24–35.

Apple, M. (1987) *Teachers and Texts*, London: Routledge & Kegan Paul.

Ball, S. J. (1994) *Education Reform: A Critical and Post-Structural Approach*, Buckingham: Open University Press.

Ball, S. J. and Bowe, R. (1992) 'Subject departments and the "implementation" of National Curriculum policy: an overview of the issues', *Journal of Curriculum Studies* 24(2): 97–115.

Barton, L., Barrett, E., Whitty, G., Miles, S. and Furlong, J. (1994) 'Teacher education and teacher professionalism in England: some emerging issues', *British Journal of Sociology of Education* 15(4): 529–43.

Bennett, N. (1992) 'Never mind the sophistry', *The Times Educational Supplement*, 14 February.

Brehony, K. J. (1990) 'Neither rhyme nor reason: primary schooling and the National Curriculum', in M. Flude and M. Hammer (eds) *The Education Reform Act 1988: Its Origins and Implications*, Basingstoke: Falmer.

Broadhead, P. (1987) 'A blueprint for the good teacher? The HMI/DES model of good primary practice', *British Journal of Educational Studies* 35(1): 57–72.

Campbell, R. J. (1990) 'Curriculum coordinators, the National Curriculum and the aims of primary education', in N. Proctor (ed.) *The Aims of Primary Education and the National Curriculum*, London: Falmer.

Campbell, R. J. (1992) Letter to *Guardian*, 19 February.

Campbell, R. J., Evans, L. St. J. Neill, S. R. and Packwood, A. (1992) 'The impact of educational reform on infant teachers' work and their perceptions of work', paper presented to the Centre for Educational Development, Appraisal and Research Conference, Warwick, April.

Central Advisory Council for Education (England) (1967) *Children and their Primary Schools*, (The Plowden Report), London: HMSO.

Consultative Committee of the Board of Education (1931) *The Primary School* (The Hadow Report), London: HMSO.

Cunningham, P. (1988) *Curriculum Change in the Primary School Since 1945*, Lewes: Falmer.

Department of Education and Science (1975) *A Language for Life* (The Bullock Report), London: HMSO.

Department of Education and Science (1982) *Mathematics Counts* (The Cockroft Report), London: HMSO.

Department of Education and Science (1983) *Teaching Quality*, Cmnd 8836, London: HMSO.

Department of Education and Science (1984) Circular 3/84 *Initial Teacher Training: approval of courses*, London: HMSO.

Department of Education and Science (1985) *Better Schools*, Cmnd 9469, London: HMSO.

Department of Education and Science (1989) *Future Arrangements for the Accreditation of Courses of Initial Teacher Training: A Consultation Document*, London: HMSO.

Department of Education and Science (1992) *Curriculum Organisation and Classroom Practice in Primary Schools: A Discussion Paper*, London: DES Information Branch.

Furlong, J. (1992) 'Reconstructing professionalism: ideological struggle in initial teacher education', in M. Arnot and L. Barton (eds) *Voicing Concerns: Sociological Perspectives on Contemporary Education Reform*, Wallingford: Triangle.

Grace, G. (1985) 'Judging teachers: the social and political contexts of teacher evaluation', *British Journal of Sociology of Education* 6(1): 3–16.

Hammersley, M. and Scarth, J. (1993) 'Beware of wise men bearing gifts: a case study in the misuse of educational research', in P. Gomm and P. Woods (eds) *Educational Research in Action*, London: Paul Chapman.

Hargreaves, A. (1989) *Curriculum and Assessment Reform*, Milton Keynes: Open University Press.

Hargreaves, A. (1994) *Changing Teachers, Changing Times: Teachers' Work and Culture in the Postmodern World*, London: Cassell.

Hayes, D. (1994) 'Teachers' involvement in decision making: a case study of a primary school at a time of rapid change', unpublished Ph.D. thesis, University of Plymouth.

Her Majesty's Inspectorate (1978) *Primary Education in England: A Survey by HM Inspectors of Schools*, London: HMSO.

Her Majesty's Inspectorate (1979) *Aspects of Secondary Education in England: A Survey by HM Inspectors of Schools*, London: HMSO.

Her Majesty's Inspectorate (1982) *The New Teacher in School*, London: HMSO.

Lawn, M. (1988) 'Skill in school work: work relations in the primary school', in J. Ozga (ed.) *Schoolwork: Approaches to the Labour Process of Teaching*, Milton Keynes: Open University Press.

Lawn, M. (1991) 'Social constructions of quality in teaching', in G. Grace and M. Lawn (eds) *Teacher Supply and Teacher Quality: Issues for the 1990s*, Clevedon: Multilingual Matters.

Lee, J. and Fitz, J. (1994) 'Inspecting for improvement: HMI and curriculum development in England and Wales', paper presented at the American Educational Research Association Annual Meeting, New Orleans.

Nias, J., Southworth, G. and Campbell, P. (1992) *Whole School Curriculum Development in the Primary School*, London: Falmer Press.

OFSTED (1993) *The Handbook for the Inspection of Schools*, London: HMSO.

OFSTED (1994) *Primary Matters: A Discussion on Teaching and Learning in Primary Schools*, London: OFSTED Publications.

Pollard, A., Broadfoot, P., Croll, P., Osborn, M. and Abbot, D. (1994) *Changing English Primary Schools: The Impact of the Education Reform Act at Key Stage One*, London: Cassell.

Pollard, A. and Tann, S. (1987) *Reflective Teaching in the Primary School: A Handbook for the Classroom*, London: Cassell.

Richards, C. (1987) 'Primary education in England: an analysis of some recent issues and developments', in S. Delamont (ed.) *The Primary School Teacher*, London: Falmer.

Sharples, D. (1980) 'Teacher development; pre- and in-service education', in C. Richards (ed.) *Primary Education: Issues for the Eighties*, London: A & C Black.

Simon, B. (1992) Review article, *The Curriculum Journal* 3(1).

Stenhouse, L. (1975) *An Introduction to Curriculum Research and Development*, London: Heinemann.

Thomas, N. (1990) *Primary Education from Plowden to the 1990s*, Basingstoke: Falmer.

Troman, G. (1995) 'The rise of the "new" professionals; the restructuring of work and occupational identities in the primary school', paper presented at the Centre for Sociology and Social Research Seminar, The Open University, March.

Vulliamy, G. and Webb, R. (1993) 'Progressive education and the National Curriculum: findings from a global education research project', *Educational Review* 45(1): 21–41.

Webb, R. (1994) *After the Deluge: Changing Roles and Responsibilities in the Primary School*, London: Association of Teachers and Lecturers Publications.

Woods, P. (1990) *Teacher Skills and Strategies*, Lewes: Falmer.

Woods, P. (1995) *Creative Teachers in Primary Schools*, Buckingham: The Open University Press.

Woods, P. (1996) Block 3 Unit 2 'Teaching', in Course EU208 *Exploring Educational Issues*, Buckingham: The Open University Press.

Woods, P. and Jeffrey, R. (1996) 'A new professional discourse? Adjusting to managerialism', in P. Woods, (ed.) *Contemporary Issues in Teaching and Learning*, London: Routledge.

Woods, P. and Wenham, P. (1995) 'Politics and pedagogy: a case study in appropriation', *Journal of Education Policy* 10(2): 119–41.

Chapter 4

A new professional discourse?
Adjusting to managerialism

Peter Woods and Robert Jeffrey

A MANAGERIALIST DISCOURSE

The last ten years have seen a concerted and determined attempt by central government to transform the school as a workplace and teachers as a workforce. Intensification has increased workloads, expanded bureaucracy, colonized teachers' time and space, reduced flexibility and separated the conceptualization of policy (made by others) from its execution (by teachers) (Apple 1986; Hargreaves 1994). The introduction of the market ideology into education has brought a new emphasis upon managerialism. Teachers' work is being more closely regulated, with a strong emphasis on accountability to the consumers – school managers, governors and parents. The 'social market' model of professional learning sees teachers as products of a training system closely geared to pre-specified outcomes and the behaviours that lead to them (Aspland and Brown 1993). New divisions have opened up among practitioners between managers and teachers. Ball (1994: 64) observes that

> the reinscription of power relations in education attempted by the ERA offers the potential of a massive over-determination of the work of teaching. In this heterotopia of reform the relationships of teachers with their significant others are changed and confused; the teacher as person and professional is both scapegoat and victim. Professionality is replaced by accountability; collegiality by costing and surveillance.

Inglis (1989) argues that managerialism retains power by suppressing moral and political argument and turns responsibility and accountability into functions of state surveillance. There is also a restructuring of teachers' skills in process, with deskilling in some areas, though enskilling in others. Ball (1990: 98) forecast that 'teachers will have less responsibility for deciding what they do, where and how', though he also noted that 'grand intentions are not always realized in practice and may actually be contradicted'. With these changes has come a shift away from the styles of teacher professionalism that have held for much of the century – those of either 'licensed' or 'regulated autonomy' (Dale 1989) – towards a new form based on a market-driven technical-rationalist ideology (Hatcher 1994). Primary teachers have thus been faced with a new form of role conflict – between their role as relatively autonomous, creative teachers and their new role as managers of a new curriculum system. The new role requires a considerable amount of administration relating to plans, assessment and record keeping. The introduction of limited devolved budgets also means teachers have to spend more time managing their school. Since primary schools typically have a small number of highly collaborative staff, this means that many teachers are involved in all kinds of decision-taking in the school.

The changes have been framed within a new legitimizing discourse involving a whole new thesaurus of terms and everyday practices, and the key concepts of choice, accountability and quality. Maguire and Ball (1994: 11–12) argue, following Foucault, that

a discourse is only ever partial, is only one stance among many variants. However, some bases for interpretation or definition become more dominant than others; power and knowledge are redistributed. Some voices, some modes of articulation and forms of association are rendered silent. Certain possibilities are offered and others are closed down, some ways of thinking are supported and empowered, others are inhibited. Actors are positioned and constructed differently within different discourses, different values and ends and purposes are operant within different discourses. The task then of the progressive educator is to reappropriate key discourses, to deconstruct dominant meanings and reassert more democratic, participatory and socially just meanings [cf. Epstein 1993].

There are some studies that suggest this can be, and is, done. Ball and Bowe (1992), for example, argue that the Education Reform Act in one respect is 'another micro-political resource for teachers, LEAs and parents to interpret, re-interpret and apply to their particular contexts' (p. 100), and that

it is in the micropolitical processes of the schools that we begin to see not only the limitations and possibilities state policy places on schools, but equally, the limits and possibilities practitioners place on the capacity of the state to reach into the daily lives of the schools.

(p. 101)

Fitz (1994: 60) comments that ' "implementation" is rendered as a complex, creative, and important "moment" in the cycle, in which practitioners are conceptualized as meaningfully interpreting, rather than simply executing, policy which has been "handed down" '. Fitz points out that the 1988 Education Reform Act is 'as much about restructuring institutions – defining new goals, delineating fields of operation and reconstituting membership of the policy community – as it is about promulgating substantive educational policies' (ibid.). Within this area of restructuring there appear to be a range of possible adaptations (Simkins *et al.* 1992; Woods 1995). Hatcher (1994:

49) observes that 'the restructuring of teachers' skills, and the extent to which teachers are retaining some control over conception as well as execution, is a matter for detailed empirical work'. He also feels that 'the struggle to create this new school culture takes place on the terrain of teachers' professionalism' (p. 55).

It is in that area that we concentrate. We draw on our research into 'creative teaching' (see Woods and Jeffrey 1996). Here, we focus on a group of teachers from two London primary schools who seemed to epitomize the 'creative' criteria – they were innovative, sought ownership of the knowledge involved in their teaching (and pupil ownership of knowledge involved in their learning), and control of pedagogical processes. We might expect such teachers to be well to the fore in the kind of struggle that Hatcher depicts. Data collection involved observation of their teaching over a two-year period, three tape-recorded interviews with each, a number of more informal discussions, taped discussions with their pupils, and documentary and photographic analysis.

We focus on the tension felt by teachers between their basic values, encapsulated in the role of 'creative teaching', and those of the new managerialist role. The substance of this tension can be summed up in terms of 'going with the flow' against 'getting done' (Apple 1986). 'Getting done' is characteristic of bureaucratic systems – an objectives-led approach, with the emphasis on outcomes and monitoring, which focuses attention on getting the prescribed task finished and records completed regardless of what other opportunities for learning occur during its course. 'Going with the flow' – a term that encapsulates our teachers' approach – puts the emphasis on process, and involves intuition, spontaneity, 'tacit knowledge', enthusiasm and fun. In speaking about the changes, teachers employ a professional discourse which is both a way of expressing their concerns and a way of handling them. It is a restatement of their values. In this way, the events of the past few years have been an opportunity – for re-examination, clearer exposition and evaluation of the practical application of those values – as well as a crisis. We shall examine the main features and characteristics of this discourse, together with teachers' experience of the new managerialism. Currently the two discourses sit side by side in their daily lives. There is a sense of struggle and conflict, of oppression and loss; but also of hope and resolution, and creative adaptation as these teachers feel their way towards a new professional discourse within which they can contextualize the changes ushered in by the 1988 Act.

Here, we consider three prominent areas of conflict suggested by our research focusing on 1) teaching approach; 2) the use of time; and 3) accountability. In each case, we note the pressures, but also the progressive adaptations, as far as they go, through which the teachers seek to re-establish their ownership and control of their own teaching. We conclude by examining the price paid for their endeavours – high levels of stress and guilt – but a continuing resolve.

TEACHING APPROACH

The pressure for 'getting done'

Our teachers, like others reported elsewhere (for example, Campbell and Neill 1994; Pollard *et al.* 1994), were in favour of balance. They welcomed a National Curriculum in principle, but were concerned at the amount of content, and the effects managing its implementation would have on their kind of teaching. Thea, for example, recognized the need for structure and progression, things that were not well in evidence before 1988, but felt things had got out of balance:

> There are certain things that you have to get done that these children have to cover during the course of their time with you. So that pressure has taken away a lot of what I consider to be our imaginative (role), the spon-taneous side of teaching and lighting a spark in children. You still do it. The National Curriculum has many good things to it as well, but you can't organise your topic in quite the same way as you could before because you have to bear in mind all the attainment targets.

Ends had come to predominate over processes. Peter, a deputy head, thought the National Curriculum

> certainly has cut down opportunities for taking an idea and developing it. I think I have more now in mind where I want to end up now in terms of ends and I'm not sure that's altogether healthy. It's certainly not healthy to say we can go anywhere – you've got to set boundaries and a sense of what is worth pursuing but much more these days I get the feeling that if a child offers something that doesn't actually fit into my National Curriculum target, then I'm more likely to say, 'yes, you've got a good idea there, it's worth pursuing but we haven't actually got the time now.'

Teachers were also torn between their concerns to provide a broad and balanced curriculum and their responsibilities towards providing children with basic language, literacy and numeric skills.

> At this age, once they've got the enthusiasm for something that's the way I like to work. Within that, one's doing one's basics, a lot of language work, literacy, and I just think we should be specialists in teaching literacy and numeracy. The National Curriculum's ignoring the fact that primary teachers are specialists in literacy and numeracy and that on top of that, we show a real interest in project learning to include history, geography, science, technology. As soon as you try to teach with the specialisms of a secondary school, what's going to happen is that you're not going to have any literacy and numeracy taught because it's not like a forty-five minute or a half hour secondary English lesson. You're teaching children how to read and write. It can be an all day process going through that with young

children. . . . There's a lot of work to be done with them, and it's not just something you do in between doing other stuff, it's something you do all the time with them whatever framework you use and you try to make that as interesting as possible and as creative as possible.

(Wendy)

Reaffirmation of 'going with the flow'

Even in the above, it is possible to detect signs of a professional discourse attempting to make sense of, and to contest, the new order. There is a recognition of the need for balance, a reflective analysis of what is involved, and a reasoned resistance. Above all, however, there is a reaffirmation of the principles in which they believe, and the kind of practice which those principles imply, that is, 'going with the flow'.

'Going with the flow' is important to our teachers for four main reasons. First, spontaneity affects the atmosphere of the classroom and the enthusiasm of child and teacher alike. As Laura said,

> If there's something there that children are really, really enthusiastically interested in, it would be so silly to ignore it. Because the motivation's there. It's already made, the eagerness, the drive to look at something, to find out about something. You don't have to stimulate it, you haven't got to set it out. It's a gift. . . . It's the energy and the curiosity, the desire to know is satisfying so they feel good about it, that they've asked the question and answered it and it stems from their need to know, and it's like saying 'Yes, what you're thinking is important, let's explore it'. It's not saying 'no, not now dear, we've got to do this, much more important, could you pay attention please' and I start complaining 'cos they're not listening.

Second, 'going with the flow' enhances the learning process for *all* children. Particular pupils need more help and assistance. Freda argues that a 'one best way' system is not effective for these children. She thinks, 'We need to ease up on them a bit and look at where they are and try to give them what's appropriate for where they are.' Theresa supports this approach in generating what she calls her 'hidden curriculum' – teaching people to be people;

> Because basically the hidden curriculum has got to do with not being too organised. . . . It's about letting go of that and letting things sort of drift. It's kind of knowing how much to let it slip. So I would have to think very much about the real quantities and the real actualities of what I do there. I have let a lot of situations ride and roll – like good referees in football matches.

Third, 'going with the flow' encourages pupil control. Marilyn explained:

I was thinking about this week's close observation art and how I got children to say how they did it, how they achieved it to the rest of the class. They're taking part in the instruction really. They're taking a role in teaching themselves, they've learnt something and they can pass it on to the rest. There's a huge value for them to know that they have that value and that you've got children who are talented in different areas. It does motivate them 'cos they will look at that and they will go away and try that or they will try another angle on that.

Fourth, 'going with the flow' enables teachers to concentrate on the learning rather than being dominated by the monitoring of a system. Terrie commented,

In times gone by you could probably be more open to just taking off at a tangent if the children were interested. Somebody brings something from home and you could develop so much around that.

Theresa also rued the threatened loss of

those spontaneous topics that you used to be able to have, say if children brought something in. . . . You could give it a certain amount of time . . . the children spurring you on, rather than you saying, 'Well, this is the way it is.'

There is an acknowledgement of threat here, and almost nostalgia for lost times. Things have certainly changed. But the educational reasons for 'going with the flow', the gains to the child, the thrill and excitement of learning at such moments stay with them. Their convictions remain. They stay devoted to the principles. In a way, the Education Reform Act might be regarded as a natural experiment, in which their values and practice have been put to the test. They have had to search their consciences, in the light not only of political rhetoric, but also of academic research, where Alexander (1992), for example, has raised questions about ostensibly child-centred practice, which, in his research, 'paid rather more attention to teachers and classrooms than to children's learning' (p. 143). There is ample testimony here to their reasons for, at times, 'going with the flow', and they are couched largely in terms of pupils' learning.

The tension between 'going with the flow' and 'getting done' is not a new one for primary teachers. They are constantly juggling a great number of demands upon both their time and expertise. However, the balance between these two demands seems to have shifted radically, and particularly with the inroads being made on teachers' time and space. 'Going with the flow' requires some flexible time and a considerable degree of mental space – time to be with children, to teach, to potter, to discuss with colleagues, to read, to listen; space to reflect, to think, and to have ideas. However, both time and space have been squeezed in the inexorable concern to 'get things done'.

THE USE OF TIME

Pressure on time

As Hargreaves (1994: 95) points out, time is a principal structurant of teachers' work, and is, in turn, structured by it. Time is a different element in 'going with the flow' than in 'getting done'. In the former, it is more flexible, multi-dimensional, people-oriented; teachers and pupils *make* time, and above all, have a sense of ownership and control of it. In the latter, it is more objective, task-oriented, compartmentalized, unidimensional, rationed in segments, controlled by others (see Woods 1993: 147–8, for further discussion). Hargreaves (1994) claims that teachers' time, which teachers previously owned and controlled, is becoming colonized by others. How much time teachers have in which to do their work is an issue, but even more important is the use to which it is put and who controls it.

Teachers employed a number of strategies in coping with the attempted 'colonization'. We noted the following:

Distancing

There were considerable pressures on teachers' time, first, in terms of sheer amount of work. Theresa, expressing the difference between technicians and professionals, argued that the National Curriculum could provide an easy way out for some teachers; but she distances herself from this adaptation, reaffirming her own professional identity, and incurring in consequence a vastly increased workload:

> It's because you've got a set parcel, haven't you? If somebody tells you what to do it's much easier than if you've got to think for yourself. Someone who has not got decisions, somebody who has not got choices to make, that's fine. The lazy teacher can get through a certain amount just as long as she satisfies the National Curriculum. The good teacher spends an awful lot of time on development, tension from the National Curriculum is undermining. They do three times as much work, fine OK. If you teach the National Curriculum you don't have to worry that much. You've cut your work in half. If you're a good teacher you're teaching the National Curriculum *and* what you were teaching before.

The perception of alternatives

Apart from the sheer load, there was a question of quality. As with Cockburn (1994: 377), our teachers found it difficult to achieve 'high quality teacher time working with their pupils'. Campbell (1993: 220) has shown that nearly 10 per cent of teachers' time is 'evaporated time', taken up by activities such as moving pupils around and supervision. However, the main threat to quality in the teachers' opinion was the intrusion of bureaucracy upon teaching. Judy expresses it here in describing how she has to fill in detailed records to obtain some government funding for new books for the school. The colonization is clear, but it is prefaced by the comment that there has to be a better way. The hard-edged intrusion upon Laura's time is thus morally undermined.

> It makes you think there's got to be another way of being alive, and of working ... where actually you know what you're doing isn't the right thing to do. Where I'm spending today and tomorrow filling in these records it's not for the children's benefit ... it's an accurate record but it doesn't enhance the children's learning. ... They want this record, we've got to do another record for our national curriculum records, make sure children have been delivered, have achieved, and then of course, we need to do another record all together that mentions that we actually taught them to read, 'cos of course, they could achieve all sorts of statements of attainment and still not be able to read which is another problem. ... I was up on Thursday night till 3 o'clock in the morning doing these and I'm not even doing as many as some other teachers. ... I don't think anybody would mind so much, spending all this time if you really felt that the children's learning was being enhanced.

The use of other resources

Marilyn told of how meetings out of school hours 'impinge on your actual teaching', and how she often 'arrived home "brain dead" ', unable to plan her teaching for the morrow, or to advise her daughter on her homework. However, at times, salvation was at hand:

> On Monday I did a piece of work on tenths and I realised that there was a group of children hadn't got a clue about tenths of something. I wanted to sit and plan some work for them. I was late on Monday, I was late on Tuesday, there were finance committee meetings and something else. Fortunately, I had the students, and I said to them, 'Can you do some work on tenths?' She went away and planned it, showed it to me, and I said 'Great! Go and do that with that group of four', which was brilliant. I only needed the time to talk to the student rather than needing time to sit down and organise it, get together the stuff I needed. She did all that.

Reaffirmation of pupil ownership of time

Teachers rehearsed the need for pupils to have time and space in which to work, as Marilyn does here:

> Knowing that they can choose to discuss work with me and being able to have time and space to discuss is important for them to know where they

are in their work, and I also think it's important to give them time to experiment. With a lot of the tasks that are set, writing for instance, if I'd been heavy about them sitting silently on their own it wouldn't have worked so well. Children need to have that space to talk to someone and very often you'd look at them and think what are they talking about? Nine times out of ten if you went over and sneaked up behind them to listen they'd be talking about writing. The book reviews done in groups was giving a kind of space as well. It certainly was a lot of time to give to one piece of work because that's very time consuming 'cos they all want to have their say. . . . All that time taken over one piece of work was incredibly valuable because it moved them on in their next piece of work. Next time they did a book review they remembered what went on in that interchange. What somebody had said, 'about your organisation, couldn't you just . . . ?', 'What about the characters?'

Contrastive rhetoric

Hargreaves (1981) has coined the term 'contrastive rhetoric' for a strategy deployed by senior managers in a school to secure collective decisions for one option by ridiculing others. In this way, the managers 'translate institutional power into interactional power' (p. 15), though it does require the acquiescence of the collective. Our teachers used contrastive rhetoric, not so much to ridicule or belittle – things were much too serious for that – but to delineate and expose.

The teachers were conscious of the need to keep records and to monitor pupil development. They were enthusiastic about innovations that improved their pedagogy or their understanding of individual pupil needs. Most of the schools, for example, used the Primary Language Record which entailed keeping detailed records of each child's language development. However, some were finding it necessary to organize their teaching materials to satisfy new, less educationally sound demands. Laura, for example, observed others teaching through the assessment worksheet and felt this narrowed the learning situation. There 'wasn't time to do anything else'.

> The reality is the teacher does a worksheet with all sorts of little drawings on it with various things which are balanced or not balanced in different ways and asks the children to check these, and if they do it all right they will be considered to have gained that concept. So the worksheet acts as the teaching implement, the assessment and the record.

Grace pointed to the loss in reflective planning time:

> In the past I would stay after school, potter around, get my resources ready, think about what I'm going to do, have everything ready, much more leisurely, and next day be well prepared and it was all nice. But the

balance is wrong, I'm doing records. This weekend I did about 7 hours work that had nothing to do with the way I was going to teach on Monday morning. I was doing minutes for language meeting, minutes for staff meeting, summary of the half term reports. I had to do a reference for a teacher who left. I had to do my reading samples and write them up, my reports, about 7 hours, and none of this was my classroom work. Monday was given 3 seconds thought.

Laura explained how the energy teachers relied on to generate a creative climate was being diverted to more bureaucratic approaches:

I feel the informal network was stronger, because there's only so much energy attached to it. Energy is limited, you just get tired after a while and because the network was stronger [in personal terms] and because there was more time to talk, you felt more relaxed about things in the past and so there was more time, not only to support members of staff who did need it, but to notice members of staff who needed it, and I think this is occasionally being misheard. I mean the support that was offered in the past was much more in the nature of a sort of informal, friendly, helping hand. Whereas now one is more likely to fill in a form and write down what the problem is and it's sometimes quite difficult for somebody to articulate what their problem is because in a sense, if you can articulate what the problem is you've solved it. So it takes quite a lot of talking around to find out what the problem even is.

REDEFINING ACCOUNTABILITY

Accountability is a principal feature of the new professional managerialism, and was something that had to be confronted by our teachers. Following Foucault (1977), Poulson (1994: 3) notes a change in the meaning of the term, being seen 'less as a moral obligation to clients and colleagues, either individually or collectively, than as an aspect of the disciplinary technology by which the work of teachers and schools is surveyed and controlled'. In the market ideology that currently prevails, education is a commodity sought by consumers, whom the producers, consequently, have to satisfy. Accountability is then used 'to establish a discursive consensus which constructs teachers and schools as being in need of external regulation' (see also Epstein 1993). Poulson (1994: 11) noticed that, in the secondary schools of her research, her examples,

which indicate how accountability is used, understood, interpreted and re-interpreted, seem to indicate that although a specific term such as accountability may recur in accounts given by different actors in relation to particular issues, meanings shift according to those specific contexts.

Our teachers sought to construct their own meanings of the term and its implications within their own preferred contexts. The sheer pressures generated led Grace to refer to it as 'heavy duty accountability'. At once, this designates it as unwarranted on workload and rational grounds:

> If you think of the last five years we've had the National Curriculum. We've had to get used to it 'cos there's millions of attainment targets, and we've had people learn how to teach science. There was so much to adapt to. Then they changed it, so then we had to change what we were doing in the class. We had to look at the way we were planning. We had to be able to include everything in a balanced way in the planning, because it was all new and the planning was all new, it was real heavy duty stuff. Then, when they [i.e. inspectors] came in we had to be able to say why we were doing this planning, . . . and then they wanted to see the records and the evidence, so we had to be able to produce the samples, umpteen million samples. For five years it's been that heavy duty way that has never really changed because we're always reviewing and evaluating and changing it. Refining it, and refining it, and even now after five years we still are haggling over the way we should collect the evidence. How we should select, how we should mark. Even now we still haven't got it right.

It was 'heavy', secondly, because teachers did feel under a kind of sinister surveillance. Terrie voiced her fears:

> I worry about the fact that somebody's going to march in and say 'Oh, what's this covering in the National Curriculum?' If you've got the gift of the gab, you can immediately call to mind the connection and defend yourself. I suppose I feel all the time that people might come and say 'Oh yes, but you haven't done this, where's all your technology, where's your science or your history, or your something', and I think it constrains you from being brave enough to actually just do what you want to do.

Grace wished that the 'checking up' and the 'appraisal' of your and others' work

> could be left and we could just get on with teaching without pressures, without demands and bring the fun back in and the relaxed way we have. We'd feel less stressed and therefore it'd affect your teaching in a more positive way. I don't mind the national curriculum.

It is a short move from here to attacking the credentials of those to whom they were accounting. It seemed to the teachers that these people lacked the knowledge and expertise to warrant their authority. This increased the sense of burden, but also aided the transformation of the exercise to one whereby they could consign this key element in the managerialist discourse to the rubbish bin. Grace inveighed against inspectors who criticized everything, but could not tell them 'what was right':

> No, we haven't had one bloody word of advice. . . . It's like a crystal maze, you're going round all and not getting anywhere. You're not getting out of this turmoil . . . this whole mesh of record keeping and mesh of paper and mesh of admin. and mesh of time-consuming wasteless, wasteless, valueless paperwork. I said to our local inspector the other day, I said, I'm so angry talking about records, I thought I can't take this any more.

Grace, like most teachers, is by no means an opponent of many of the reforms. She spends a considerable amount of time on records. She is instrumental in co-ordinating and attending a vast range of meetings in her school and she uses the National Curriculum as the cornerstone of her curriculum planning. The root of her anger lies in the perceived uselessness of so many of these procedures. She asked one inspector, to no avail,

> Why do we have to collect these bloody samples? Just go and look in their books for God's sake. Why are we photocopying out of the books to stick in the bloody folders so that when you come in you've got to look there, and you've got to look there, and you've got to look over there. We collect all this stuff, we put it in folders and none of us look at it.

Grace keeps her folders amongst her shoes because she wants to 'trample them to death'.

> Why am I spending Saturdays doing records and writing them out, why? The only thing I think is worth while is the reading and writing records. I don't mind doing them, but all the other stuff, taking out samples of this and that, no way, and I'd say most teachers feel exactly the same . . . because heavy duty accountability is destructive. We all come in on Monday and we're as ratty as hell because we're too tired.

The inability, in her terms, of the inspector to answer her question satisfactorily, plus her observation (backed up by other teachers, Laura specifically), that nobody actually checks on the records they make, further undermines the educational legitimacy of this form of accountability.

Finally, there is the question of to whom teachers are accountable. The new order put the emphasis on parents as the main consumers of the new education. This is acceptable up to a point, but again, there is a taste of the 'heavy duty' about it. Terrie expressed a typical attitude, reaffirming their view of professionalism:

> Parents know a lot about education but I like the kind of attitude of listening to what you do and commenting and adding things like that, but I think because the debate has been shifted out so much to the public I can't bear the idea that I'm being utterly accountable to parents. I'm sure you are to a certain extent and I respect a lot of people who have advocated that but again the feeling that people are standing in the playground and talking about teaching methods I should adopt that come from on

high is a bit much. I mean doctors and solicitors don't get told how to do their job by their patients and clients.

By designating the process as 'heavy duty', identifying and reacting to the implications of surveillance, attacking the credentials of the monitors, denying the usefulness of the exercise, and reaffirming their own professionalism, the teachers were reconstructing the notion of accountability in their own discourse. They are under pressure, but fighting to retain the moral ground.

EMOTIONAL CONFUSION

The result is, despite mental clarity, considerable emotional confusion. Teaching is not a well-remunerated job in terms of salary. Hence the importance of intrinsic rewards (Lortie 1975; Nias 1989), and the necessity of 'feeling right' (Riseborough 1981). Many teachers have not 'felt right' for some time. For many, the 'fun' has gone out of teaching (see Campbell *et al.* 1991). For example, Sandra commented,

> I don't think there is as much. It's still there, but it's artificial. Everything seems much more artificial than it used to be. As a staff we don't really discuss the deep seated issues as far as education is concerned, but a lot of my time is spent chivvying along, calming people down, trying to make things sound a bit more positive, just generally humouring people.

Laura stayed in teaching because

> I actually enjoy it, but I think sometimes the frustration level is such – the paperwork and the record keeping – wonder whether I should move on to something else. . . . The frustrating thing is, having done it, you don't even feel that slight glow of pleasure when like you've done an essay . . . you think 'Oh wow! I've done it at last!', even if it's tortured you. You know it's been a waste of time.

The fact that these teachers were so emotionally involved with their work and felt so passionately about it, meant that they were highly vulnerable. They felt these tensions deeply, and, though imaginative and innovative people, did not always see a way forward. This is a classic recipe for the generation of guilt and the onset of stress. Hargreaves and Tucker (1991: 495) note that teaching is attended by 'guilt traps', many of them deriving from the fact that

> in the context of teaching, doing or failing to do what is right is more than a matter of personal moral choice. It also involves the context of caring and the extent to which that context enables or restricts the exercise of such choice. Teachers may, for instance, be prevented from doing what is right as they wish by insoluble dilemmas or impossible constraints.

Grace argued that the process of record keeping was eroding confidence:

> I used to feel a much happier, comfortable confident teacher and now I think I've become uptight. Now I feel I've got to get this done, I've got to get that done, don't talk to me, go away, you know, and I hate it. Yet I put in more effort, I'm working harder than I've ever done before. I'm working harder and yet spending a lot more hours doing school work but not doing class work.

Nadine illustrated how the tension between her conception of teaching and 'heavy duty accountability' produced guilt feelings:

> I will always decide how I teach, I know they don't dictate that and I'll always do it the way that I think is best for them but I don't like the guilt feelings. I don't like the thought that if I, say, spent a whole term on doing something that we all really enjoyed and it's not in the National Curriculum, at the end of the year I have no box to tick and people will say I'm not accountable. I haven't covered subjects that I'm supposed to have done, I haven't planned a topic that's covered enough.

Nadine looked forward to seeing her children in the morning and 'having a chat. . . . Listening to their stories about things which I don't always have enough time to actually listen to what they want to tell me'. She felt that to some extent you can still 'go with the flow', but 'you feel guilty about doing it because you feel that you're not doing the other things that you should be doing'. If you concentrate on 'getting done', however, you feel that 'it's eroding what children want to do, what they enjoy, how they learn through their own experiences'. Nadine had got to the heart of this tension by indicating that whichever way teachers went they would feel guilty.

The sense of guilt derived from a profound feeling of moral and social responsibility. For Terrie,

> Part of it is feeling that you can never do enough for them. You haven't got enough time to see everyone and do Maths with everyone. Also it's to do with the National Curriculum in that you feel that to give them the best chance, you have to do as much of the National Curriculum as possible, whereas the other half of you says that you know that what you are doing is better for educational reasons. It's all about the aims and purposes of schooling – the government's imposition of the product model. It's under-valuing exactly what teachers do. It's almost saying to us, 'you haven't been doing it right, you're not doing it right. This is what you should be doing.' What teachers do is just say we are doing it right, we can do it right, we're going to do what you're asking us to do in our way, but it won't stop us feeling guilty about not doing enough. All the time there's a mismatch between what you want and what you think is best and what they're imposing. It's like you're being pulled in different directions.

This is a classic stress syndrome (Woods 1990). That most of these teachers do remain in the system and manage the guilt in some form or another is a credit to their powers of survival. However, it is achieved at some cost. Theresa talked evocatively about her teaching experience and how managerialism was affecting her:

> Before not too long I will have spent twenty-five years in teaching, and it just seems ludicrous that one's burning so hard and so bright after twenty-five years. After twenty-five years one should be honed and it should be skilled and effortless as if you were watching a kind of blacksmith. . . . They wouldn't be putting such strain on their heart or such emotional effort into what's happening. It's almost like sulphur burning. It's frightening. . . . Every year we end up giving more to children and having to give more to children and every year the job gets wider and more diffused. There is inevitably an end to the elasticity of what teachers can give.

Laura, on the other hand had managed to fight off feelings of guilt about doing something different to the National Curriculum, seeing this as an exclamation of her humanity:

> I want a world where we live in some sort of mutual respect, and I want it for my sons and my daughter and for me and for all the children. There's got to be humanity and part of the humanity of it [teaching] is that sometimes I've had enough, but I still feel OK about saying to the children, 'I'm sorry I can't.' It's not often I do it but I do feel if I do it, it's OK. I don't feel guilt about this.

There is anger, frustration, stress and guilt here in teacher reactions. There is also a sense of deprivation. But running through the comments is a sustained commitment, resolve and sense of moral purpose: 'I actually enjoy it . . .', 'I will always decide how I teach . . .', Nadine 'looking forward to having a chat with her children . . .', Sue 'burning bright . . .', Laura's insistence on 'humanity' . . . At times, they are run a bit ragged by the new demands, but this thread of positive emotional reactions buttresses the mental aspects of the new professional discourse – at least for the moment.

A NEW PROFESSIONAL DISCOURSE

We would argue that there is a more positive outcome here than simply feelings of exhaustion, frustration, rage and stress, though those are real enough. What is being generated is a new professional discourse to combat that of professional managerialism. Foucault (in Weedon 1987: 108) defines discourses as 'ways of constituting knowledge, together with the social practices, forms of subjectivity and power relations which inhere in such knowledge and the relations between them'. They are based in institutions and realized in practice, but 'these institutional locations are themselves sites of contest, and the dominant discourses governing the organization and practices of social institutions are under constant challenge' (p. 109). Professional managerialism may still be the 'dominant discourse', but there is sufficient discursive space to allow resistance, and 'resistance to the dominant at the level of the individual subject is the first stage in the production of alternative forms of knowledge' (p. 110). This is a 'complex and unstable process whereby discourse can be both an instrument and an effect of power, but also a hindrance, a stumbling block, a point of resistance and a starting point for an opposing strategy' (Foucault 1981: 101).

The new professional discourse may be embryonic at this stage, but there has been an easing of the government's position since 1988, and we might expect a concomitant strengthening of the alternative professionalism (see Hatcher 1994). Its main features as manifested in our teachers are, first, reaffirmation of the principles that underpin teachers' practice. Second, there is resistance to those elements in the changes that run counter to those principles. There is a reasoned opposition, again at the level of values, on both pragmatic and moral grounds (Bridges 1994). Some of the changes do not work, like, for example, much of the bureaucracy and the overloaded curriculum. But they are wrong anyway in trying to run education like a business. A feature of the resistance is taking the attack to the enemy, as in, for example, Grace's assault on the inspectorate. There is, third, no blanket condemnation, however, of the changes. They give a balanced verdict, one that acknowledges the educational benefits in the National Curriculum. They are aware of the dangers of returning to a 'free-for-all', and admit to some of their own previous inadequacies. Fourth, a number of strategies are employed to counter and neutralize the effects of managerialism, such as distancing, perceiving alternatives, and the use of contrastive rhetoric. Fifth, there is a transformation of some of the main tenets of professional managerialism, namely choice, quality and accountability. Choice becomes professional choice, especially with regard to teaching methods. Quality is a matter of 'teachable moments', framework, some records, balance and adjustment, emotional attachment and moral worth. Accountability under professional managerialism becomes, in the new discourse, 'heavy duty', a short-hand description for time-consuming, stressful, and useless activity. They prefer an accountability located within professional values, best judged by their peers. Sixth, the emotional character of some of the responses indicates both their passionate commitment to their work, and the recognition of the part played by the emotions in the teaching and learning process. This is in stark contrast to the technical-rationalism of parts of the National Curriculum and particularly of its assessment, which seems guided by behaviourist principles (Pollard 1991). It is certainly out of tune with professional managerialism.

Finally, there is an articulation of solutions. In amongst the pressures, there were signs of confidence, optimism, and opportunities. Terrie, for example, was striving for a 'happy medium' and noted that 'as you go on a bit, you feel more confident about doing this and doing that'. Nadine noted that, intrinsically, it was possible to do adventurous topics *and* meet the requirements of the National Curriculum. For example, 'The stuff we did on giants doesn't fit anywhere into anything but it does fit into bits of everything.' Similarly, she wouldn't have chosen to do 'electricity' 'the very first year of Year 2 if I hadn't had to'. But she 'worked it all around my own way by using a story about who'll be the sun'.

Theresa had made a resolution about her management style if she were to become a head. She would spend her time 'making sure that people were able to do some of the exciting things that we have lost'. If she were to continue in classroom teaching, she would hope to be a 'good teacher' and become 'even more and more selective as to what I do and what I don't do'. Laura found a way of resisting increasing bureaucratization by a new kind of collaboration. She engaged in team teaching with a close colleague and found this liberating. It 'spread the load tremendously' on things like record keeping, and, most importantly, provided enormous support at a time of extreme vulnerability.

There need not, of course, be a clear-cut solution for a discussion to be helpful. As Laura astutely observes, 'If you can articulate what the problem is, you've solved it.' Though the teachers bemoan the pressures on their time, the heavy accent on 'getting done' and new forms of accountability, it could be argued that their formulation of the problems constituted a step forward. They are with the 'significant minority' of Pollard *et al's.* (1994) teachers who felt that 'a new professionalism involving creative ways of working with individual children was possible, provided they had the confidence to shape the imposed changes to more professionally accepted ends' (p. 99). There is a kind of political activism here, not one characterized by attempts to engage directly in trying to change policy, but as articulated in the course of everyday interaction. Its importance lies in this exercise of power, and in the production of a 'truth' and 'knowledge' within which their professional selves can work. As Ball (1994: 22) notes,

> We do not speak a discourse, it speaks us. *We are* the subjectivities, the voices, the knowledge, the power relations that a discourse constructs and allows. We do not 'know' what we say, we 'are' what we say and do. . . . This is a system of practices . . . and a set of values and ethics.

In this way, these teachers were not only coming to terms with the reforms, but finding their own way through them.

REFERENCES

Alexander, R. J. (1992) *Policy and Practice in Primary Education,* London: Routledge.
Apple, M. W. (1986) *Teachers and Texts: A Political Economy of Class and Gender Relations in Education,* New York: Routledge and Kegan Paul.

Aspland, R. and Brown, G. (1993) 'Keeping teaching professional', in D. Bridges and T. Kerry (eds) *Developing Teachers Professionally*, London: Routledge.

Ball, S. J. (1990) *Politics and Policy Making in Education*, London: Routledge.

Ball, S. J. (1993) 'Education markets, choice and social class: the market as a class strategy in the UK and the USA', *British Journal of Sociology of Education* 14(1): 3–19.

Ball, S. J. (1994) *Education Reform: A Critical and Post-structural Approach*, Buckingham: Open University Press.

Ball, S. J. and Bowe, R. (1992) 'Subject departments and the "implementation" of National Curriculum policy: an overview of the issues', *Journal of Curriculum Studies* 24(2): 97–115.

Bridges, D. (1994) 'Education and the market place: the nature of the argument', paper presented at the British Educational Research Association Conference, Oxford, September.

Campbell, R. J. (1993) 'The broad and balanced curriculum in primary schools: some limitations on reform', *The Curriculum Journal* 4(2): 215–29.

Campbell, R. J. and St. J. Neill, S. R. (1994) *Curriculum Reform at Key Stage 1 – Teacher Commitment and Policy Failure*, Harlow: Longman.

Campbell, R. J., Evans, L., St. J. Neill, S. R. and Packwood, A. (1991) *Workloads, Achievement and Stress: Two Follow-up Studies of Teacher Time in Key Stage 1*, Policy Analysis Unit, Department of Education, University of Warwick.

Cockburn, A. (1994) 'Teachers' experience of time: some implications for future research', *British Journal of Educational Studies* 42(4): 375–87.

Dale, R. (1989) *The State and Education Policy*, Buckingham: Open University Press.

Dearing, R. (1994) *Review of the National Curriculum: Final Report*, London: School Curriculum and Assessment Authority (SCAA) Publications.

Epstein, D. (1993) 'Defining accountability in education', *British Educational Research Journal* 19: 243–59.

Fitz, J. (1994) 'Implementation research and education policy: practice and prospects', *British Journal of Education Studies* 42(1): 53–69.

Foucault, M. (1977) *The Archeology of Knowledge*, London: Tavistock.

Foucault, M. (1981) *The History of Sexuality*, Harmondsworth: Penguin.

Hargreaves, A. (1981) 'Contrived collegiality: the micropolitics of teacher collaboration', in J. Blase (ed.) *The Politics of Life in Schools*, London: Sage.

Hargreaves, A. (1994) *Changing Teachers, Changing Times*, London: Cassell.

Hargreaves, A and Tucker, E. (1991) 'Teaching and guilt: exploring the feelings of teaching', *Teaching And Teacher Education* 7(5/6): 491–505.

Hatcher, R. (1994) 'Market relationships and the management of teachers', *British Journal of Sociology of Education* 15(1): 41–62.

Inglis, F. (1989) 'Managerialism and morality: the corporate and the republic school', in W. Carr (ed.) *Quality in Teaching: Arguments for a Reflective Profession*, London: Falmer.

Lortie, D. C. (1975) *Schoolteacher*, Chicago: University of Chicago Press.

Maguire, M. and Ball, S. J. (1994) 'Discourses of educational reform in the United Kingdom and the USA and the work of teachers', *British Journal of Inservice Education* 20(1): 5–16.

Nias, J. (1989) *Primary Teachers Talking*, London: Routledge.

Pollard, A. (1994) *Learning in Primary Schools*, London: Cassell.

Pollard, A., Broadfoot, P., Croll, P., Osborn, M. and Abbott, D. (1994) *Changing English Primary Schools? The Impact of the Education Reform Act at Key Stage One*, London: Cassell.

Poulson, L. (1994) 'The discourse of accountability: analysis of a key word in the process of implementing national curriculum policy in a core subject', paper presented at BERA Annual Conference, Oxford.

Riseborough, G. F. (1981) 'Teacher careers and comprehensive schooling: an empirical study', *Sociology* 15(3): 352–81.

Simkins, T., Ellison, L. and Garrett, V. (eds) (1992) *Implementing Educational
Reforms: The Early Lessons*, Harlow: Longman/BEMAS.

Weedon, C. (1987) *Feminist Practice and Poststructuralist Theory*, London: Basil
Blackwell.

Woods, P. (1990) *Teacher Skills and Strategies*, Lewes: Falmer Press.

Woods, P. (1993) *Critical Events in Teaching and Learning*, London: Falmer Press.

Woods, P. (1995) *Creative Teachers in Primary Schools*, Buckingham: Open University
Press.

Woods, P. and Jeffrey, R. (1996) *Teachable Moments: The Art of Teaching in Primary
Schools*, Buckingham: Open University Press.

Chapter 5

In search of good primary practice[1]

Robin Alexander

'Good primary practice': the ubiquitous phrase begs questions nearly every time it is uttered. What is the substance behind the slogan? The following examples from the Leeds research[2] (Alexander 1992), not untypical of their time, provide one obvious starting point.

Why do we do it this way? Well, it's good primary practice, isn't it?

We don't adopt the old-fashioned method of keeping [the curriculum] in little boxes. It's unnatural – children don't see the world that way, so why should we impose our adult views on them?

We apply all the basic principles of good practice here – a stimulating environment with high quality display and plenty of material for first hand exploration; a flexible day in which children can move freely from one activity to the next without the artificial barriers of subjects; plenty of individual and group work.

We don't believe in teaching here. The job of the teacher is to create the environment in which children can find things out for themselves, not to tell them what they should know.

The successful candidate will be familiar with good primary practice. A belief in a child-centred approach is essential.

Plowden is still my Bible, whatever the government or any airy-fairy academics say. They are not the practitioners – I am!

I have terrible problems planning, because we're all supposed to use topic webs and show them to the head, and I'm not very good at them, and find them impossible to use, especially as now I have to add all the attainment targets. So what I do is a topic web to satisfy the head, and my own planning for me.

When I go into one of my classrooms I don't expect to see all my children sitting down. I expect movement. I expect them to be busy. A quiet classroom is a dull classroom.

If you don't have drapes and triple mounting, you won't get on here.

It is, of course, not only appropriate but necessary that professionals should have clearly articulated convictions about what counts as quality in their day-to-day practice, but the examples above illustrate some of the immediate problems: the appeal to authority rather than argument, whether that authority be provided by a leading report or figures higher up in the professional hierarchy; the tendency to tautology and dichotomizing; the intolerance towards alternative viewpoints; the emphasis on belief as the ultimate touchstone of good practice; the context of power and patronage; above all, the assumption of consensus over matters where consensus cannot – and arguably should not – be presumed.

Each of these tendencies has its counterpart outside the teaching profession, illustrated in the examples which follow, all from the period immediately after the publication of the Leeds research. By then, the matter of good practice was firmly on the national political agenda in the run-up to the 1992 general election.

> Child-centred education . . . part of a deliberate political project to undermine the respect the young should have for the achievements of those who went before them.
>
> (Anthony O'Hear in the *Daily Telegraph*, 12.2.91)

> A generation of wasted time. . . . The education of millions of children has been blighted in the name of an anarchic ideology, says a new study.
>
> (*Daily Telegraph*, 19.9.91)

> Children spend more time with paint pots than mastering the three Rs, said Schools Minister Michael Fallon. . . . They should get back to basics and teach the whole class in an organised way.
>
> (*Daily Mail*, 2.11.91)

> At its worst, current practice hinders concentration, disguises time-wasting, lack of real learning and superficial questioning; and provides little useful contact between the teacher and the individual pupil.
>
> (former Secretary of State Kenneth Clarke, in a circular to all primary schools, 3.12.91)

> We will take no lectures from those who led the long march of mediocrity through our schools. . . . I will fight for my belief. My belief is a return to basics in education. The progressive theorists have had their say and, Mr President, they've had their day.
>
> (Prime Minister John Major, Conservative Party Conference, October 1991)

> Look on your works, Lady Plowden, and despair.
>
> (*Daily Telegraph*, 7.11.91)

The 'back to basics' rhetoric above, of course, is entirely lacking in novelty.

The media and political reactions to the Leeds research closely resembled those provoked by Bennett's earlier teaching styles study (Bennett 1976) and were repeated in connection with the 1992 primary discussion paper (Alexander, Rose and Woodhead 1992), the OFSTED follow-up reports to that document and the 1995 HMCI annual report on the state of the nation's schools (OFSTED 1993, 1994, 1995).

A rather different style of pronouncement on the good practice question, more extended and descriptive though no less suffused by values, can be found in official reports. Thus, for example, the 1967 Plowden Report portrayed three schools 'run successfully on modern lines', whose characteristics are captured in these extracts:

> The children . . . spread into the hall, the corridors and the playground. The nursery class has its own quarters and the children are playing with sand, water, paint, clay, dolls, rocking horses and big push toys under the supervision of their teacher. This is how they learn. . . . Learning is going on all the time, but there is not much direct teaching. . . . The class of sevens to nines had spread into the corridor and were engaged in a variety of occupations. One group were gathered round their teacher for some extra reading practice, another was at work on an extraordinary structure of wood and metal which they said was a sputnik, a third was collecting a number of objects and testing them to find out which could be picked up by a magnet and two boys were at work on an immense painting of St Michael defeating Satan. They seemed to be working harmoniously according to an unfolding rather than a pre-conceived plan. . . . As he leaves the school and turns into the grubby and unlovely street onto which it abuts, the visitor passes a class who, seated in a quiet, sunny corner, are listening to their teacher telling them the story of Rumplestiltskin.
>
> (CACE 1967: 103–5)

Twenty years later, the agenda had changed somewhat, though its antecedents were still discernible, as the following extracts from HMI's direct encounter with the good practice problem show.

> First impressions were of an informality which typifies many primary classrooms. Closer investigation revealed that the freedoms were not there merely by chance. . . . The children were keenly interested in their work. Their commitment to what they were doing extended beyond the more obviously enjoyable aspects of their practical activities. . . . The children were being taught to listen carefully and speak clearly and articulately. . . . Their written work caused them to use a variety of styles. . . . The high quality of teaching was the strongest feature common to all the examples . . . there were variations in the teaching styles reflecting the needs of the situation and the personality of individual teachers. . . . Teachers had a sound knowledge of their pupils' social and cultural

backgrounds. . . . A dominant factor in the achievement of high standards was the strength of commitment on the part of the teachers to ensure that pupils were making progress. . . . Challenges were set so that the work was neither too difficult not too easy. . . . The overriding characteristic is that of agreed, clear aims and purposeful teaching.

(DES 1987: 32–4)

Thus, the appearance might be that of a Plowden classroom, but the teacher had by now become considerably more prominent, and the organic model of an unfolding sequence of intrinsically educative experiences had been replaced by a firm emphasis upon detailed prior planning. This theme was also taken up at school level, underscoring the way that serendipity was to be replaced by management, and individualism by collective endeavour.

In each school the head and staff had agreed aims . . . a shared sense of purpose . . . curricular guidelines which had been carefully thought out. . . . These guidelines had been written after staff discussions. . . . Schools were exploring ways of deploying the staff so that more effective use was made of their abilities and curricular strengths. . . . Schools were making positive efforts to strike the delicate balance which is involved in making the best use of the curricular expertise of a primary school staff as a combined teaching unit.

(DES 1987: 31–2)

September 1989 saw the start of the phased introduction of the National Curriculum, which carried its own clear messages about good practice, at least where conceptions of curriculum and assessment were concerned. Yet the National Curriculum Council at that point felt it important to combine the reassertion of traditional values with a synthesis of Plowden and HMI:

The aims of the National Curriculum are more likely to be achieved where . . . pupils are properly equipped with the basic tools of learning. In particular, where numeracy, literacy and oracy are given highest priority by teachers and are soundly taught. These skills form the basis of a proper and rigorous education to the highest standards which parents and public expect. . . . Due recognition is given to the importance of first-hand experience and practical tasks. . . . Pupils are led to ask questions and seek answers. . . . Teachers' expectations of what pupils are capable of achieving are high and pupils' learning is structured, relevant and stimulating. . . . Pupils are encouraged to become self-confident, self-disciplined and courteous.

(National Curriculum Council 1989: 2)

With the debate about the content of the curriculum apparently closed, the focus of concern shifted to pedagogy, especially during the highly-charged period 1991–2 which saw the publication of the Leeds research and the commissioning and publication of the DES primary discussion paper. The latter trawled the by then extensive body of research on teaching and learning in primary schools, much of it grounded in systematic classroom observation, and under the heading 'Improving classroom practice' offered a set of 'propositions about aspects of classroom practice to which the evidence suggests particular attention should be devoted . . . not as a definitive checklist but as the basis for open and constructive discussion' (Alexander, Rose and Woodhead 1992: 37). The propositions related to the themes of teacher knowledge, planning, curriculum balance, the classroom context, teacher expectations of pupils, the management of classroom time, differentiation in learning tasks, assessment and diagnosis, feedback, teaching strategies and techniques. In respect of all of these, and of the many alternative possibilities for action which they suggest, the document identified 'fitness for purpose' as the key principle for deciding what course of action to take in particular circumstances (Alexander, Rose and Woodhead: chapters 4 and 6).

The notion of 'fitness for purpose' was central. Good practice, the document suggested, resides in the teacher having a clear sense of educational purpose, reflected in his or her planning and the context in which teaching and learning are to take place; a well-developed range of pedagogical skills, firmly grounded in appropriate knowledge of children, curriculum and pedagogy; and the capacity to judge how and when this repertoire should be exploited.

The specific research on which the 1992 primary discussion paper drew included several studies which themselves had addressed the good practice question, albeit from the restricted standpoint of a concern with effectiveness (see p. 69). Thus, Mortimore *et al.* (1988: 250–6) identified 'twelve key factors for effective junior schooling', several of which accorded with the conclusions of the earlier studies of Galton *et al.* (1980a, 1980b), Bennett *et al.* (1984) and others. The Leeds project, evaluating the impact of an ambitious initiative to improve primary education across an entire LEA, highlighted fifty-five issues arising from the initiative which merited local attention, and twenty-four priorities for improving educational practice which were deemed to have national relevance (Alexander 1992: 155–60 and 195–6). The 1992 primary discussion paper itself spawned a succession of annual follow-up reports from OFSTED which identified six 'factors associated with better topic work' and twenty-one 'factors associated with better classroom practice' (OFSTED 1993), then six 'factors associated with high standards of achievement', eight which in contrast were 'associated with poor standards of achievement' and a further six 'associated with successful topic work' (OFSTED 1994). Whatever the limits of each such study, collectively they did at least offer clearly enunciated propositions of value in the quest for good primary practice, and, it must be said, a fair degree of consensus arrived at by different methodological routes. But was this enough?

The most important point to make, and the most obvious, is that any notion of good practice presupposes criteria for judgment. While some of the published extracts above make criteria explicit, they remain tacit or only partly explicated in others, and in some of the statements from teachers, the press and politicians with which this article started there is a clear assumption that criteria are not needed at all – either because good practice is about belief rather than justification, or because the presumed consensus makes their explication unnecessary. In general, good primary practice discourse has tended to be strong on assertion and weak on justification. As a result, the necessary task of defining and defending criteria is frequently neglected.

When we say of teaching which we do, see or wish to commend 'this is good practice', what are we really asserting? There seem to be several possibilities, of which four should be noted:

- This practice is in line with what I, or others in authority, define as good practice.
- This teaching works in as far as teachers and children seem to be appropriately and gainfully occupied.
- This teaching demonstrably leads to effective learning along lines which can be made, or have been made, explicit.
- This teaching is consistent with my values and beliefs about the proper purposes and conduct of education.

Though there is inevitable overlap between the statements – notably in the sense that each of them, notwithstanding the use of supposedly neutral words like 'effective', is grounded in values of some kind – their status is nevertheless somewhat different. Thus, the first, being about the exercise of power, is a *political* statement. The second is essentially a *pragmatic* statement. The third, being grounded in experience and observation and being concerned with verification, is an *empirical* statement. The fourth is *evaluative* in the sense of expressing, and being explicitly validated by, values and beliefs.

If we now return to the quotations, it is possible to classify them in terms of these categories. Sometimes the classification is clear-cut, as in the case of several of the assertions by teachers and politicians, where a firm value-stance is adopted, but no justification, evidential, ethical or otherwise, is offered. Sometimes the exercise of classification shows, notwithstanding the apparent certainty of the judgement being offered, how the ostensible neutrality of the empirical statement is usually nothing of the sort, being on the one hand necessarily and inevitably underpinned by values, and on the other sustained by a sense of its own (methodological or academic) authority.

There is a further difficulty. So far, we have considered one word in the phrase 'good practice' – the epithet 'good'. What of the other one, the notion of 'practice' itself? Is it reasonable to assume that when we speak of good primary practice we are all talking of the same phenomena, and the only problem concerns the basis on which we rate them as good, bad or indifferent? Though we recognise that 'education' is a pluralistic concept, is 'teaching' significantly less so?

The quotations above indicate that it is not. Of course, none of the statements made by teachers, journalists or politicians was intended to be anything other than selective in its focus, though the nature of that selectivity is of considerable interest. However, even the ostensibly more comprehensive statements display somewhat different conceptions of, as well as different values about, teaching. Thus, the Plowden extracts are preoccupied with the use of time and space, relationships, children's motivation, attitude and behaviour, the school and classroom context, pedagogic processes, the whole rather than the parts, evolution rather than structure, and especially with the needs of the child, defined developmentally and motivationally. In contrast, the 1987 HMI extracts imply a very different agenda: aims, planning, curriculum content, staff expertise and deployment, challenge in learning experiences, diagnosis and assessment, matching of child and curriculum task, structure, progression and continuity, the parts as well as the whole, and the needs of the child, defined in relation to societal realities and expectations. Or consider this statement from an HMI report on an initial teacher training institution:

> The college declares publicly its philosophy of good primary practice. This is stated in all substantial course documents. The philosophy has several key elements. These are stated to include: the recognition of the uniqueness of the individual child; the importance of first-hand experience; the value of an attractive and stimulating learning environment.

The problem here is not so much the substance as the scope of this statement. Few would dissent from the three principles thus enunciated, and many would applaud them. But as a philosophy of good primary practice this is surely deficient. It is rather like a play with scenery but no actors or text, or a concert with orchestra but no music, or the National Gallery bereft of its pictures. It provides the context for education and gently hints at its conduct, but it indicates nothing of its purposes, scope, content or outcomes.

The problem with many such everyday accounts or definitions of good practice is that not only do they leave unexplored vital questions of justification, but they also focus in a frequently arbitrary way upon particular aspects of practice which are then elevated to the status of a complete and coherent 'philosophy'. More often than not, they are merely philosophical fragments or preliminary clearings of the throat. In its everyday usage, therefore, the phrase 'good primary practice' is deeply flawed, both ethically and conceptually. Some who use the phrase are intuitively aware that this is so, and in writing adopt the apologetic device of placing the words in inverted commas, providing the digital equivalent in conversation. This is rarely more than a tic, since having made this passing acknowledgement that the phrase is problematic they invariably go on to treat it as though it were not.

In order to judge the adequacy of a good practice claim, therefore, we need not only to examine the criteria by which practice is judged to be good, but also to be clear about which aspects of practice are defined in this way and which aspects are ignored. There is, of course, no reason why a good practice statement should not be selective and sharply focused, and indeed every reason why sharpness of focus is desirable: it is difficult to talk meaningfully about teaching unless we engage with its specifics. The problem comes when over time, or within a statement purporting to stand as a complete educational rationale, some aspects of practice are consistently emphasised while other aspects are consistently ignored. The underlying message of selectivity in this context is that what is emphasised is all that matters, whether it be – to draw on contrasting selections – display, group work, thematic enquiry, the subject-based curriculum, whole-class teaching or the basics. Thus, in the words of the third respondent at the beginning of this paper, before staking out his/her own somewhat incomplete map of the territory, 'We apply *all* the principles of good practice here.'

How, to tackle this problem, can we begin to draw up a map of the vast territory of educational practice? In absolute terms it is an impossible enterprise. However, there may be a level at which such a map is not only possible but might also serve as a useful prompt to those involved in the examination, execution and judgement of practice.

My own shot at such a framework starts with what one encounters on entering a classroom: a context comprising first the physical and organizational features of furniture, resources and participants, and second the relationships observable as existing among and between these participants. Looking closer, one notes that most of the relationships and interactions are not random, but are framed by pedagogic process: teachers adopt particular strategies, particular combinations of class, group and individual work, particular patterns of interaction; and pupils are organized so as to facilitate these. Next, we note that these processes are focused upon specific tasks and the acquisition of specific knowledge, skill, understanding or attribute: the content of teaching and learning. Finally, we recognize that what we see and what the participants experience is subject to the teacher's management: it is planned, co-ordinated and evaluated.

Thus far, we are dealing with what can be observed. However, to make sense of what we see we need to encounter the educational ideas and values in which the observable practice is grounded. Without them practice is purposeless and random. It is reasonable to assume that although we may not necessarily agree with such ideas as a teacher puts forward to explain and justify what he or she does, ideas and values of some kind are the basis for all observable practice.

Listening to teachers talking about their practice I find I can group such ideas and values under three broad headings. The first concerns children. All teaching rests on assumptions about what children can or cannot do, what they need, how they develop, how they learn, how best they can be motivated and encouraged, about their rights and entitlements, and, more generally, about the nature of childhood itself. The second area concerns society. Teachers invariably have some sense of the demands and expectations which emanate from outside the school, of the needs of society or particular sections of it, and of the needs of the individual in relation to that society. Finally, most teaching rests upon views of the nature of knowledge: its structure, its character, its source and its content, what is important, what less so.

It will be apparent that this is to telescope a line of analysis which deserves to be greatly extended. However, for present purposes the intention is not to provide in fine detail a fully-comprehensive framework for analysing and exploring classroom practice, but simply to illustrate that some such framework is feasible. Thus the present framework has two main dimensions and seven main components, as shown in Figure 5.1. The categories are, of course, not discrete, but are simply presented as such for analytical purposes. More important, the two dimensions, here presented as a sequential list, interact: each aspect of practice is to a greater or lesser extent informed by one, two or all of the areas of ideas, values and assumptions.

These seem to constitute not so much the totality as the minimum: whatever else classroom practice encompasses, it contains these elements. Armed with such a framework we can return to any good practice statement, test its emphasis and scope, and examine the thrust of the ideas and justifications, if any, in which it is rooted. The model, incidentally, has its parallel version at whole-school level. There the observable practice components include context, management, and external relations, but because the focus of this discussion is the classroom, I am not elaborating that part of the framework in the same way.

Applying such a framework to the various examples given earlier, and to the wider context of the National Curriculum, we can venture some basic propositions. Plowden, for example, tended to focus on context and pedagogy rather than content and management. Its vision was firmly grounded in views of the child, especially the child's development and learning. About society and its needs it had relatively little to say, while its view of knowledge was an extension of its analysis of the nature and needs of childhood. In contrast, HMI from 1978 onwards began to develop a view of practice which dealt with all four elements of practice in the framework, but focused particularly on content and management, with a relatively subsidiary interest in pedagogy. The justificatory basis had less to do with children's inherent characteristics as learners than with a quasi-legal notion of entitlement to breadth, balance and challenge in the curriculum, and was firmly guided by a sense of knowledge as cultural artefact, handed on from one generation to the next and providing an essential tool for the individual to make sense of, participate in, and act upon society and to respond to its needs. In turn, the National Curriculum is even more distant from Plowden. The emphasis

ASPECTS			CENTRAL EDUCATIONAL QUESTIONS
OBSERVABLE PRACTICE	CONTEXT	physical interpersonal	
	CONTENT	whole curriculum subjects/areas	WHAT should children learn?
	PEDAGOGY	teaching methods pupil organization	and
	MANAGEMENT	planning operation assessment of learning evaluation of teaching	HOW should children learn and teacher's teach?
IDEAS VALUES BELIEFS	CHILDREN	development needs learning	WHY should children be educated in this way?
	SOCIETY	needs of society needs of the individual	and
	KNOWLEDGE	children's ways of knowing culturally evolved ways of knowing	WHAT is an educated person?

Figure 5.1 Educational practice: a framework

here (at least until the interventionist rumblings about pedagogy in late 1991) is almost exclusively on content and management – or rather those aspects of management which are concerned with delivery of content and proof of such delivery, planning and assessment. (The postal nuances of the language of the National Curriculum are startlingly pervasive, and have built remorselessly on former Secretary of State Keith Joseph's initial concept of the curriculum as educational package.) The justificatory basis is unambiguously societal, or rather economic.

To take stock: 'good practice' statements come in different forms. Some are statements of value or belief; some are pragmatic statements; some are empirical statements; some are political statements; most combine more than one of these characteristics, which are themselves neither discrete nor

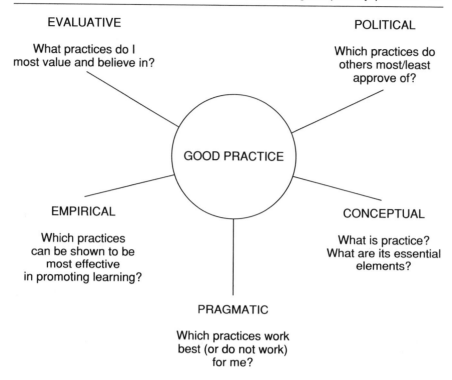

EVALUATIVE

What practices do I
most value and believe in?

POLITICAL

Which practices do
others most/least
approve of?

GOOD PRACTICE

EMPIRICAL

Which practices
can be shown to be
most effective
in promoting learning?

CONCEPTUAL

What is practice?
What are its essential
elements?

PRAGMATIC

Which practices work
best (or do not work)
for me?

Figure 5.2 Good practice 1: reconciling competing imperatives?

one-dimensional; and all presuppose a concept of practice itself. Pursuing our quest for good primary practice in this way, therefore, we can see that while in a physical sense it resides in primary schools and classrooms, to know what we are looking for and to begin to understand how we might define and judge it, we need to recognize that it lies, conceptually, somewhere at the intersection of the five considerations or dimensions which we have explored: evaluative, pragmatic, empirical, political and conceptual. Figure 5.2 represents this relationship.

The quest for good primary practice, then, is as much a conceptual as a physical one. However, the point at which the various overlapping considerations meet is an arena of conflict as much as of resolution. Our own values may lead us in one direction; alternative values in another; practical constraints may make neither course of action in its pure form possible without modification; we may know of evidence which makes us doubtful about the wisdom of adopting the compromise position to which we find ourselves being steered; our decisions may be further shaped by external pressures or expectations; and so on.

Primary practice – any educational practice – requires us to come to terms with and do our best to reconcile competing values, pressures and constraints.

It is about dilemma no less than certainty (Alexander 1995: chapter 2). If this is so of practice in general, it must also be the case, *a fortiori*, with practice we wish to define as 'good'. Far from being an absolute, therefore, as it is frequently treated, good primary practice entails an almost inevitable element of compromise, for however firm our intention and however consummate our professional skill, beliefs and actions in teaching are seldom consistently congruent with each other, and consensus in matters of belief can rarely be assumed.

However, there has to be a qualitative difference between practice and good practice if the latter notion is not to become redundant. Or is it the case that good practice is no more than the best we can do in the circumstances? Is our quest for educational quality to run into the morass of relativism? I believe not. Through in the diagram the five considerations or dimensions appear to have equal weight, the pursuit of good practice has to move beyond a mere balancing of competing imperatives. There have to be superordinate reasons for preferring one course of action to another, which enable education to rise above the level of the merely pragmatic.

The five considerations, therefore, are not in any sense equivalent. Each set of questions is wholly different from all the others. However, it is possible to order and group them. Thus, the conceptual questions stand apart from all the rest as being concerned with the scope and comprehensiveness of our definition of practice: before we consider judgements of quality we must be clear what it is that we are talking about. Next, the political and pragmatic questions remind us of the pressures and constraints of the circumstances in which practice takes place. Such pressures and constraints cannot be ignored, and they may yield practice which is as likely to be bad as good. There remain the value and empirical dimensions. In the end, it seems to me, close attention to these two is what distinguishes good practice from mere practice. Education is inherently about values; it reflects a vision of the kind of world we want our children to inherit; a vision of the kinds of people we hope they will become; a vision of what it is to be an educated person. Whatever the other ingredients of good practice may be, they should enable a coherent and sustainable value-position to be pursued. Values, then, are central.

Yet, in teaching, values have to be be made manifest as learning contexts, tasks and encounters, and while, obviously, such activities must be congruent with the values they seek to realize, such congruence is of itself no guarantee of success in terms of the specific learning goals which give the broader vision practical meaning. We need to go one step further, therefore, and to couple with the commitment to values and value-congruence a clear awareness of the strengths and weaknesses of the various teaching strategies open to us, in order that we can construct, ideally, learning tasks and contexts which are not just consistent with the values but also will translate them into meaningful learning for the child. It is for this reason that the empirical dimension is so critical an adjunct to matters of value, belief and purpose.

It is also clear that the pursuit of 'effectiveness' *per se*, a popular quest among educational researchers during the 1980s and 1990s, can produce versions of good practice which are incomplete or untenable in the same way that value statements detached from empirical understanding may be inoperable. Those who presume that the inconveniently untidy value problems in the good practice question are resolved at a stroke by talking of 'effective' practice (or the effective teacher/effective school) are engaging in mere sleight of hand: practice which is effective in relation to what? In relation, of course, to a notion of what it is to be educated. Good practice, then, is intrinsically educative as well as operationally effective. Effectiveness as a criterion existing on its own is meaningless.

The relationship between the evaluative and the empirical in defining good educational practice is thus a particularly difficult one, operationally and conceptually. Indeed, it is possible to explain some of the well-documented problems in primary classroom practice in terms of a failure to hold the two in proper balance: the problems, for example, of individualized learning (Galton *et al.* 1980a, 1980b), multiple curriculum focus teaching (Mortimore *et al.* 1988), and classroom questions and questioning (Alexander 1992). The tension between the evaluative and the empirical may also help to explain the apparently pervasive gap between the progressive claim and classroom realities in the 1970s and 1980s (DES 1978; Alexander 1988; Simon 1981).

In any event, while beliefs and actions need to be consistent, they are not synonymous. Thus, a belief in co-operation and a distaste for competition might imply and seem to justify group work, but does the belief of itself make such a strategy effective as a tool for the acquisition of knowledge, understanding and skill? Or a belief in the unity of knowledge might imply and appear to justify an integrated curriculum, but does it follow that this is the most effective way for children to come to know? Or a belief in the importance of an enquiring mind might imply and justify asking questions but never providing answers, but does it follow that through this strategy children themselves will learn to question what they experience?

We are now in a position to sum up. Figure 5.2 represented good practice as existing at the intersection of the five considerations and as a matter of reconciling competing imperatives. I have now suggested that this approach does not take sufficient note of what the 'good' in 'good practice' might dictate, and that although all the considerations are important, they are not equivalent. The pursuit of good practice sets the considerations in a hierarchical relationship with ethical and empirical questions pre-eminent, and both dependent on a prior conceptualization of the nature of educational practice itself. This alternative relationship, a development of the initial idea, is shown in Figure 5.3.

When this approach to the good practice question was first presented (in Alexander 1992) some took it to espouse a narrowly technicist view of teaching, in which the identified considerations bearing on the good practice

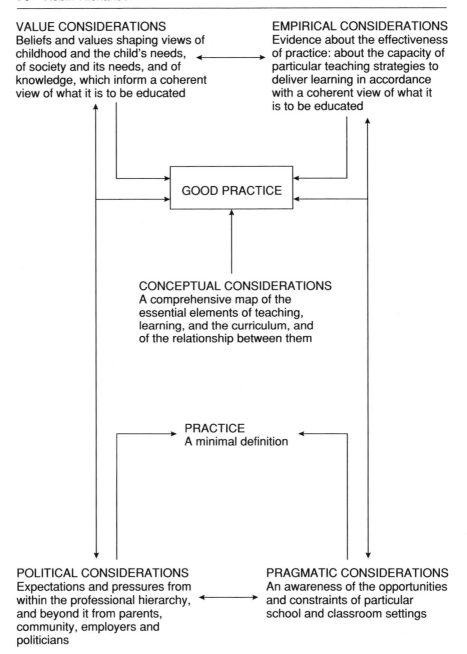

VALUE CONSIDERATIONS
Beliefs and values shaping views of
childhood and the child's needs,
of society and its needs, and of
knowledge, which inform a coherent
view of what it is to be educated

EMPIRICAL CONSIDERATIONS
Evidence about the effectiveness
of practice: about the capacity of
particular teaching strategies to
deliver learning in accordance
with a coherent view of what it
is to be educated

GOOD PRACTICE

CONCEPTUAL CONSIDERATIONS
A comprehensive map of the
essential elements of teaching,
learning, and the curriculum, and
of the relationship between them

PRACTICE
A minimal definition

POLITICAL CONSIDERATIONS
Expectations and pressures from
within the professional hierarchy,
and beyond it from parents,
community, employers and
politicians

PRAGMATIC CONSIDERATIONS
An awareness of the opportunities
and constraints of particular
school and classroom settings

Figure 5.3 Good practice 2: beyond relativism?

question – evaluative, empirical and so on – were seen as discrete, mutually exclusive and equivalent (Drummond 1993; Carr 1994). This misreading I find inexplicable, except perhaps as a response to the bizarre political climate of the time, in which academics no less than politicians and journalists sometimes indulged in the polarized rhetoric of 'them' and 'us'. But because this misreading exists I must emphasize again that the intention was precisely the opposite: to argue for more comprehensive versions of both practice and good practice than some of those on offer; and to insist that however hard the task of reconciling the various competing demands, pressures and considerations to which the teacher is subject, the primacy of values and a clear and explicit value-orientation in teaching must always be asserted, for without them all notions of being educated, let alone any versions of good practice, become, in an exact literal sense, meaningless.

Similarly, the 1992 primary discussion paper's emphasis on the principle of 'fitness for purpose' was not, as some suggested, an invitation to the unprincipled pragmatism of 'anything goes', but a different kind of attempt to underline this paper's concern with the quest for congruence between classroom action and educational values. It is the challenge of attaining this congruence which makes the notion of good primary practice, like education itself, as much an aspiration as an achievement. But the other message of 'fitness for purpose' is that good practice, created as it is in the unique setting of the classroom by the ideas and actions of teachers and pupils, can never be singular, fixed or absolute, a specification handed down or imposed from above in the manner charted in the Leeds research and illustrated in the quotations at the beginning of this chapter. Good practice is plural, provisional and dynamic: there are thus as many versions of good practice as there are good teachers striving to attain it.

NOTES

1   This chapter is a revised version of chapter 11 of R. J. Alexander (1992) *Policy and Practice in Primary Education,* London: Routledge.
2   The Leeds research referred to in this chapter was a five-year study (1986–91) of primary education in one of England's largest cities. The project's final report (reprinted as part of Alexander 1992) examined issues and practices ranging from LEA policy, resourcing, advice and support to school management, the deployment of staff, the curriculum, teaching methods and relationships between schools and parents. The report received considerable publicity and provoked a certain amount of controversy. Its political potential, especially vis-a-vis 'progressive' methods and the power of LEA's, was eagerly exploited in the run-up to the 1992 general election. It also led to the commissioning of the DES discussion paper on curriculum organisation and classroom practice in primary schools (Alexander, Rose and Woodhead 1992), referred to in this chapter.

REFERENCES

Alexander, R. J. (1988) *Primary Teaching*, London: Cassell.

Alexander, R. J. (1992) *Policy and Practice in Primary Education*, London: Routledge.

Alexander, R. J. (1995) *Versions of Primary Education*, London: Routledge.

Alexander, R. J., Rose, A. J. and Woodhead, C. (1992) *Curriculum Organization and Classroom Practice in Primary Schools: A Discussion Paper*, London: DES.

Bennett, S. N. (1976) *Teaching Styles and Pupil Progress*, London: Open Books.

Bennett, S. N., Desforges, C., Cockburn, A. and Wilkinson, B. (1984) *The Quality of Pupil Learning Experiences*, Hove: Erlbaum.

Carr, D. (1994) 'Wise men and clever tricks', *Cambridge Journal of Education*, 24: 1.

Central Advisory Council for Education (CACE) (England) (1967) *Children and their Primary Schools* (The Plowden Report), London: HMSO.

Department of Education and Science (1978) *Primary Education in England: a survey by HM Inspectors of Schools*, London: HMSO.

Department of Education and Science (1987) *Primary Schools: Some Aspects of Good Practice*, London: HMSO.

Drummond, M. J. (1993) *Assessing Children's Learning*, London: David Fulton.

Galton, M., Simon, B. and Croll, P. (1980a) *Inside the Primary Classroom*, London: Routledge.

Galton, M. and Simon, B. (1980b) *Progress and Performance in the Primary Classroom*, London: Routledge.

Mortimore, P., Sammons, P., Stoll, L., Lewis, D. and Ecob, R. (1988) *School Matters: The Junior Years*, London: Open Books.

National Curriculum Council (1989) *Curriculum Guidance 1: A Framework for the Primary Curriculum*, York: NCC.

Office for Standards in Education (1993) *Curriculum Organisation and Classroom Practice in Primary Schools: A Follow-up Report*, London: OFSTED.

Office for Standards in Education (1994) *Primary Matters: A Discussion on Teaching and Learning in Primary Schools*, London: OFSTED.

Office for Standards in Education (1995) *Standards and Quality in Education 1993–4: The Annual Report of Her Majesty's Chief Inspector of Schools*, London: HMSO.

Simon, B. (1981) 'The primary school revolution: myth or reality?', in B. Simon and J. Willcocks (eds) *Research and Practice in the Primary Classroom*, London: Routledge.

Chapter 6

Responding to pressures: a study of four secondary schools

Sally Brown, Sheila Riddell, and Jill Duffield

INTRODUCTION

The study which we describe in this paper explores features associated with pupil progress in four secondary schools differing on measures of SES and effectiveness. The questions which we address are the following:

- What are the characteristics of the four case study schools in terms of political and historical background; goals; curriculum; relationships with pupils and parents?
- How do these characteristics relate to the effectiveness and SES profile of the schools?
- What are senior managers' perceptions of policies designed to encourage a managerial and market-oriented climate? Do these views vary according to the schools' effectiveness and SES?

Data were drawn mainly from accounts offered by members of senior management teams and analysis of school policy documents. The aim was to consider the schools as reflexive and evolving institutions, shaped by their own histories and the political and social context in which they operated. This, we suggest, is a more subtle view of institutional culture than has sometimes been reflected in school effectiveness studies, which have tended to detach schools from their political and cultural context.

THE TREATMENT OF SOCIAL CLASS IN SCHOOL EFFECTIVENESS AND IMPROVEMENT RESEARCH

Although sweeping claims have been made for the importance of school effectiveness findings, on closer scrutiny they may appear somewhat disappointing. Despite the use of sophisticated statistical techniques, debates continue concerning the size and significance of school effects (Scheerens 1989), the extent to which the principal variance is to be found at the level of the department or classroom rather than the school (Fitzgibbon 1993) and the extent of stability within the system (Gray, Jesson, Goldstein and

Hedger 1993). Furthermore, it has been suggested that, in proposing lists of process factors associated with greater effectiveness, important context variables such as SES may have been neglected. Hallinger and Murphy (1986), for instance, investigated school processes in effective elementary schools in the State of California which varied on the dimension of SES. The authors concluded that although there were some similarities, there were also some striking differences between the high and low SES institutions. For example, whereas parents were centrally involved in the life of the higher SES schools, in those of lower SES, parents' values were regarded as incompatible with those of the school and therefore the heads attempted to limit their involvement. This implies that the compilation of a list of effectiveness factors of universal applicability may well remain a pipe dream, since different approaches 'work' in different settings.

A general problem of large-scale studies is the limited extent to which they are able to explain the relationships between educational outcomes and other variables and, where correlations are apparent, the direction of causality. If we take the matter of schools of different SES, for example, explanations of apparent links between high expectations and pupil performance may vary with context. In high SES schools it may be the high levels of pupil performance and parents' aspirations that lead to (rather than are caused by) high expectations among teachers. If that is so, then it is not necessarily the case that a direction to a low SES school to raise its expectations would result in any substantial improvement in pupil performance unless accompanied by a much more radical change in the social and economic circumstances of pupils and parents.

For some, problems with school effectiveness research are endemic to the paradigm. Angus (1993), in a critical review of three recently published texts, suggested that school effectiveness research was characterized by atheoreticism, failure to understand schools as operating within a given political context and an obsession with discovering what works rather than why it works. He commented:

> Family background, social class, any notion of context are typically regarded as 'noise' as 'outside background factors' which must be controlled for and then stripped away so that the researcher can concentrate on the important domain of school factors.

> (p. 361)

Neither has school improvement research escaped critical commentary. Although school improvers have focused their interest on processes and have been less concerned about outcomes, they too have tended to ignore the variability of social contexts of institutions. By concentrating their efforts on producing change in individual institutions, they have limited the extent to which understanding of both positive and negative outcomes has been advanced.

THE LOCATION AND NATURE OF THE PRESENT STUDY

A key feature of our study, then, was to include social class as well as level of measured effectiveness in the framework for the selection of our cases. In addition, rather than engaging in a programme of intervention in line with the school improvement paradigm, we wished to investigate naturalistically the culture of four case study schools.

The data used in identifying the sample of schools were gathered by the Centre for Educational Sociology at Edinburgh University. The SES information on the schools was the most recent available for pupils in their fourth year of secondary school (S4, age 16) from the region in which the schools were situated (1987/88). It was based on data about work (separately for mothers and fathers), parental education and household structure. The parents of pupils in the two schools identified as of lower SES had relatively low participation in paid work, their jobs were of relatively low status and they had left school at a relatively early age. In contrast in the two 'high SES' schools, parents had relatively high work participation, were in high status jobs and substantially more stayed on longer at school.

The statistical regression analysis of attainment in the schools was based on data from S4 in session 1990/91. Attainment on entry to secondary school was estimated by the performance in the Edinburgh Reading Test at the end of primary school. Estimates of attainment at S4 were carried out for eight measures: overall Scottish Certificate of Education Ordinary or Standard Grade awards at levels 1 to 3, and the average grade of award within each of seven curricular modes defined by the Scottish Consultative Committee on the Curriculum (science, English, mathematics, languages, social studies, aesthetic studies and technology).

In comparison with the region as a whole, one each of the 'high SES' and 'low SES' schools had (1) at least three modes on which statistically significant figures suggested the average pupil would have higher attainment if he or she attended that school and (2) no modes with statistically significant negative figures. The other two schools had no significant positive figures and at least three significantly negative ones. For the rest of this paper, they are referred to as follows:

School A	High SES, higher effectiveness
School B	High SES, lower effectiveness
School C	Low SES, higher effectiveness
School D	Low SES, lower effectiveness

We were particularly interested in the way in which the teachers construed progress and support and the actions they took to achieve their aims. Classroom observation and post-lesson interviews were used to gather data. We also interviewed pupils to gain insight into aspects of pupil culture. In order to develop a picture of school culture at a more general level, we drew upon interviews with members of the senior management team and school policy documents. The interviews with members of the senior management team in the school were semi-structured and included questions on the following: schools' recent history; pupil environment; school goals; school development planning; relationships with parents and pupils; the guidance system and support for pupils with behavioural and learning difficulties; teaching and assessment strategies; impact of recent innovation including the 5–14 programme, publication of league tables, parental choice of school and devolved school management.

As indicated earlier, the research had a reflexive dimension in that we were not simply interested in school culture in relation to measures of effectiveness and SES, but also in the way in which the school was evolving within a management- and market-oriented climate.

THE CULTURES OF THE FOUR SCHOOLS

If we turn to some of the early findings of the research at school as well as classroom level, there are some interesting points to be made in looking at various aspects of the individual schools which relate to their cultures. Perhaps somewhat alarmingly, the most apparent distinction between the two more effective schools (high and low SES) and the two less effective schools is their history, and the high level of awareness of that history, as senior secondary (grammar) and junior secondary (secondary modern) schools respectively prior to comprehensivization in the 1960s. Many of the parents of the pupils now in the schools will have had their own secondary education in the decade following the move towards comprehensive schooling. Their own experiences and views may well have been influenced by the expectations and prejudices which at that time focused on the earlier status of the newly formed comprehensive institutions. Despite the fact that the significance of former school status is well documented in the literature, we are surprised at the extent to which the history, in the minds of some people at least, is thought to affect current decision making and parental choice.

Some of the other broad features of the schools' culture, as seen through the eyes of their senior management and other teachers, show contrasts between the schools which reflect their differences in SES status. It is more difficult, however, to identify contrasts (apart from their histories) that distinguish between the measured high and low effectiveness institutions (we have been careful, of course, to try to avoid pre-judging the effectiveness of any activity within schools, especially in the so-called 'less effective' pair). Our strategy is to work with the four schools as separate case studies, but to keep looking across the studies for similarities and differences. At this stage we can offer some preliminary portraits of each school and a comparative commentary.

HIGH SES, HIGH EFFECTIVENESS (SCHOOL A)

As in the other schools, staff in School A were concerned about academic, personal and social development goals. Somewhat surprisingly, given that this school had the highest examination results, academic achievement was regarded as by no means the only, nor necessarily the most important, aspect of the school's work; the other schools, in contrast, were giving academic goals increasing pride of place. School A was a large, well-established, high achieving former senior secondary school which was built in the nineteenth century in a university town. It was secure, therefore, in the privilege it was able to confer on its pupils and the variety of experiences it could offer them so they could fulfil their academic potential. Given its high levels of performance over most of its pupil population, it had the space to turn its attention to personal growth and the development of confidence among its pupils to enable them to cope with whatever they had to face in life.

Teaching time and homework hours were greater than those in the other three schools. The comparisons were particularly marked with the low SES schools where pupils had the equivalent of eight school days less of teaching time per year and about two-thirds the hours of homework set by School A. Like the other schools, School A felt itself under pressure from the 5–14 Programme (Scotland's national curriculum) with the requirement for greater differentiation in the early years of secondary. There was, therefore, a continuing acceptance of setting within subjects (especially mathematics) at this stage. However, this was of some concern in School A, as it was in School B, the other high SES school, because it was seen as requiring predictive judgements that might be unrealistic and involve premature labelling of pupils. These views contrasted with those in the low SES schools which saw considerable advantages in setting in terms of improving the performance of the relatively small number of pupils likely to perform well in external examinations.

The content of the curriculum in this school was generally similar to that in the others. However, one interesting divergence was shared with School C, the other high effectiveness (but low SES) school: the opportunity of Latin or a second modern foreign language was offered to some pupils at the end of the first year in the school. This appeared to be a vestige of the senior secondary tradition which was still apparent in the more academic curriculum offered to higher achieving pupils. No such offer was available in the former junior secondaries which comprised our ineffective schools (B and D).

A striking feature of senior management in all the schools was their view that parents had a profound influence on the school's culture. School A, like the other high SES school, was aware that most of its parents appreciated academic success and other spheres of the school's activities, were demanding and conscious of their children's rights, would be prepared to exert pressure elsewhere (e.g. with the regional authority) and expected the very best for their children. As such they were extremely supportive but could take up a great deal of staff time in the school and might even interfere with its smooth running. The influence of these middle-class parents was evident in the support for lower achieving pupils in both the high SES schools. Dyslexia (or specific learning difficulties) had a salience in parents' thinking about their children's learning difficulties that had no place in the low SES schools. School A, with the most extensive learning support staff of the four schools, had one half-post above normal allocation which was designated to provide support for pupils with specific learning difficulties.

The general comparative pattern of learning support deserves some comment. School A was by far the largest of the four schools and so had the largest allocation of learning support staff, since allocations were related to the size of school roll. It also appeared to have a substantially lower proportion of pupils with learning difficulties. As a result of these circumstances and the extra half-time post, learning support staff were more likely to be available for co-operative teaching. The contrast with the two low SES schools was particularly marked. Their much higher proportions of pupils with learning difficulties made more stringent demands on learning support and it appeared to us that co-operative teaching, with mainstream and learning support teachers collaborating in the classroom, was spread much more thinly than in School A. Our work has been in only a minority of classrooms, however, and conclusions about higher levels of learning support in high SES mainstream classrooms have to remain tentative. It was clear that School A's current strategy was to employ a large measure of co-operative teaching, but a view was expressed that primary schools should be offering more learning support so that the resources at secondary could be focused on those with the greatest needs through, for example, individualized tuition.

The pupil culture in School A reflected its high SES status and had clear similarities with School B. Positive attitudes to school, especially in the early years, enthusiasms and appreciation of the efforts made by the staff were apparent. The programme of extra-curricular activities in School A was very extensive and, unlike many schools in Scotland, revived immediately after the long period of teachers' industrial action in 1986. Even for second year pupils (14 year olds), a Council was established by the Deputy Headteacher and consulted on organizational matters, and several third year pupils acted as prefects, assisting in various ways with the running of the school. Problems, such as they were, seemed to arise mainly from parental pressure and high expectations, although pupils from working-class families might sometimes feel alienated. Low achievers appeared just as committed as high achievers and the interactions between the school and families had the effect of positive reinforcement of shared values.

An important focus of the research was schools' responses to educational changes such as the introduction of development planning, the publication of league tables, marketing of the school and parental choice of school. These are regarded by the government as central to the thrust for improvement in the effectiveness of schools. School A, together with the other high SES school and the other high effectiveness (low SES) school, although not antagonistic to development planning, was conscious of the constraints which might be put on schools' own wider creative ideas by the emphasis on priorities determined externally by the region or SOED. The style of leadership cultivated by the Headteacher, inherited from his predecessor, was described as 'listening', 'consensual' and 'discussion-based'. The reaction to league tables of raw results was, as in the other high SES school, relaxed – high SES ensures good examination results. Value-added measures were also regarded with satisfaction as evidence to counter any suggestion that this privileged school was less successful with lower achieving pupils. None of the other schools said anything in favour of value-added measures. The issue of parental choice had scant significance for School A; its geographical position made it relatively inaccessible from other areas and there were no other secondary schools in the same town to provide competition. Although the school was one of those piloting the region's scheme for devolved school management of resources, there was no sense in which this was construed as some great leap forward with possibilities for increased resources. Indeed, the decision to take part seemed to relate more to the prospect of an enhanced independence rather than to money.

School A had the self-confidence and familiarity with high levels of performance that enabled it to reflect on the wider goals of education and to focus a substantial part of its energies on lower achieving pupils. It did not have to strive as hard as other schools to improve the academic achievements of a large proportion of its pupils; they and their parents were already well-motivated, accustomed to longer working hours and ambitious. The absence of local competition from other schools added to the 'space' available to the staff to think about the quality of education rather than the marketing of their wares. Its history and the nature of its local community, of course, bestowed real advantages on this school. Innovations like development planning and marketing of the school seemed irrelevant in explaining its effectiveness.

HIGH SES, LOW EFFECTIVENESS (SCHOOL B)

As we have seen, the high SES status of this school suggested similarities with School A in such matters as parental influence on the school's culture, some aspects of support for low achievers, pupils' attitudes to school, opinions about development planning and reactions to raw results league tables. It also displayed similar attitudes to the other high SES school in its reservations on the value of setting. Indeed, of the four schools it appeared the most committed to mixed ability teaching and individualized learning and least likely to be observed using whole class teaching. It was only the incompatibility of this school's preferred practices with the differentiated Standard Grade (Scottish Certificate of Education) mathematics course at Credit level that resulted in some reorganization within mixed ability classes at the end of the second year to introduce some differential grouping. In almost all these respects it displayed differences from the two low SES schools (C and D), but it was similar to those schools in its increasing emphasis on academic achievement (even at the expense of social and personal goals). It was also closer to schools C and D than to A in teaching time available and homework hours. Like the other low effectiveness (low SES) school, before comprehensivization its history was as a junior secondary although it opened as a purpose-built comprehensive.

School B had been involved in the region's pilot phase of school development planning, and was further advanced in this activity than the other three. Many committees relating to this had been set up within the school, although some teachers suggested there was sometimes a reluctance on the part of the Headteacher to act on staff views and that the committee structure was over-elaborate. Another distinctive feature of School B was its particularly active marketing strategy in direct competition with other schools in the locality. Cultivation of the school's public image, an agenda driven by media concerns, operating the school as a business with the parents as customers, ensuring that school events were reported in local papers and planning to place leaflets advertising the school in banks and building societies were all part of the strategy. Gratification was apparent when preference over other schools, including the private sector, was displayed by parents. Considerable comfort was drawn from the school's relatively good showing on raw results league tables and sympathy was expressed for other local schools where such results looked like 'a disaster'. School B's relatively poor performance in value-added terms, however, seemed to generate little concern; the assumption seemed to have been made that negative value-added measures were unlikely to be understood or criticized by the general public. In contrast, high raw results seemed to be attracting more middle-class parents which, in turn, boosted those raw results. The school was quite clear that to sustain this it should not advertise itself as being good with low achievers, though it was pleased to be regarded as a caring institution.

This high SES but low effectiveness school, therefore, was the most market-oriented of our case study institutions. Its SES associated it in many respects with School A, but it was less assured of its academic standing and so put very great emphasis on academic goals in the light of what it saw as parents' demands. It could be described as the school which, more than our other case studies, had responded to the government's directives for educational innovations. That and its history as a junior secondary were the most obvious contrasts with the two more effective schools (A and C). Whether its market-oriented approach would pay off in improved value-added measures of effectiveness in the future remained to be seen.

LOW SES, HIGH EFFECTIVENESS (SCHOOL C)

In common with the other high effectiveness school, School C was a former senior secondary school though in its establishment as a comprehensive it incorporated a nearby junior secondary with a progressive ethos. The school consciously nurtured its roots in the community by, for example, helping parents to organize a successful School Reunion leading to the foundation of a Friends of [School C] Association. Although the school occupied an open site, it was surrounded by local authority housing and the marks of the collapse of heavy industry, and the buildings had many of the disadvantages of early post Second World War construction. Like the two less effective schools, increasing emphasis was being placed on academic achievement, not least because an HMI report had stressed the need for this (whether HMI had access to the relatively high value-added measures we cannot say). Although there was a view in the school that academic awards were a crucial 'passport' for pupils to take on and that this must be the priority, the Headteacher showed considerable concern for a greater focus on personal and social development and on dealing with problems like bullying.

Like the other low SES (low effectiveness) school, School C was conscious of the preponderance of low achieving pupils in mixed ability classes who 'had a dragging' effect on the rest. Setting in mathematics was welcomed as providing opportunities for those who had the potential to achieve academic goals. In these circumstances, the need to target learning support on those with the greatest need was regarded as more important than the thin spread of learning support across mixed ability classes. In both low SES schools parents were less demanding, less supportive, less likely to attend parents' evenings, more inclined to leave decisions to the school and more likely to have values different from the school (e.g. with regard to physical violence) than in the high SES schools. Similar contrasts were apparent in the pupil cultures. The low SES schools' populations had significant numbers of disaffected, academically unmotivated pupils. School C placed considerable emphasis on trying to convince these young people that academic success was in their grasp, rewarding good behaviour, attendance and punctuality, and exploring ways of involving pupils in their own assessments to encourage more constructive thinking and activity. The Headteacher bemoaned the demise of extra-curricular activities, particularly school sport, which had not been revived after the 1986 dispute over teachers' pay and conditions. The activities were seen as important in helping pupils develop self-discipline and a commitment to the school; their disappearance had had a negative effect on pupil morale. Such circumstances were also indicative of low teacher morale and the Headteacher was well aware of the frustrations associated with working in an institution like School C. In the light of this, he endeavoured to support all teacher-led initiatives, even if they were costly, and urged the staff to seek support from their colleagues.

In considering school development planning the school was concerned, like the high SES schools, that the process was a mechanism for exerting too much external control and stifling a more creative and collegial system that was already operating in the school. Like the other low SES school, there was also anxiety about the unmanageable amount of paperwork and about the damaging effect of raw results league tables. School C saw such tables as essentially destructive with no constructive explanations of why things were the way they were or of action that might be taken to improve things. Despite the school's good showing on value-added measures, these were more or less discounted as incomprehensible to parents and likely to add to the confusion. Nor was there great rejoicing at the extra 200 pupils admitted as a result of parents' placement requests. This addition made little difference to the school's academic profile, and enlarged the school population in ways that have ensured even greater practical problems, especially of space and stress on teachers. Devolved school management was seen as providing opportunities to target extra resources on lower achieving pupils, especially those with learning difficulties, but there was an awareness that this might damage the school's public image in the current climate that puts so much emphasis on performance of the more able. The fear of the re-emergence of 'fast-track' and 'sink' schools haunted the low SES institutions and made them wary of promoting too enthusiastically their work with lower achieving pupils.

School C's value-added measures identified it as a successful school that was working in difficult circumstances. Its senior secondary history was to its advantage and it might have benefited from an initial upheaval twenty years ago as it was incorporating a progressive junior secondary school. The substantial task of establishing shared understanding from two different traditions might, in the longer term, have established what seemed to be a reflective and creative tradition of collegial management and opportunities for staff to identify and develop their own priorities, opting into developments of their choice. Part of this tradition had included particular concerns for low achievers who formed a substantial proportion of pupils. More recently, the tradition seemed to be at some risk from central planning developments, concentration on the publication of performance measures and increases in the pupil population brought about by parental choice. As in the other high effectiveness (high SES) school, therefore, we had little evidence that these innovations were likely to have increased the school's effectiveness. Paradoxically, because that effectiveness might depend on the school's creative response to its role in a difficult environment, the innovations might have had a negative influence.

LOW SES, LOW EFFECTIVENESS (SCHOOL D)

School D, the smallest of the four, served a socially disadvantaged area of villages/small towns with high unemployment and increasing crime and family breakdown. Its raw examination results were very low indeed. Despite admirable policies to fulfil the comprehensive school ideal, and a new, purpose-built and lavish building, the school had difficulties in attracting pupils. It had replaced a number of former junior secondaries and that replacement did not please all of the villages which had lost their local schools.

As we have seen, it had many similarities with the other low SES school. It had a preponderance of low achieving pupils, somewhat alienated characteristics among the parent population, low motivation among many pupils, concern that a move away from mixed ability teaching towards setting and individual tuition was probably necessary to support both those with academic potential and those with the greatest problems, a belief that insufficient account was taken of social deprivation factors in the regional allocations of learning support staff and a concern that it should not present itself as a school for the less-able.

This school currently placed very heavy emphasis on academic goals. This was not necessarily of the school's own choosing, given its circumstances, but it was seen as the only performance measure that 'counts'. Within this, however, School D was committed to general improvement in its performance rather than what it saw as currently unattainable targets of excellence. It was frustrated that in a norm-referenced system (whether based on raw results or value-added measures) improvement on the school's own base-line measure of achievement seemed to count for little. Creative developments, such as the removal of barriers between a special needs unit attached to the school and the learning support department in order to provide opportunities for special unit pupils to integrate into mainstream classrooms and curricula (a beneficial spin-off from this allowed children in mainstream access to specialist teachers), received little recognition in a climate that lays so much stress on achievements that are relevant, for the most part, to the more able. Pipe bands and successful dramatic productions were probably of major importance in the achievements of a school of this kind, but the effectiveness measures that are in vogue are destined to ignore these and concentrate on those that rub the nose of School D in the bottom of the heap of failure. It felt crucified by the local press and frustrated that some parents and associated primary schools continued to prefer to send their children to a neighbouring and former senior secondary (but less well-appointed) school. The morale of enthusiastic young teachers recruited when the school opened was seen by some as having been sapped both by its poor academic performance and by the low expectations of older teachers who spent much of their earlier working lives in junior secondary environments. It is difficult to see how the recent government innovations could be regarded as a constructive way of improving this school's effectiveness.

DISCUSSION OF THE FINDINGS

Any aspiration to identify a straightforward common set of factors to account for the differences in value-added measures between the pairs of more and less effective schools seems destined to disappointment. At this stage we have only two factors which appear to be associated with higher effectiveness (Schools A and C). The first of these relates to the history of the institution as a senior (grammar) rather than junior secondary (secondary modern) school before comprehensivization. No doubt that history influences the way parents, and perhaps pupils, still regard the school and what they expect of it. Furthermore, and more surprisingly, it seems also to affect the ways in which at least some staff think about it. This 'senior secondary effect', however, is mediated by social class. In School A the very high commitment of the middle-class parents is channelled directly, and indirectly through the school, to influence the regional authorities to provide, for example, additional specialized learning support or to improve transport arrangements. The pattern in School C is for parents to express their support by choosing it for their children over other local schools and engaging in activities like fundraising. But the school is conscious that it has continually to encourage parental support and involvement. Indeed, even when they do become involved parents still do not expect to participate in the educational decision making; that they regard as the province of the professionals in the school.

The second factor is less clear-cut and must be tentative at this stage. It seems to relate to the efforts made by the more effective schools to incorporate pupils into aspects of the running of the school and to establish a collegial atmosphere among the teachers. The two schools have, of course, very different social environments and this affects the ways in which this factor is manifest. Thus School C (low SES) concentrates on tangible rewards for pupils; School A (high SES), in contrast, can rely on existing high levels of motivation for involvement among pupils. School C has to put energy into cultivating teacher morale and be ready to use its resources to respond to teachers' ideas in order to cultivate a collegial atmosphere in what is basically a very difficult environment. School A is also concerned to cultivate a collegial atmosphere but is in the position of being able to assume a relatively high morale among staff. In both schools, however, there appears to be evidence consistent with the hypothesis that ownership (a word that seems to survive derision heaped upon it) of their activities on the part of teachers and pupils is an important ingredient of effectiveness, in a way that proactive decision making by the Headteacher and strength of line management is not. We did not find significant evidence of similar beliefs and practices in the less effective schools. Neither of the two factors identified here seem to be particularly salient for most school effectiveness studies, although Reynolds (1991) in summarizing work carried out over a decade in Welsh schools has pointed to high levels of pupil involvement, as prefects or class monitors, as features associated with being an effective school.

Perhaps more important than this, however, are the striking contrasts between schools of different SES. The fact that these differences are so much more marked than those associated with differences in effectiveness, suggests that any notion that there is a common set of management reforms, that would be expected to enable schools of all SES levels to become more effective, must be misguided (this is not to deny, of course, that there may be some innovations that are of value to all schools).

The most obvious contrast between the high and low SES pairs of schools is their achievement profiles. While for the great majority of pupils in the high SES schools the goals of good certificate examination results seem entirely appropriate, in the low SES schools there is a substantial proportion of pupils for whom other goals would seem to have higher priority and who might well be seen as impeding the progress of the higher achievers.

Although in all schools it could be argued that there is a continuum of achievement, in practice the high SES schools are able to take for granted the motivation of the great majority of the pupils and their parents towards awards for academic achievement; the minority for whom this is not the case (or have other reasons for differing from the majority) can then be given special attention. Because learning support staffing is based on the size of school rolls, and middle-class parents can make effective representations for special provision (e.g. for those deemed to be dyslexic), the high SES schools are able to provide effective help for those with learning difficulties. The task for the low SES schools appears to be quite different. Here there is a tendency to see two populations of pupils: those for whom the pursuit of certificate awards is a priority and those for whom other kinds of goals are seen as having much greater urgency. Because the proportions of pupils with learning difficulties are substantial, and parents are less articulate in their demands for specific resources, learning support tends to be spread much more thinly than in the high SES schools. It seems very likely that the most effective structures and strategies for improving the effectiveness of schools in relation to low achievers would vary quite markedly among schools serving different SES populations.

Complementing the contrast of achievement profile in schools of different SES is one of motivation. A very great deal of effort in low SES schools has to be devoted to improving the morale of teachers, the attitudes of pupils towards learning and the level of involvement of parents in their children's education. High SES schools can to a far greater extent take these matters for granted and can expect an annual boost from the publication of raw certificate results which everyone understands; such results offer little comfort for the low SES schools. High SES schools may, of course, have problems such as excessive demands from parents, but these are *different* problems. While the low SES schools may put a priority on, say, the elimination of bullying and the persuasion of parents that physical violence cannot be condoned as 'standing up for yourself', the high SES schools may be more concerned about 'unreasonable' requests from parents for greater shares of resources for their children.

A third contrast relates to the marketing of schools. For both those serving low SES communities, this is a source of anxiety. A principal responsibility which they must accept is to provide support for low achievers, yet they are clear that in the current culture of achievement they cannot advertise themselves as specializing in education for those with learning difficulties. Furthermore, the marketing game is very much one of competition on the basis of raw examination results, and low SES schools have little chance of winning. The school with high value-added effectiveness would welcome recognition of that measure, but it is convinced that the complexity of such information will not be grasped by many parents. In any case, it has no wish to increase the school population which is already of a size that produces considerable stresses and strains. For the high SES school with high effectiveness, marketing appears irrelevant. For the other high SES school, with low effectiveness, it is a principal thrust of policy. It could be seen as a satisfactory strategy, based as it is on good raw examination results and leading to more parents choosing to send their children to the school. But this diverts attention from the less favourable value-added measures which, not surprisingly, are ignored in the marketing; this school, like the low SES schools, assumes that parents will be unaware of, or fail to understand, such measures.

IN CONCLUSION

This study sets out to investigate to what extent school effectiveness research, in its familiar forms, could play a leading role in bringing about school improvement. It started from the assumption, based on past experience, that in presenting findings from school effectiveness studies account has to be taken of the ways in which teachers and schools already make sense of their educational endeavours. In so far as school effectiveness surveys construe the world in ways that are different from those of the people with responsibility for bringing about the improvements, the probability of change (of the kind desired by the proponents of school effectiveness) is slight.

Our empirical findings and examination of school effectiveness studies support six broad propositional points.

1   The ways in which teachers conceptualize pupils' progress and the kind of classroom support that is needed to promote that progress, are much more complex and rich than the conceptions of progress and support implicit in school effectiveness research. The latter operationalizes progress very largely in terms of achievement and easily measurable non-cognitive criteria; support variables are for the most part management structures

and practices, or broad-brush judgements about, for example, teaching methods. As our research proceeds, we expect to say more about whether the relatively crude and management-oriented variables of school effectiveness research can engage with teachers' frameworks of constructs and, indeed, whether there is enough in common among teachers (let alone among countries) to be able to see such engagement as a possibility. We are not suggesting, of course, that the discourse of school effectiveness is unintelligible to teachers. In in-service staff development or at conferences they can patently hold their own in debate; but their thinking about their own teaching and their pupils' learning appears not to have a predominantly management/achievement orientation. (Evidence from other Scottish research (Brown and Swann 1994) suggests a similar split between teachers' external public dialogues about the 5–14 Programme, Scotland's national curriculum, using the language and concepts of that programme and their internalized ways of thinking about their classroom teaching.)

2   The well-meaning efforts of school effectiveness studies to incorporate qualitative data collection to complement the quantitative are unlikely significantly to bridge the gap between school effectiveness and school improvement. Their basic problem is that they are still dependent on researchers' frameworks (theoretical or political) and not on the practitioners' implicit theories about what they are trying to do. Until the latter are taken into account the chances of real understanding of why things turn out the way they do (effective, not effective, improving, deteriorating) are negligible. It might be possible, of course, to change the ways practitioners think to bring them more in line with researchers, but to do that a start would have to be made from where the practitioners are now. As long as the qualitative approach or paradigm is essentially the same as the quantitative (but with less precise data, of course) and based on earlier research of the same kind, it is unlikely to advance our understanding.

3   Identification of the characteristics of the most effective schools has been the meat of school effectiveness research. The variables that are explored, however, arise from researchers' and policy-makers' ideas about 'what will work' and, as we have said, emphasize management features. Our research has looked at how four case study schools view their own distinctive management structures and practices. A striking finding has been the paucity of commonalities between, on the one hand, the more effective and, on the other hand, the less effective pairs of schools. The two characteristics which distinguish the more effective schools are their histories as senior secondaries (grammar schools), and the opportunities they give to staff and pupils to make decisions influencing their lives in school. However, much more marked are the differences between pairs of schools identified as high and low SES. That implies that strategies

for improvement are likely to be highly dependent on the social class of the school population.

4   Among the most salient differences among the schools are the differences in achievement profile between the high and low SES pupil populations. In the high SES schools the majority of pupils are well motivated and able to achieve substantial academic awards at Standard Grade. The learning support staff can focus their attention, therefore, on the minority with learning difficulties. Other research (Willms 1986; Paterson 1992) suggests that this minority, even if their own social background is disadvantaged, can benefit from the higher cultural resources of socially advantaged peers. The low SES schools have much more substantial proportions of children with learning difficulties, but similar levels of learning support staff to the high SES schools. (Some authorities make extra staffing allowances for social deprivation, but these do not match the differences in requirements.) Furthermore, as well as the support being more thinly spread, the schools have to deal with large numbers of young people whose self-esteem does not relate to academic achievement and motivation to learn is low. It is on matters of this kind that teachers see efforts for improvement as having to focus. Telling them that effective schools are associated with strong and competent leadership, particular patterns of punishment and reward systems, management structures, committed staff with high expectations and standards, and so on is likely to be greeted with 'that's all very well but somewhat distant from what faces me as a teacher'. Even within the framework of the characteristics that school effectiveness researchers emphasize, the questions of those in low SES schools may well be asking how on earth teachers' morale and high expectations are to be sustained in very difficult and unrewarding circumstances.

5   There is no evidence that management innovations, like school development planning and the competitive marketing of schools, are improving school effectiveness. School development planning seems to be somewhat sidelined, though there is some feeling that it constrains schools' own creative planning. The context in which it is most clearly implemented is the school with the only significant involvement in marketing itself; this is one of the less effective schools.

6   Publication of raw results is seen as a benefit only by the high SES schools, particularly the less effective one. For the latter, the raw results have contributed to the increase in the numbers of parents choosing the school for their children, but they have also allowed the school to discount the value-added findings. Value-added measures, supported by critics of the government and many academics as potentially beneficial to schools serving disadvantaged populations, are seen as irrelevant by the low SES schools; none regard them as having meaning for parents. The norm-referenced nature of both kinds of performance measures do nothing for the incentive to improve.

Finally, we hope that in the future both school effectiveness and improve-ment researchers will pay more attention to the issue of social class. As our case studies demonstrate, this element is crucial to the development of an understanding of individual pupils' attainment and progress and the wider backcloth of their social experiences. Rather than developing evermore elab-orate lists of factors promoting effectiveness across cultures, it may be more fruitful to develop grounded theory based on close study of critical cases.

ACKNOWLEDGEMENT

The researchers would like to express their gratitude to the Economic and Social Research Council, who funded this research (award R 000 233906).

REFERENCES

Angus, L. (1993) 'The sociology of school effectiveness', *British Journal of Sociology of Education* 14(3): 333–45.

Brown, S. and Swann, J. (1994) 'Teachers' classroom thinking: the impact of the 5–14?', paper presented to the annual conference of the Scottish Educational Research Association, 29 September to 1 October 1994 in St Andrews.

Fitzgibbon, C. (1993) 'Differential effectiveness: implications for monitoring', paper presented to the ESRC Seminar Series on School Effectiveness and School Improvement.

Gray, J. Jesson, D. Goldstein, H. and Hedger, K. (1993) 'The statistics of school improvement: establishing the agenda', paper presented to the ESRC Seminar Series on School Effectiveness and School Improvement.

Hallinger, P. and Murphy, J. F. (1986) 'The social context of effective schools', *American Journal of Education* 9(4): 328–55.

Paterson, L. (1992) 'Socio-economic status and educational attainment: a multi-dimensional and multi-level study', *Evaluation and Research in Education* 6(2): 97–121.

Reynolds, D. (1991) 'School effectiveness in secondary schools: research and its policy implications', in S. Riddell and S. Brown (eds) *School Effectiveness: Its Messages for School Improvement*, Edinburgh: HMSO.

Scheerens, J. (1989) *Effective Schooling: Research, Theory and Practice*, London: Cassell.

Stoll, L. (1993) 'Linking school effectiveness and school improvement: issues and possibilities', paper presented to the ESRC Seminar Series on School Effectiveness and School Improvement.

Willms, J. D. (1986) 'Social class segregation and its relationship to pupils' exami-nation results in Scotland, *American Sociological Review* 51: 224–41.

Chapter 7

The challenge of turning round ineffective schools[1]

John Gray and Brian Wilcox

INTRODUCTION

In September 1994 Fairfax Community School in Bradford was reported to be 'the first casualty among local authority schools of the new inspection system launched by the Office of Standards in Education' (reported in the *Guardian*, 7 September 1994). Senior education officers within the authority had recommended it be closed.

The previous autumn the school had been judged by OFSTED inspectors who had produced a series of strongly worded criticisms as well as recommendations for its improvement. Unusually, the school had also featured in a High Court case when a group of (mainly Bangladeshi) parents had tried unsuccessfully to get their children places at other schools in the area. A second visit by OFSTED inspectors during the summer of 1994 had 'found little improvement and made further criticisms'.

The acting headteacher was said to be 'shocked and horrified by the (closure) decision. The staff's hard work seemed to have been ignored and wasted.' A leader of the Bangladesh community meanwhile was reported as saying: 'if this means all other schools have to improve their standards, it will have been justified. The parents feel that it shows their stand was right.'

In the same article a second school, St Mark's Church of England comprehensive in Hammersmith and Fulham LEA, was reported to have been 'condemned by Ofsted inspectors as a failing school'. The inspectors said that 'a plan drawn up by the head and governors after an adverse report in December 1993 had not improved teaching'.

A mere fortnight after their initial recommendations Bradford LEA had had second thoughts about closing Fairfax, stepping back from their initial decision (BBC Breakfast TV News, 20 September 1994). The school had the chance to fight on.

Both cases underline how high the improvement stakes have become. Ineffective schools, which fail to improve rapidly, run the risk of being simply closed down. Rarely can knowledge about how to improve have been at more of a premium.

CASE STUDIES OF CHANGE IN 'INEFFECTIVE' SCHOOLS

In fact there is very little research, especially in Britain, which is explicitly about 'turning round' so-called 'ineffective' schools. This is not to say that no research has been done on this topic but rather that, in the search for the correlates of effectiveness, the correlates of ineffectiveness have been assumed to be the same. It is by no means clear, however, that they are. How an 'ineffective' school improves may well differ from the ways in which more effective schools maintain their effectiveness.

Most of the work which has been undertaken to date has been in the form of case studies and it is to some of these that we now turn.

Charismatic leadership on the 'wrong side of the tracks'

The story of improvement at George Washington Carver High School in Atlanta is told in Lightfoot's study *The Good High School* (1983, chapter 1). It is the first of six case studies she presents of 'good' American schools and the only one relating to an inner-city area. Its claim to a place in the book rests on the extent to which a new leader had secured sufficient changes within a relatively short space of time to bring the school back from the brink. Lightfoot clearly felt that such a school deserved a place in her catalogue of excellence as much, if not more than, more traditional examples.

The school's story of change revolved around just one figure, the new principal Dr Norris Hogans. Hogans was in his late forties, a former American football player; 'powerful in stature and character, he dominated the school':

> a man of great energy he walked about the campus in perpetual motion, looking severe and determined, always carrying his walkie-talkie. Through the walkie-talkie he barked orders and made enquiries. His requests sounded like commands. There was an immediacy about him, an unwillingness to wait or to be held back.

Atlanta's school superintendent, Dr Alonzo Crim, had turned to Hogans when he had contemplated closing the school which was, at the time, 'an ugly reminder of the deterioration, chaos and unrest that plagues many big-city schools' (Lightfoot, 1983, p. 31 and ff.). Crim saw Hogans as 'a diamond in the rough, a jock who made good . . . and a man who learnt and grew every day'. In Crim's view Hogans had done a good job in a short space of time (just three years): 'he had gotten the kids to listen (and) disrupted the inertia'.

Opinions about Hogans amongst the staff were more mixed.

> 'Everyone agreed he was powerful. Some viewed his power as the positive charisma and dynamic force required to turn an institution around and

move it in a new direction. These enthusiasts recognised his abrupt, sometimes offensive style, but claimed that his determined temperament was necessary to move things forward. They willingly submitted to his autocratic decisions because they viewed his institutional goals as worthy and laudable.

His detractors, on the other hand, had been around in the school for long periods of time and were used to policies which had permitted considerably more autonomy. Now they 'tended to keep their complaints to themselves, forming a covert gossip ring and passively resisting [Hogans'] attempts to make changes by preserving their own inertia'.

Lightfoot felt there were three key thrusts to Hogans' interventions: the need for discipline; the need for a new image for the school; and the need for better and closer links with the community. 'Discipline and authority had become the key to gaining control of the change process.' Hogans passionately believed that the school 'must provide the discipline, the safety and the resources that students were not getting at home and that it must demand something from them'. 'A chaotic school setting and a permissive atmosphere could only lead to ruin and failure so there was a preoccupation with rules and regulations at Carver.' 'Visible conformity, obedience and a dignified presence were critical concerns.'

Reflecting in a concluding chapter on why Carver might deserve the accolade of 'excellence', Lightfoot was clearly concerned to present both the pros and the cons. On the positive side she identified several areas where Carver had made 'great strides'. 'School people focused on the measurable, visible indices of progress: steady attendance rates, fewer disciplinary problems, a decline in acts of vandalism to property, and more jobs filled upon graduation.' On some other 'standards of goodness', however, such as the 'more psycho-social, less measurable qualities of civility, poise and ambition' she was less certain. And on a number of indices which 'reflected the substance of education including curricular design and structure, and pedagogical processes', Carver lagged behind many other Atlanta high schools. Many of the staff were committed to tackling 'the educational malaise' but 'the school had a long way to go before it could claim that most of its students were receiving a good education'. The school had 'progressed from terrible to much better' and it was this progress which was impressive. But, in the round, it had only achieved the 'minimal standards of goodness which [she] envisioned as a first stage of movement towards higher goals'.

'Hostility and conflict' on the road to change

Most case studies of improving schools report that some improvement (eventually) occurred. In our view such studies, biased as they tend to be towards the change efforts that worked, probably give too rosy an impression of how much change can take place over relatively short periods of time. More work on the myriad efforts which probably 'failed' is required.

One of the few pieces of research which reports an attempt to tackle this issue suggests that we may be looking at a rather different set of factors from those which emerge in the successful cases. In an all-too-brief account of a project which failed to turn around an ineffective Welsh school Reynolds (1991 and 1992, pp. 178–82) argues that the 'deep structures' of ineffective schools may have been inappropriately ignored.

A variety of factors were observed to be at stake in the school he worked in. Individual teachers, he suspected, were projecting their own deficiencies as teachers onto the children or the communities from which they came, claiming that the latter were the reason for the school's ineffectiveness. They 'clung on' to past practices, arguing that things had always been done the way they were doing them. They had, at the same time, built up defences to keep out threatening messages from outsiders. They were reluctant to attempt change 'for fear that it might fail and were convinced that change was someone else's job, not theirs'. They sought 'safety in numbers', retreating into a ring-fenced mentality. Finally, the staff were organised into strongly-demarcated sub-groups, with sometimes hostile relationships between them.

Reynolds goes on to describe some of the issues he encountered which the 'school improvement literature had given [him] no warning about'. Attempts to get the staff to discuss the educational problems facing the school, rather than the personal deficiencies of individual children, often resulted in 'increased interpersonal conflicts amongst staff, a breakdown of some pre-existing relationships and much interpersonal hostility'. An attempt to get teachers to understand the nature of pupils' experiences by shadowing them during the course of a morning or afternoon produced a situation in which many staff 'realised for the first time the incompetence of their colleagues, having experienced it at first hand rather than merely encountering it through rumour or innuendo'.

The account Reynolds offers is not uniformly pessimistic. Eventually some of the change efforts began to penetrate the school's management structures, encouraging more openness and sharing on the part of the management team. These changes, in turn, influenced the staff who began to 'solidify in terms of interpersonal relationships'. None the less, there were casualties including, in this particular case, the headteacher who retired from a nervous breakdown.

Eventually, Reynolds reported, the school emerged through these processes as a 'more effective institution ... more able to handle the complex inter-personal difficulties that school improvement brings'. Summing up, he concluded that 'knowledge of the rational-empirical paradigm encountered irrationality, emotionality, abnormality and what can only be called personal and group disturbance' (Reynolds, 1992, p. 182).

Reynolds' account opens up the dark side of school improvement efforts and exposes the naive optimism on which much of the current literature is premised. In particular it encourages us to read the major studies with a more discerning eye whilst paying greater attention to what they don't say as well as what they do.

A recent British 'success story'?

The story of change at Newall Green High School on the Wythenshawe estate in Manchester is told in the OFSTED study, *Improving Schools* (OFSTED, 1994). The school serves one of the most disadvantaged areas of Manchester with high rates of unemployment in the locality. The extent of its 'improvement' appears to offer significant messages for all those involved in providing for the educationally disadvantaged.

At the time when the school was inspected there were a wide variety of issues which apparently required attention. These included:

> improvement in the quality of classroom experience; greater use of assessment to set expectations and to raise standards; adoption of a wider range of teaching styles; improvement in the effectiveness of departmental management; reorganisation of support for low-attaining pupils; improvement in vocational and educational guidance; and the continued development of the transitional arrangements between primary and secondary school.
>
> (OFSTED, 1994, p. 9)

Standards of achievement, at least as measured by public examinations, were low: only six per cent of the year group (some 8 or 9 pupils) were obtaining five or more A–C passes.

The most striking thing about the school's subsequent experience was the very short period from the time of the first inspection within which, it is claimed, the improvements took place. First inspected in October 1991 and revisited just over a year later (in January 1993) 'there was no mistaking the fact that the issues identified in the inspection had been addressed and that this was an improved and improving school; there were clear advances on many fronts' (OFSTED, 1994, p. 10).

Amongst the 'tangible improvements' HMI cited was the increase in pupils gaining five or more A–C passes at GCSE.

From six per cent in 1991 it had jumped to 18 per cent by 1993 representing, as HMI observed, 'a three-fold improvement in two years' (OFSTED, 1994). In some department the changes had been 'astonishing'. In Science, for example there had been 'a five-fold improvement' in the grades obtained over the two years and History had also secured very considerable gains. Improvements were not confined to those taking exams either. 'In 1992–93 53 per cent of entrants had a reading age below nine years [but] by Christmas every child had improved measurably and some had made enormous gains.' At the same time 'unusual methods' for handling the processes of transition from primary to secondary school had produced 'unmistakable improvements in pupils' attitudes, confidence and motivation to learn' (op. cit., p. 11). Commenting on the school's ethos, 'an area where the measurement of improvement by objective yardsticks is most difficult', HMI identified a 'brightening, school-wide picture' of 'better relationships, better behaviour, better attendance and better attitudes'.

The report went on to ask 'what was special about the way this school achieved the improvements?' It identified five main areas in which there had been significant developments. The first was in relation to school develop-ment planning. 'Successive plans had built carefully on earlier ones, rearranging priorities, ensuring continuity and progression and the rescue of any neglected or uncompleted initiatives'. The second was the 'regularity with which various kinds of review were undertaken'. These took place between the SMT and faculty heads; between faculty heads and individual teachers; and between subject teachers and individual pupils. The third was in the 'sharing of aspirations and criteria for success'. This had included making pupils aware of what constituted progress in their work and developing innovative arrangements for pupils' transition from primary to secondary school. The fourth related to quality control. 'The school understood the need to monitor its work, to maintain momentum and to keep standards up' through a wide variety of arrangements. Fifth, and finally, there was the 'hard work and dedication' the school staff had put in.

Important changes were undoubtedly taking place at Newall Green between the time of the first inspection and the second. Whether they were as substan-tial as the report suggests seems, however, more doubtful. School development planning, for example, has some potential but no previous studies have envis-aged success on the scale reported here. And other institutions have sought to bring about changes in the ways teachers review their work and counsel students but again with more limited success.

It may, of course, be that Newall Green was already successful in certain key respects and that the 'improvements' described were consequently devel-oped over the following year from already solid foundations. Returning to the original inspection report, there are signs that, whatever the list of areas identified as requiring further action, much was already going well in the school. Indeed, at the time of the first inspection 'standards of work were satisfactory or better in three-quarters of lessons seen' (a figure, we note, that was around the national average for all schools), 'relationships in the classroom (were) generally very good', 'behaviour around the school (was) courteous and orderly' and teachers already 'worked hard to provide a stim-ulating environment for learning'. Finally, the school was 'well led' by the headteacher and deputies who gave 'a clear sense of direction and purpose' through 'concise and realistic' aims and objectives which 'linked effectively with the school development plan and faculty/departmental schemes of work' (Newall Green, 1991, p. iv). Indeed, with the benefit of hindsight, the only features of the school that seem out of place within a general story of success were the extremely low exam results (which were rather generously described in the initial report merely as being 'below the national and Manchester averages') and the attendance of Year 11 pupils.

None the less there is a problem in interpreting what caused what. If all these positive features were already in place at the time of the first inspection, then it is more difficult to see how the particular factors identified in the case study made the 'extra difference' that brought about the improvements which were noted. If school development planning, for example, was already an established part of school practice (as it seems to have been), then it must have been some additional and notable aspect of the plan(s) that made the additional difference. If relationships in the classroom were already 'generally good' then teachers would surely have had difficulty in improving them much further; and if teachers already 'worked hard', then they would have had to work still harder.

Another possible explanation is that, at the time of the first inspection, the school had undertaken much of the groundwork needed for improvement to flourish but had not yet seen the more tangible benefits which began to emerge shortly afterwards. On another tack, the study does not rule out the possibility that the improvements in measured performance could have been brought about by other means. The better results in GCSE might, for example, have come about through the school targeting a rather small number of 'borderline' pupils and giving them extra help to get them over the five A–C hurdle, as has happened in a considerable number of other schools nationally. Starting from a very low base one can make considerable progress in percentage terms by improving the performance of rather small numbers of pupils. On the question of whether the school succeeded in improving the attendance of boys in Years 10 and 11 (a concern that was singled out for comment in the first inspection) the account is simply vague.

The purpose of this critique is not to suggest that there were *no* important changes at Newall Green over the period between the two inspections. We doubt, however, whether the school's experience was typical of improvement efforts in similar schools. A sense of realism about what schools can be expected to achieve over periods as short as a year is required. If a 'failing' school's fate is to be judged simply by the distance the most successful have travelled then most will be damned.

WHAT'S IN IT FOR TEACHERS?

Most studies agree that, by one means or another, teachers' enthusiasm and commitment to change must be captured. The task of mobilising them, however, may be more difficult in some circumstances and cultures than in others. For example, in her study, *Teachers' Workplace*, Rosenholtz (1989) identifies two kinds of schools at opposite ends of a continuum. One group she describes as 'high consensus' schools. In these principals and teachers 'appeared to agree on the definition of teaching and their instructional goals occupied a place of high significance' (Rosenholtz, 1989, pp. 206–8). There were numerous other ways in which the teachers in these schools created an educative environment. 'They seemed attentive to instructional goals, to evaluative criteria that gauged their success, and to standards for student conduct that enabled teachers to teach and students to learn.' In low-consensus schools, by contrast, 'few teachers seemed attached to anything or anybody, and they were more concerned with their own identity than a sense of shared community'. Teachers in such schools talked of 'frustration, failure, tedium, though not in their own person; they managed to transfer those attributes to the students about whom they complained, themselves remaining complacent and aloof'. In these latter schools 'no-one, not even the principals, lay claim to the responsibility for helping struggling teachers improve'. Again, by way of contrast, 'in learning-enriched settings an abundant spirit of continuous improvement seemed to hover school-wide because no-one ever stopped learning to teach'.

Rosenholtz's attempt to capture the spirit of these two ideal-types led her to characterise them as 'stuck' and 'moving' schools, terms which have proved sufficiently illuminative for them to have achieved wider adoption since then. Teachers from 'moving' schools held an ideology that was 'the reverse of fatalism – everything was possible'. Teachers in 'stuck' schools, on the other hand, created environments in which they were 'unfree'. 'Boredom, punitiveness and self-defensiveness resulted.' To free themselves from 'their distressing work' they took days off, with obvious consequences for their schools and their colleagues. Unfortunately the study has little to say directly about schools which actually improved over the course of time but the implications would appear to be largely self-evident. Improvement efforts which duck the question of what's in them for teachers are likely to fail.

SEARCHING FOR SOME BROADER LESSONS

How much improvement can schools be expected to achieve in the medium-term? One of the leading North American contributions is Louis and Miles' (1990) study *Improving the Urban High School*. In it they try to trace the longer-term outcomes in over one hundred schools which implemented 'effective school' programmes during the mid-to-late eighties.

The basic tenets of such programmes have usually been summarised in five- or seven-point plans. These have tended to emphasise the importance of such factors as strong administrative leadership; the creation of a safe and orderly climate for teaching and learning; an emphasis on the acquisition of basic academic skills; the generation of higher teacher expectations; and constant monitoring of pupils' performance. Interventions along these lines were pioneered in New York by Ron Edmonds (1979) in the late seventies and early eighties, although the extent to which they have been firmly-grounded in the research evidence has since been questioned (see, for example, Ralph and Fennessey, 1983).

Louis and Miles contacted participating schools several years after they had embarked on their reform programmes. Principals in each school answered a variety of questions put to them by the researchers. Of particular interest are the principals' assessments of the outcomes.

Most change was claimed in the areas of student attitudes and behaviour. Half the principals (49%) reported 'greatly improved' outcomes in terms of student behaviour whilst over four out of ten (43%) reported 'greatly improved' student attitudes. Just under four out of ten (38%) reported 'greatly improved' student attendance. However, only a small minority (12%) reported 'great improvements' in the employment of their students upon graduation and a similarly small minority (15%) reported that student dropout rates were 'greatly improved'. These findings would suggest that it is relatively easy to improve the things which are directly under the schools' control but more difficult in some other respects.

The final area considered in the research was the central one of student achievement. It is reasonable to suppose that all the programmes sought improvements in this area as one of their main objectives. Only one in four (24%) principals, however, reported that student achievement had 'greatly improved'. The majority were frank enough to report only modest improvements. Taken as a whole the study reminds us forcibly of the extent to which schools have to struggle for progress without guarantees of success.

The detailed case studies Louis and Miles provide of individual schools which claimed to have improved are sufficiently varied to offer little prospect of common findings across cases. In their quantitative review of the data from interviews with the principals, however, one major factor survived their statistical analyses and emerged as influential. This was the school's capacity for what they termed 'deep coping'. It is interesting that this notion has some of the social-psychological dimensions Reynolds identified in his study. Whether it is an empirically-realisable concept, however, is more doubtful. Amongst the features Louis and Miles identified as examples of 'deep coping' were 'vision-building and sharing; rolling planning; substantial restaffing; increasing school control over the environment; empowering people; and redesigning the school organisation' (Louis and Miles, 1990, p. 281). Each of these seems to us, however, to represent a substantial agenda in its own right. To simply sweep them into a single factor, as Louis and Miles attempted to do, is to take the process of simplification a stage too far.

We suspect the attempt to distil the 'lessons' of school improvement into a rather small (and manageable) number of 'factors which work' is unlikely to be convincing as anyone who has attempted to follow Fullan's comprehensive reviews of the change process will testify. As Fullan himself has remarked: 'It is so easy to underestimate the complexities of the change process' (Fullan, 1991, p. 350).

SOME COMMON ELEMENTS OF THE CHANGE PROCESS

Any attempt to identify 'key factors' in the change process is likely to mushroom rapidly. In our own reading of the literature, however, there were only a handful which survived across context and circumstance.

First, there is the question of time-scales. These are best summarised as medium-to-long-term. Hardly any studies have seen time in terms of months.

Second, there is the question of ownership. For improvement to take off a body of staff within a school need to agree amongst themselves (and with 'the management') that there is 'a problem' which needs to be tackled, that there are some strategies which could be explored and that they will search out the solutions for a while.

Third, there is the question of prioritising. For the space to be created for a significant body of staff energy to be targeted towards change, some 'problems' need to be identified as more important than others. By their nature, however, schools seem to be organisations in which it is difficult to focus and prioritise – one concern invariably seems to compete with another.

These three concerns will strike many as being rather obvious. We would merely observe that they would appear to have challenged, at times, even the most experienced school leaders. There is also an additional factor at play in 'ineffective' schools. If we believe the research the skills that are required to bring these key factors into play are likely to be in short supply. Time and resources are often seen as fully committed already; views about what the staff see as the problems and are willing to take on will vary; and the capacity to prioritise is seen as lacking. First, teachers will need to be convinced – and then pupils (Rudduck, 1991). It is no surprise, therefore, that a common piece of advice about how to get things moving in such circumstances has been to 'do and then plan' hoping, in the process, that something will take root. As Louis and Miles put it:

> In 'depressed schools' one of the few ways of building commitment to a reform programme is for successful action to occur that actualises hope for genuine change. Effective action by a small group often stimulates an interest in planning rather than vice versa.
>
> (Louis and Miles, 1990, p. 204)

Co-ordinating such change efforts frequently challenges the 'leadership' of 'effective' schools; in 'ineffective' schools the problems posed may prove insurmountable.

CLOSURE: THE UNTHINKABLE ALTERNATIVE?

We are very reluctant in Britain to close schools down; it also happens to be rather difficult to do this. However, if we allow ourselves, for a moment, the possibility of a 'symbolic' closure it becomes much easier to see how the various factors which have been identified in the school improvement literature might be allowed to flourish.

First, there is the question of staffing. A new headteacher in a 'new' school is probably in a much better position to build a senior management team and teaching staff who are prepared to work together within a collaborative culture. The current practice of simply replacing the headteacher (and other staff as and when 'natural wastage' allows) merely places the same 'problems' in another set of hands. Few can single-handedly rise to the challenge.

Second, there is the possibility of creating a new vision of what the school might be about whilst sharing it with the school's community. In a new institution the need to deconstruct one set of messages and concerns whilst, simultaneously, fostering another is lessened; people expect there to be some changes.

Third, there is the prospect of mounting a mutually consistent set of curriculum practices. Traditions associated with the teaching of different subjects may linger on. With the whole approach up for review, one is likely to be in a better position to break through the varying and uneven patterns pertaining within different departments.

Fourth, there is the possibility of deploying resources in different ways. It is a feature of most school improvement efforts that they are perched on the backs of staff whose goodwill is, almost certainly, stretched already. Within a new institution there is the possibility of some re-examination of prevailing assumptions about resourcing.

The most likely outcome for any institution that has been newly-created is that it would start life as a school of 'average effectiveness'.

Although there is much interest amongst policy-makers in the problems of closing 'ineffective' schools, there is not much prospect of them doing so as a direct response to the problems posed by research on school improvement. 'School closure' will, doubtless, continue to be a last resort when all other efforts have failed – a long, drawn-out and painful experience for all concerned.

BETTING ON CHANGE

In the early-to-mid nineties a number of school improvement projects have been launched in Britain, each in its different way claiming to build directly upon previous research. Such projects are of interest insofar as they represent different 'bets' on the importance of the various starting points we have discussed.

The largest to date is, undoubtedly, that on *Improving School Effectiveness*, launched by the Scottish Office Education Department involving some 60 Scottish schools (see MacBeath and Mortimore, 1994). Three candidates for action have, in the Scottish view, emerged.

One is the process of school development planning. This is an area which has been given some prominence in recent reports by Scottish HMI (SOED, 1990). There has been a good deal of interest in the potential of planning processes in schools in recent years (see Hargreaves and Hopkins, 1991) although, as yet, only limited direct evidence that it brings about significant improvements in children's learning.

Another thrust is a concern to improve schools' 'culture and ethos', a theme which has dominated earlier research on school effectiveness. The conditions within which educational activities are conducted are seen as generating crucial conditions for learning. By working on teachers' and pupils' expectations of the learning environment the project hopes to make the development of school cultures more tangible in their contribution to pupils' learning.

The third area concerns the view that the methods of teaching and learning that schools are employing need to be examined and possibly changed. This is the most challenging and potentially controversial of the three concerns. Interventions in the classroom have hitherto seldom been undertaken as part of school improvement efforts. It is also likely to be the one with the greatest pay-off from successful intervention.

The Schools Make A Difference (SMAD) project launched by the Hammersmith and Fulham LEA in 1993 is another example of a school improvement project in action, albeit on a somewhat smaller scale than the Scottish one. The main aim has been 'to lay the foundations for raising student levels of attainment, achievement and morale' in eight secondary schools within the authority (see Stoll, Myers and Harrington, 1994). One of the original schools involved was, in fact, St Marks which we noted earlier had been severely criticised by OFSTED's inspectors.

SMAD is of particular interest because it has been relatively well-resourced albeit over a relatively short, two-year period. Like an earlier project in Sheffield LEA (Rudduck and Wilcox, 1988) the project team has paid particular attention to ensuring staff 'ownership' of the action. Much of what the schools have been doing will seem familiar: sharing theories about change, views of school culture, value-added approaches to measuring progress, and the need for some monitoring and evaluation. But there are also some elements which suggest a more fundamental and innovative review of prevailing practices has taken place: course-work clinics outside school time for pupils taking public exams; mentoring of Y8 students in relation to their literacy skills; and the formation of a group of teachers in one school to act as 'critical friends' in each other's classrooms.

Another project which has claimed considerable success in raising achievement is the Two Towns School Improvement Project in Staffordshire (reported in *The Times Educational Supplement*, 5 June 1994, and Barber *et al.*, 1994). The head of one school is quoted as saying that prior to the project 'the school had gone through a hasty reorganisation and was on a downward spiral . . . staff were demoralised and credibility was declining'. The head had taken over shortly before the project had begun and its involvement had helped to remotivate the school. She partly attributed the school's improving staying on rates, falling truancy rates and better exam results (up over three years from 19 per cent achieving five or more A–C passes to 26 per cent) to the project's influence.

These three projects do not exhaust the range of possibilities. Others of which we have some personal knowledge have started in Birmingham, Bradford, Lewisham, Nottinghamshire, Shropshire and Suffolk; and there are doubtless many more.

ESTABLISHING THE EXTENT OF 'REAL CHANGE'

When industrial psychologists first began to experiment with the conditions of the workplace they believed that it was the specific initiatives they had introduced which made the difference. It was only later that they discovered so-called 'Hawthorne' effects. Most changes made some difference to workers' productivity – but not for very long. Their experiences prompt the question whether the 'successes' claimed by improvement projects, especially in 'ineffective' schools, are just a more sophisticated version of Hawthorne effects played out in educational settings?

There are several ways in which we could guard against this possibility. The first is the need to scrutinise external reviews closely. They may capture the issues but they should be treated, initially at least, as only one account of what needs to be fixed; insiders' views need to be treated equally seriously. We have to find better ways of 'listening in' on a school's 'discussions' about change. Who saw things this way? What was and wasn't on the agenda? What ideas got tossed around and thrown out? And, crucially, whose view(s) of the 'problems' eventually prevailed?

Second, we need better accounts of what actually went on. Over twenty years have passed since the early studies of implementation taught us that what gets planned and what gets put into practice can differ, sometimes alarmingly. How far did the initiative penetrate and influence classroom practice? Did anyone, for example, broaden their repertoire of teaching styles? Did anyone eventually succeed in shifting their dominant pedagog(ies)? And could any of them explain how? Much of this evidence is likely to be qualitatively-based but could be powerfully complemented by some quantitative evidence as well.

Third, we need to keep reminding ourselves of the importance of taking the longer view, by which we mean considerably more than a twelve-month period. The educational world is full of initiatives (and their attendant evaluations claiming 'success') which were still up-and-running three months after the funding and/or energy were withdrawn but which disappeared a short while later. The only really longer-term follow-up we have of TVEI, for example, suggests that a project's survival chances are not always that good (William and Yeomans, 1993). It is hard to keep momentum going and rather too easy to help an initiative change direction and fade away. We must expect to plough our way through numerous cases which claim to have been successful to find those which probably have.

IN CONCLUSION

We began by asking whether the existing evidence on how to improve 'ineffective' schools pointed the way ahead. The traditions of research conducted within the school effectiveness paradigm encouraged us in our belief that there might be some 'common messages'. In the event we encountered two stumbling blocks. The first was the rather small number of studies from which to generalise. Most are not specifically about how 'ineffective' schools improve but about the more general processes of improvement *per se*. We still suspect that there are problems and barriers to change which are specific to 'ineffective' schools but which the research has not teased out as yet. The second was more fundamental. As Andy Hargreaves has noted: '*faith* in generalised and scientifically known principles of school effectiveness has begun to be superceded by commitments to more ongoing, provisional and contextually sensitive processes of school improvement' (1994, p. 54).

The national and international press towards 'raising achievement' is something that can engage the professional commitment of teachers. It is potentially a powerful enough rallying cry to allow schools to review their routine ways of going about things. Ultimately a school's staff are and feel accountable to their pupils who must eventually leave, capable of taking their place with confidence in the world beyond. The commitment to 'raising achievement' (broadly construed) could be one expression of the 'visible ideology' which Lightfoot discovered in all her 'excellent' schools; and it evokes the *professional* 'inspiration' which Bryk argued animated his. It can encourage teachers to explore the possibilities of real change. However, as Rosenholtz warns us, 'there is no easy formula . . . there are [only] clues and guidelines' (1989, p. 216). Teachers will have to interpret the clues and adapt the broad guidelines in the light of the demands of their own setting and situation. The success of any given strategy depends in large part upon its context and the sensitivity with which each individual institution can, as Richardson put it, 'creatively reconcile its newness and its oldness' (1973, p. 330), relinquishing some of the pull of the past in the endless pursuit of understanding and improvement.

NOTE

1   This chapter was first published as chapter 12 in J. Gray and B. Wilcox (1995) *'Good School, Bad School': Evaluating Performance and Encouraging Improvement*, Buckingham: Open University Press.

REFERENCES

Barber, M., Collarbone, P., Cullen, E. and Owen, D. (1994) *Raising Expectations and Achievement in City Schools: The Two Towns School Improvement Project*, University of Keele.

Bryk, A., Lee, V. and Holland, P. (1993) *Catholic Schools and the Common Good*, Cambridge, Mass.: Harvard University Press.

Edmonds, R. (1979) 'Effective schools for the urban poor', *Educational Leadership* **37**: 15–27.

Fullan, M. (1991) *The New Meaning of Educational Change*, London: Cassell.

Fullan, M. (1992) *Successful School Improvement: The Implementation Perspective and Beyond*, Milton Keynes: Open University Press.

Hargreaves, A. (1994) *Changing Teachers, Changing Times* London: Cassell.

Hargreaves, D. H. and Hopkins, D. (1991) *The Empowered School: The Management and Practice of Development Planning*, London: Cassell.

Lightfoot, S. L. (1983) *The Good High School: Portraits of Character and Culture*, New York: Basic Books.

Louis, K. S. and Miles, M. B. (1990) *Improving the Urban High School: What Works and Why*, London: Cassell.

MacBeath, J. and Mortimore, P. (1994) 'Improving school effectiveness: a Scottish approach', paper presented to the Annual Conference of the British Educational Research Association, Oxford.

Newall Green (1991) *Newall Green High School: A Report by HMI*, London: DES (reference 67/92/SZ).

OFSTED (1994) *Improving Schools*, London: HMSO.

Ralph, J. and Fennessey, J. (1983) 'Science or reform? Some questions about the Effective Schools Model', *Phi Delta Kappan* **64**(10): 689–94.

Reynolds, D. (1991) 'Changing ineffective schools', in M. Ainscow (ed.) *Effective Schools For All*, London: David Fulton.

Reynolds, D. (1992) 'School effectiveness and school improvement in the 1990s', Chapter 10 in D. Reynolds and P. Cuttance (eds) *School Effectiveness: Research, Policy and Practice*, London: Cassell.

Richardson, E. (1973) *The Teacher, the School and the task of Management*, London: Heinemann.

Rosenholtz, S. (1989) *Teachers' Workplace: The Social Organisation of Schools*, New York: Longmans.

Rudduck, J. (1991) *Innovation and Change: Developing Involvement and Understanding*, Milton Keynes: Open University Press.

Rudduck, J. and Wilcox, B. (1988) 'Issues of ownership and partnership in school-centred innovation', *Research Papers in Education*, **3**(3): 157–79.

Scottish Office Education Department (SOED) (1990) *The Role of School Development Planning in School Effectiveness*, Edinburgh: HMSO.

Stoll, L., Myers, K. and Harrington, J. (1994) 'Linking school effectiveness and school improvement through action projects', paper presented to the Annual Conference of the British Educational Research Association, Oxford.

Williams, R. and Yeomans, D. (1993) 'The fate of TVEI in a pilot school: a longitudinal case study', *British Educational Research Journal*, **19**(4): 421–34.

Chapter 8

Piagetian theory and primary school physics[1]

Christine J. Howe

Piagetian theory predicts that group work between children whose initial understanding differs will be beneficial to conceptual knowledge in physics. If correct, this prediction offers reassurance to primary school teachers who are currently charged with conveying physics to children with a disparate range of background skills and knowledge. It is particularly reassuring given current attempts to integrate special needs children into mainstream schools. Recognising this, the paper starts by summarising three studies which investigate whether the prediction is, in fact, correct. Although the studies have a consistent (and encouraging) message as regards differing conceptions, they raise a number of questions about the optimal group design. These questions led to two further studies which are also summarised.

INTRODUCTION

Within Psychology, there has been a long tradition of research into the conceptions of the physical world that primary school children hold. Piaget's (1930) classic book on children's notions of physical causality has stimulated a stream of studies (for example, Laurendeau and Pinard, 1962; Piaget, 1974; Driver and Easley, 1978) which have replicated, extended and, in some cases, qualified the basic message. The psychological significance of the research is not in doubt, but recent developments in educational policy render it potentially applicable in a wider context. The developments relate to the National Curriculum for Science (Department of Education and Science, 1989) and Environmental Studies 5 to 14 (Scottish Office Education Department, 1993), the National Curriculum's Scottish equivalent. These documents require a substantial enhancement of the physics teaching that is offered at the primary school level, with conceptions of the physical world being a focal concern. In particular, the documents specify conceptions which primary teachers are expected to cover in areas as diverse as force and motion, floating and sinking, heat and temperature, electricity and magnetism, and light and sound. Furthermore, via their levels of attainment, the documents also set out standards of conceptual understanding which primary children are supposed to achieve.

There is reason to believe that, in pinpointing conceptual knowledge, the policy developments have occasioned considerable disquiet in the teaching profession. It is not simply that the national media have carried numerous reports to this effect. It is also that research (for example Her Majesty's Inspectors, 1984) has revealed widespread anxiety amongst primary teachers about conceptually-based instruction in the specified areas. . . . Presuming disquiet, the question is whether anything can be offered by way of support, and it is here that the psychological research has its potential new role. The trouble is that it seems at first sight to have little to offer. Certainly, the research provides evidence that even before they receive formal instruction in physics, primary school children evolve strong conceptions of the physical world. However, since the conceptions are usually at variance with the received wisdom of science, evidence for their existence can only add to the anxieties that teachers feel. A more constructive contribution would be guidance about the interventions that would improve conceptual knowledge, but neither Piaget's (1930) work nor its follow-ups address this topic directly.

However, while the traditional research may appear initially to have little to say, careful reading should yield a message that is more encouraging. Irrespective of its conclusions over matters of detail, the research gives credence to a Piagetian gloss regarding the broad process of change, and this gloss has strong implications for educational intervention. In particular, the research is consistent with change involving a process which Piaget (for example Piaget, 1985) has termed 'equilibration'. This means the reconciling of conflict between existing and newly experienced conceptions via some higher synthesis, a process which of necessity involves both gradual change and personal construction. The educational implications are, of course, that children should be provided with conceptions which conflict with their existing ones but which, by virtue of not being too advanced, are assimilable to them. As Piaget himself recognized (Piaget, 1932), one context in which this might be achieved is group work between children who hold differing conceptions about the issue at stake. So long as the children are given tasks which tease the differences out and motivate their resolution, the synthesising of new and existing ideas should be a real possibility.

If Piaget's argument is correct, it would, of course, allow teachers to make a virtue out of the necessity of involving children with a range of differing competencies. Indeed, the specific requirement to include special needs children should become a strength. However, accepting the argument as correct requires directly relevant evidence, and until recently little was available. Piaget himself never studied group work, and sorties into this field by his associates (for example Doise and Mugny, 1984) have emphasised logico-mathematical reasoning and spatial relations, and not the physical world. During the 1980s, there were some attempts to redress the situation by focusing on physical conceptions, for instance studies by Nussbaum and

Novick (1981), Forman and Cazden (1985), Forman and Kraker (1985), Osborne and Freyberg (1985) and Gilbert and Pope (1986). However, with these studies, it is frequently impossible to differentiate the effects of group work from the effects of expert (usually adult) intervention. Moreover, although the studies all claim to address conceptual conflict, the guarantees that the children's conceptions differed were often far from convincing. Even when these difficulties were avoided, the studies rarely had control groups of children with similar conceptions to differentiate the effects of group composition from the effects of task, and they seldom considered whether the beneficial effects survived over time.

Recognising the need for further research, a group of us at Strathclyde University have embarked on a series of studies which, we hope, will be seen as employing a more systematic methodology. These studies will be summarised below. As will be seen, they give a reasonably consistent message as regards differing conceptions. However, while this is so, they also raise a number of questions about the optimum task design, and these questions have led to a further series of studies which will also be summarised. Again, the message is clear. . . .

COMPARISON OF GROUPS WITH DIFFERING AND SIMILAR CONCEPTIONS

The studies in the first series were concerned with children's conceptions of why some objects float in freshwater while others sink (hereafter 'Study I'); why some objects float in freshwater but sink in other liquids (hereafter 'Study II'); and why some objects roll a considerable distance off inclined planes while others do not (hereafter 'Study III'). The studies all began with individual pre-tests where the initial conceptions of primary school children were systematically appraised. Based on these appraisals, the children were assigned to groups such that conceptions were either similar or different, the groups subsequently working on tasks which required conceptions to be made explicit. Some weeks after the group tasks, the children's conceptions were appraised once more via individual post-tests to compare the consequences of differing and similar groups. A full report of Studies I and II appears in Howe, Rodgers and Tolmie (1990); a full report of Study III in Howe, Tolmie and Rodgers (1992).

In each of the studies, the pre-tests were given to around one hundred and twenty Glasgow school children aged eight to twelve. The pre-tests involved the children making and/or explaining predictions about physical events but not, to any serious degree, testing these out. The predictions/explanations in Studies I and II focused on the propensity of objects to float or sink; the predictions/explanations in Study III on the likelihood of objects travelling specified distances. About half of the pre-test items related to physically present apparatus, like toys to be immersed in fluids of varying density and model vehicles to be rolled down slopes of varying incline, friction and length. The other half related to descriptions of real-world instances, like icebergs floating in the sea or skate boarders speeding down a slope. The pre-tests always took the form of semi-structured clinical interviews, with standard openings but flexible follow-ups. The children's responses were always recorded in note form.

Although many responses contained both predictions and explanations, it was the latter that were seen as the key to initial conceptions. Thus, using the explanations, an attempt was made to group the children such that their conceptions were either different or similar. The children's conceptions differed in varying ways both within and between the studies, and the composition of the groups reflected this. Full details of group composition can be obtained from Howe *et al.* (1990, 1992), but Table 8.1 presents a summary. The main point to note is that, as signified by the DD label, half of the differing groups in Studies I and II and all of the differing groups in Study III contained children at different *levels* of understanding. Approximately 25% of the pre-tested children were excluded from the groups. This was partly because, as Table 8.1 shows, the criteria of difference and similarity were extremely stringent, partly because group membership was restricted to classmates, and partly because, in contrast to research cited earlier which focused on pairs, the groups were always foursomes. The use of foursomes was motivated both by pilot work and by Her Majesty's Inspectors (1978) which reveals that groups smaller than four are rare in primary classrooms. There were no sex differences between the different and similar groups. . . .

The tasks were presented to the groups between four and six weeks after the pre-tests. At the start, each child in the group was given a set of cards. Apparatus similar to the pre-test was displayed and the children were asked to make private predictions by ticking the correct answers from choices on their cards. Once they had done this, they moved to the group phase proper. They were given workbooks which were attractively illustrated and written in a simple style. The workbooks invited the groups to compare their predictions and come to an agreement where they differed. Pilot work had revealed that comparing predictions when each child is committed to a position in writing is an excellent incentive to lively discussion. The workbooks specified that once the predictions had been agreed, they were to be tested using the apparatus. The outcomes were to be observed, and the children were to agree explanations of what they saw. In addition to items relating to the predictions, the workbooks also contained descriptions of real-world instances for which children were invited to agree explanations.

The group tasks were presented by researchers who took the children through the first two items of the workbooks, refraining from giving feedback on the decisions but checking that the procedure (especially the need to discuss and agree) had been properly grasped. Once the first two items had been completed, the researchers withdrew, with the children being

Table 8.1   Composition of the groups in Studies I, II and III

	*Differing groups**	*Similar groups**
Study I	7 × DD Groups** 4 children who were more or less advanced than each other in their conceptual understanding 7 × DS Groups** 4 children who had different conceptions but could not be said to be more or less advanced than each other	7 × SS Groups 4 children who had similar conceptions
Study II	6 × DD Groups 4 children who were more or less advanced than each other in their conceptual understanding 6 × DS Groups 4 children who had different conceptions but could not be said to be more or less advanced than each other	6 × SS Groups 4 children who had similar conceptions
Study III	6 × LowDD Groups 2 children holding very low level conceptions and 2 holding conceptions at moderate levels of understanding 6 × HighDD Groups 2 children holding very high level conceptions and 2 holding conceptions at moderate levels of understanding	6 × LowSS Groups 3 groups with 4 children whose conceptions were all low level; 3 groups with 4 children whose conceptions were all moderate 6 × HighSS Groups 3 groups with 4 children whose conceptions were all high level; 3 groups with 4 children whose conceptions were all moderate

* Children assigned to differing groups were required to have given different responses from all other group members to at least two-thirds of the pre-test items. Children in similar groups were required to have given the same responses as all other group members to at least two-thirds of the items.

** DD means the children differed by Virtue of being at different levels of understanding. DS means that they differed despite being at the same level of understanding.

videotaped as they proceeded through the workbooks. The children had been told by the researchers to read the workbooks out loud before following the instructions. However, they were not told whether the reading was to be shared or whether one child could monopolize. Thus, the groups made their own arrangements as regards the reading, as indeed they did as regards the administration of testing. The researchers returned at the end of the tasks and enquired what some of the decisions had been, once more without giving feedback. In all three studies, the tasks lasted between forty-five and seventy minutes.

In Study III only, a randomly pre-selected 25% of the children were given immediate post-tests within a day of the group tasks. These post-tests contained items equivalent to the pre-tests, as did the delayed post-tests that were given to all group participants in all three studies. In Studies I and III, the delayed post-tests were administered between four and five weeks after the group tasks. In Study II, the time interval was two weeks. In Study III only, the delayed post-tests had additional items which asked whether more could be discovered about 'rolling down slopes' from direct observation, from reading books and from asking other people, and if it could, whether the children had tapped the source after the group task. The procedures for administering the post-tests and for identifying conceptions in the responses were identical to the pre-test. Having been identified, pre- and post-test conceptions were scored in preparation for statistical analysis.

In fact, scoring was not just applied to the conceptions which had been identified in the pre- and post-test responses but also to the conceptions which, as far as could be judged from the videotapes, individual children were advancing at the conclusion of each group task item. For Studies I and II, scoring was on a scale from 0 to 4, with conceptions receiving a score of 0 if they omitted physical factors (for example, 'things float when they want to') and a score of 4 if they included relative density (for example, 'things float when they're lighter than the same volume of water'). Inter-judge reliability over pre- and post-test scoring was 99% in Study I and 96% in Study II. Interjudge reliability over group task scoring was 78% in Study I and 76% in Study II. For Study III, scoring was on a scale from 1 to 4, with conceptions receiving a score of 1 if they showed confusion over the factors (for example, 'steep slopes slow things down') and a score of 4 if they co-ordinated the factors adequately (for example, 'the higher things start, the further they go'). Here interjudge reliability was 88% over pre- and post-test scoring and 80% over group task.

Mean scores per item for pre-test, group task, delayed post-test and, in Study III, immediate post-test were computed for each group participant, pre-test means being subtracted from each of the other means to yield measures of change. T-tests were then carried out to compare the change in the children from the differing and similar groups. The main results are summarised in Table 8.2. From Table 8.2, it should be clear that, firstly, the

Table 8.2 Mean conceptual change in Studies I, II and III

		Differing groups				Similar groups		
		Pre-test	Change from pre-test to group task	Change from pre-test to delayed post-test		Pre-test	Change from pre-test to group task	Change from pre-test to delayed post-test
	DD (N=28)	1.55	−0.07	+0.31**				
Study I					SS (N=28)	1.50	−0.07	+0.07
	DS (N=28)	1.43	+0.02	+0.27*				
	DD (N=24)	1.15	+0.18	+0.42**				
Study II					SS (N=24)	1.03	−0.07	+0.05
	DS (N=24)	1.05	+0.40***	+0.32*				
	LowDD (N=24)	2.12	−0.01	+0.56**	LowSS (N=24)	2.21	−0.06	+0.33
Study III								
	HighDD (N=24)	2.56	−0.42	+0.19	HighSS (N=24)	2.54	−0.37	+0.22

NB: When the mean change of a Differing Group is marked with an asterisk, it was significantly higher than the mean change of the corresponding Similar Group on a two-tailed-test (* $p < .05$, ** $p < .01$, *** $p < .001$).

change from pre-test to group task in the children from the *DD* and *DS* groups of Study 1 and the *LowDD* and *HighDD* groups of Study III was negligible, often regressive and certainly no greater than the change in the children from the corresponding similar groups. The change from pre-test to group task in the children from the *DD* and *DS* groups of Study II was both progressive and far from negligible. However, it was only significantly greater than the change in the children from the similar groups for the *DS* groups. Secondly, the change from pre-test to delayed post-test in the children from the *DD* and *DS* groups of Study I, the *DD* and *DS* groups of Study II and the *LowDD* groups of Study III was considerable, progressive and significantly greater than the change in the children from the corresponding similar groups. It was only the children from the *HighDD* groups of Study III that failed to differ from their similar counterparts.

In these results, there is, then, little evidence for group work where initial conceptions differ having an instant impact, and the data from the immediate post-test of Study III endorse this. Here, neither the *LowDD* children nor the *HighDD* changed appreciably from pre-test, and in neither case was their performance significantly different from their SS equivalents. By contrast, there is in the results considerable evidence for group work where initial conceptions differ *having a longer-term impact*, with five of the six comparisons producing supportive results. Even the exception may not be too significant. It became clear in the course of Study III that although the children in the *HighDD* groups differed in their underlying conceptions, they did not vary to any extent in the predictions they made. This may have reduced the likelihood of their conceptual differences becoming explicit during their interactions. If this is what happened (and subsequent work by Howe, Tolmie, Anderson and Mackenzie (1992) renders it highly probable), the implication is that minor changes to the task items would eliminate the problem.

Whatever the truth about the *HighDD* children, it is clear that *the data as a whole strongly endorse the value of group work where initial conceptions differ*. However, they suggest that the full benefits may take time to appear. This is theoretically gratifying from the Piagetian perspective, for it is readily interpretable in terms of the sorting out of conflicts. In addition though, it is also gratifying from the perspective of educators for, as mentioned already, it turns the contrasting competencies of children into a teaching resource. . . .

INFLUENCES OF TASK DESIGN ON CONCEPTUAL DEVELOPMENT

Although the benefits from working in differing groups took time to show, it was nevertheless clear that they were a direct consequence of the dialogues that took place while the groups were interacting. There were correlations between aspects of the task-related dialogue and pre- to post-test change (see Howe, Tolmie, Anderson and Mackenzie (1992) for details). . . . Dialogue was clearly important, and this raised an intriguing possibility. If dialogue is important, perhaps it can be *shaped* in an even more productive direction. Shaping might be achieved by teacher behaviour, but it might also be achieved by modification of the task design.

Certainly, the task design in Studies I to III had potential shortcomings. In the first place, the items typically involved isolated objects, for example one toy which may or may not float and one vehicle which may or may not roll a specified distance. It could have been better to use a series of objects, with the objects carefully chosen to vary along one dimension while holding the others constant. This, after all, might have encouraged the children to engage in *critical testing* and hence to focus more readily on which conceptions are relevant to the issue at stake. In addition, the tasks in Studies I to III exerted limited pressure on the children to survey their activities and draw general conclusions. The emphasis was on the specific predict–test–interpret cycles. It might have encouraged the children to evaluate more carefully the conceptions they were considering if they were asked to *abstract rules* which applied across cycles. This might be achieved by instructions to specify on the basis of all previous observations 'things which are important' and/or 'things which don't matter'.

Recognising the potential contribution of critical testing and/or rule abstraction, the second series of studies was designed to explore them further. Two studies were conducted. The first (hereafter 'Study IV') was concerned once more with children's conceptions of why some objects float in fresh-water while others sink. The second (hereafter 'Study V') was concerned with why liquids heat/cool quickly in some containers while they heat/cool slowly in others. As before, the studies began with pre-tests to children whose ages ranged from eight to twelve. The pre-tests were administered in individual interviews which in the case of Study V, also included training with the ther-mometer to be used in group task testing. Subsequent to the pre-tests, the children were assigned to groups of four, with all groups this time containing children whose conceptions were different. Groups were assigned to work through different versions of the task, with the versions designed to allow exploration of the focal issues. Post-tests were administered at an interval after the group tasks. Study IV is described in detail in Tolmie, Howe, MacKenzie and Greer (1993), and Study V in Howe (1993). Thus, although the studies will be presented below, presentation is in summary form.

One hundred and forty-three Glasgow school children were pre-tested in Study IV, and one hundred in Study V. In Study IV, the pre-tests were iden-tical to Study I: identical materials were used and identical procedures followed. In Study V, the pre-tests involved showing the children containers which varied in thickness, material, surface area and colour (that is white, grey or black), asking them whether liquids held in them would heat/cool quickly or slowly, and inviting them to explain why that would be. The pre-tests also included items where the children were asked to account for real-world instances, for example the overnight cooling of hotwater bottles. Pre-test responses were noted *in situ*, and scored subsequently. In Study IV, conceptual level was ascertained using the Study I principles. In Study V, it was ascertained by coding pre-test responses along two dimensions, factors and processes. Factor scoring involved calculating the proportion of pre-test items on which thickness, material, surface area and colour were each mentioned and used relevantly (that is, four scores per child). Process scoring involved assigning each item a score from 0 to 3, depending on the apparent knowledge of how heating occurs. Failure to mention a process led to a score of 0, appreciation of conduction, convection and/or radiation a score of 3. Inter-judge reliability over scoring was 92%.

There was no intention with Studies IV and V to contrast differing and similar groups. Rather, the plan was to hold difference constant by, as mentioned already, ensuring that all the groups were different. This was one principle underlying the grouping that took place on completion of the pre-tests. The other was to ensure that all group members came from the same school class. Once the groups had been formed, each was assigned at random to work on a particular version of the task, the number of groups assigned to each version being shown in Table 8.3. The versions were all variants on the basic theme. In other words, they all involved apparatus similar in form to the pre-test. This apparatus was the subject of, first, private predictions indicated on cards, and second, discussion, agreement and testing of predictions and interpretation of outcomes. The versions all included some real-world instances. The difference between the versions was, as Table 8.3 shows, over the steps taken to promote critical testing and/or rule abstraction. Four versions were used in each of the studies. However, while the *Random, Critical Test* and *Critical Test + Rule Generation* versions featured on both occasions, the *Critical Test + Rule Selection* was limited to Study IV and the *Random + Rule Generation* to Study V. Study IV was conducted before Study V, and at the time it was unclear which would be preferable,

Table 8.3 Versions of the group task in Studies IV and V

Task versions	Study IV	Study V
Random: Similar to Studies I, II and III except that the objects were presented in unordered sets rather than as individual items	8 groups of 4 children	6 groups of 4 children
Critical Test: The objects were presented in controlled sets, e.g. wooden, plastic and metal boxes of identical shape, size and weight	8 groups of 4 children	6 groups of 4 children
Critical Test + Rule Generation: As Critical Test, but supplemented by instructions to abstract rules by writing down, e.g. 'The thing that is important for floating and sinking'	8 groups of 4 children	6 groups of 4 children
Critical Test + Rule Selection: As Critical Test, but supplemented by instructions to abstract rules by ticking the most important statement in a pair, e.g. 'How heavy an object is doesn't matter to floating and sinking' vs. 'An important thing for floating and sinking is how heavy an object is'	8 groups of 4 children	Not included
Random + Rule Generation: As Random but supplemented by the Rule Generation instructions	Not included	6 groups of 4 children

the open-ended format of rule generation or the pre-chosen options of rule selection. As the results of Study IV came down in favour of the former, it was decided to exclude rule selection in Study V and explore rule generation more thoroughly by introducing a version that lacked critical testing.

The group tasks were presented to the children between two and five weeks after the pre-tests. As with the first series of studies, the tasks were described in workbooks, but introduced by researchers who monitored the initial discussion. In total, the tasks lasted between sixty and ninety minutes, and were videotaped throughout. . . . In Study IV, all group participants were post-tested about four weeks after the tasks. A randomly chosen 25% also received a further post-test about seven weeks after the first one. In Study V, there was a single post-test to all group participants administered between three and eight weeks after the tasks. In both studies, the post-tests were equivalent in structure to the pre-tests and presented in an identical fashion. They did, however, contain some novel items. Post-test responses were scored in the same fashion as pre-test.

In Study IV, two measures of change were computed; first post-test score less pre-test (pre- to first post-test change) and second post-test score less first (first to second post-test change). Table 8.4 shows the mean values produced by the measures for the four versions of the task. It is clear from Table 8.4 that although pre- to first post-test change was progressive, it was modest in absolute terms, and more or less equivalent across the versions. An analysis of variance revealed no significant differences as a function of version. First to second post-test change was, however, more variable. With the *Random* version and the *Critical Test + Rule Generation*, change was still progressive but this time considerably greater than between pre- and first post-test. With the *Critical Test + Rule Selection* change was also progressive but no different from pre- to first post-test. With the *Critical Test*, there was regression to pre-test level. An analysis of variance with follow-up Scheffe tests revealed significantly more progress with the *Random* and *Critical Test + Rule Generation* versions than with the others. It is important to note that this cannot be attributed to the use of a 25% subsample for the second post-test. Analysis of pre- to first post-test change for this subsample revealed no differences from the other participants. The differences between the versions genuinely emerged between the two post-tests, a finding that is once more encouraging from the Piagetian standpoint.

Although there was only one post-test in Study V, its administration could occur up to eight weeks after the group tasks. Thus, it was reasonable to look for parallels of the Study IV results, and these to some extent were found. The parallels were not so much with the factor scores. Here, as Table 8.5 shows, there was little difference between task versions over pre- to post-test change, a conclusion confirmed by analysis of variance. The only feature reminiscent of Study IV was a slight tendency for the *Critical Test* children to lag behind over surface area. Apart from this, the picture is consistency

Table 8.4 Mean conceptual change in Study IV

Group task	Pre-test	Change from pre-test to 1st post-test	Change from 1st to 2nd post-test
Random	1.72$_a$	+0.07$_a$	+0.69$_b$
Critical Test	1.84$_a$	+0.12$_a$	−0.07$_a$
Rule Generation + Critical Test	1.78$_a$	+0.09$_a$	+0.28$_{ab}$
Rule Selection + Critical Test	1.92$_a$	+0.10$_a$	+0.06$_a$

NB: Where subscripts in a column differ, means are significantly different ($p < 0.05$).

across versions, with substantial gains for thickness and surface area and little change for material and colour. Where the parallels occurred was with the process scores, for here the *Random* version and the *Critical Test + Rule Generation* were once more in the ascendancy. Indeed, the results from the *Critical Test + Rule Generation* version were particularly impressive, for not only was the progress greatest here in absolute terms. It was, in contrast to all the other versions, closely associated with understanding of factors. The correlation between process change and a composite measure of factor change was +0.51 ($p < 0.05$) for *Critical Test + Rule Generation* while the corresponding values for the other versions were non-significant. The importance of this is that it signifies a relatively co-ordinated approach to knowledge, where factors were arguably dictated by processes rather than separated from them.

Because Study IV did not include coding for process, it was not possible to look for equivalent co-ordination in its results. Nevertheless, there were indirect signs that something similar may have been happening. The pre- to first post-test progress of the *Random* children in Study IV was marked not just by the introduction of relevant ideas (which ensured their higher scores) but also by a substantial increase in the number of irrelevancies. Thus, their first to second post-test progress was characterised by a laborious process of sifting out. By contrast, the *Critical Test + Rule Generation* children showed greater selectivity. This selectivity was directly attributable to the rule generation exercise, and suggests that the force of the exercise was to impose some discipline on the children's thinking. In view of this, it is tempting to argue that the *Critical Test + Rule Generation* version is the preferable one, even though the conceptual change that it generated was never significantly different from its *Random* equivalent.

However, while the superiority of *Critical Test + Rule Generation* could be argued in theoretical terms, it is less clear what practical consequences follow. There is no doubt that the inclusion of rule generation both lengthened the task and made it more complex. Thus, questions must be asked about the ability of all children to benefit from it, even if the results averaged across

Table 8.5 Mean conceptual change in Study V

Group task	Thickness		Material		Surface area		Colour		Process	
	Pre-test	Change from pre-test to post-test	Pre-test	Change from pre-test to post-test	Pre-test	Change from pre-test to post-test	Pre-test	Change from pre-test to post-test	Pre-test	Change from pre-test to post-test
Random	0.25_a	$+0.34_a$	0.56_a	-0.01_a	$+0.27_a$	$+0.64_a$	$+0.03_a$	$+0.01_a$	$+0.31_a$	$+0.42_b$
Critical Test	0.32_a	$+0.38_a$	0.57_a	-0.03_a	$+0.21_a$	$+0.28_a$	$+0.01_a$	-0.01_a	$+0.42_a$	$+0.24_a$
Random + Rule Generation	0.22_a	$+0.35_a$	0.72_a	-0.07_a	$+0.21_a$	$+0.60_a$	$+0.01_a$	$+0.01_a$	$+0.50_a$	$+0.27_a$
Critical Test + Rule Generation	0.41_a	$+0.46_a$	0.67_a	-0.14_a	$+0.21_a$	$+0.54_a$	$+0.04_a$	-0.00_a	$+0.41_a$	$+0.53_b$

NB: Where subscripts in a column differ, means are significantly different ($p < 0.05$).

the sample appear encouraging. Faced with such questions, it is gratifying to note that the children's initial conceptual level was unrelated to their propensity to benefit from the *Critical Test + Rule Generation* version. In Study IV, the correlation between pre-test score and pre- to first post-test change was +0.07 for the *Critical Test + Rule Generation* children. The correlation between pre-test score and first to second post-test change was zero. In Study V, the correlations between pre-test score and factor change for the *Critical Test + Rule Generation* children ranged from zero to −0.18. The correlation between pre-test score and process change was +0.34. In no case were conventional levels of statistical significance even approached.

[The original article goes on to consider the implications for special needs education – ed.]

NOTE

1   This chapter was first published in *Early Child Development and Care*, **95**, 23–39, 1993.

REFERENCES

Ashman, A. F. and Elkins, J. (1990). Cooperative learning among special students. In *Children Helping Children*, edited by H. C. Foot, M. J. Morgan and R. H. Shute. Chichester: John Wiley and Sons Ltd.

Department of Education and Science. (1989). *Science in the National Curriculum*. London: HMSO.

Driver, R. and Easley, J. (1978). Pupils and paradigms: a review of literature related to concept development in adolescent science students. *Studies in Science Education*, 5, 61–84.

Doise, W. and Mugny, G. (1984). *The Social Development of the Intellect*. Oxford: Pergamon.

Forman, E. A. and Cazden, C. B. (1985). Exploring Vygotskyan perspectives in education: the cognitive value of peer interaction. In *Culture, Communication and Cognition: Vygotskyan Perspectives*, edited by J. V. Wertsch. Cambridge: Cambridge University Press.

Forman, E. A. and Kraker, M. J. (1985). The social origin of logic: the contribution of Piaget and Vygotsky. In *Peer Conflict and Psychological Growth*, edited by M. W. Berkowitz. San Francisco: Jossey–Bass.

Gilbert, J. K. and Pope, M. L. (1986). Small group discussions about conceptions in science: a case study. *Research in Science and Technological Education*, 4, 61–76.

Guralnick, M. J. (1990). Peer interactions and the development of handicapped children's social and communicative competence. In *Children Helping Children*, edited by H. C. Foot, M. J. Morgan and R. H. Shute. Chichester: John Wiley and Sons Ltd.

Her Majesty's Inspectors. (1978). *Primary Education in England*. London: HMSO.

Her Majesty's Inspectors. (1984). *Science in Primary Schools*. London: HMSO.

Howe, C. J. (1993). Conceptual change in science: optimising the design of group tasks. Paper presented at InTER Seminar on 'Collaborative Learning', Moat House, Oxford.

Howe, C. J. Rodgers, C. and Tolmie, A. (1990). Physics in the primary school; peer interaction and the understanding of floating and sinking. *European Journal of Psychology of Education*, **V**, 459–475.

Howe, C. J., Tolmie, A., Anderson, A. and MacKenzie, M. (1992). Conceptual knowledge in physics: the role of group interaction in computer-supported teaching. *Learning and Instruction*, **2**, 161–183.

Howe, C. J., Tolmie, A. and Rodgers, C. (1992). The acquisition of conceptual knowledge in science by primary school children: group interaction and the understanding of motion down an incline. *British Journal of Developmental Psychology*, **10**, 113–130.

Laurendeau, M. and Pinard, A. (1962). *Causal Thinking in the Child*. New York: International Universities Press.

Nussbaum, J. and Novick, S (1981). Brainstorming in the classroom to invent a model: a case study. *School Science Review*, **62**, 771–778.

Osborne, R. and Freyberg, P. (1985). *Learning in Science*. Auckland: Heinemann.

Osguthorpe, R. T. and Scruggs, T. E. (1990). Special education students as tutors: a review and analysis. In *Explorations in Peer Tutoring*, edited by S. Goodlad and B. Hirst. Oxford: Blackwell Education.

Piaget, J. (1930). *The Child's Conception of Physical Causality*. London: Routledge and Kegan Paul.

Piaget, J. (1932). *The Moral Judgment of the Child*. London: Routledge and Kegan Paul.

Piaget, J. (1974). *Understanding Causality*. New York: Norton.

Piaget, J. (1985). *The Equilibration of Cognitive Structures*. Chicago: University of Chicago Press.

Scottish Office Education Department. (1993). *Environmental Studies 5–14*, Edinburgh: HMSO.

Strathclyde Education. (1991). Meeting Special Educational Needs. Unpublished policy document for consultation, Strathclyde Regional Council.

Thomson, A. (1993) Communicative competence in 5- to 8-year olds with mild or moderate learning difficulties and their classroom peers: referential and negotiation skills. *Social Development*, **2**, 3, 260–278.

Tolmie, A., Howe, C. J., MacKenzie, M. and Grerr, K. (1993) Task design as an influence on dialogue and learning: primary school group work with object flotation. *Social Development*, **2**, 3, 183–201.

Chapter 9

Communities of learning and thinking, or a context by any other name[1]

Ann L. Brown and Joseph C. Campione

Why Johnny can't read was one of the central questions raised about American education in the 1970s. Why Johnny can't think replaced it in the 1980s. In the last decade, interest in how one might teach students to think more critically has increased for both pragmatic and theoretical reasons (Glaser, 1984; Resnick, 1987). American schools in the latter part of the twentieth century face dramatic change in the population they must serve, at the same time that the demands of the workplace require complex forms of literacy – those that go beyond simple rote acts of reading and calculating. Increasingly, educated graduates need to be able critically to evaluate what they read, express themselves clearly in verbal and written forms, understand scientific and mathematical thinking and be comfortable with various forms of technology that can serve as tools for thinking. . . . In short, we would like our graduates to be independent, self-motivated critical thinkers able to take responsibility for life-long learning. Easier said than done! . . .

Higher-order thinking skills are often contrasted to basic skills, leading to the perception that such entities are not for all. Younger and more disadvantaged students are held accountable for basic skills, whereas higher-order thinking skills are seen as part of upper school curricula or, worse still, optional extras. We argue that this is absurd; thinking and reasoning should be part of the curriculum from the earliest years, and indeed fostering effective reasoning should be the main responsibility of schools. Ideally, students should develop a belief system based on rationality and sensitivity to evidence; they should acquire a general attitude to learning that is based on reasoning in all areas of the curriculum and from the earliest age. It is for this reason that our work has primarily addressed academically at-risk elementary school children.

For several years, we have been studying the reading comprehension activities of academically marginal children. . . . Our more recent work concentrates on classrooms as communities of learning where critical thinking is practised in the service of learning coherent content.

HIGHER-ORDER THINKING SKILLS IN READING

Texts are a major source of information available to a literate society. In order to enter that society fully, students must know how to learn from reading. Much of what is called reading in the later grades is indistinguishable from critical thinking and studying. Students are not only required to decode, they are also required to understand the meaning, critically evaluate the message, remember the content, and apply the new-found knowledge flexibly and creatively. The premium placed on understanding and using information gleaned from texts increases through the high school and college years when texts, to a large extent, take the place of teachers as the primary source of knowledge. Students who have not honed the necessary critical reading skills suffer a considerable and cumulative disadvantage.

More than ever before, schools must equip people to deal with facts that they never encountered in school. In a scientific and technological society based on an increasingly complex and rapidly changing information base, a productive member of society must be able to acquire new facts, evaluate them critically, and adapt to their implications. Reliance on remembered facts and fallacies from outmoded past schooling will not suffice. Schools, therefore, need to develop *intelligent novices* (Brown *et al.*, 1983). Intelligent novices are those who, although they may not possess the background knowledge needed in a new field, know how to go about gaining that knowledge. Intelligent novices have learned how to learn from texts, rather than merely to memorize facts. . . .

Intelligent novices possess a wide repertoire of strategies for gaining new knowledge from texts. Critical reading demands a divided mental focus whereby readers both concentrate on acquiring knowledge and simultaneously monitor their level of understanding. These 'metacognitive skills' of reading include (a) clarifying the purposes of reading, i.e., understanding the task demands, both explicit and implicit; (b) spontaneously making use of relevant background knowledge; (c) allocating attention so that concentration can be focused on the major content at the expense of trivia; (d) critically evaluating content for internal consistency and compatibility with prior knowledge and common sense; (e) monitoring ongoing activities to see if comprehension is occurring, by engaging in such activities as periodic self-review; (f) drawing and testing inferences of many kinds, including interpretations, predictions, and conclusions; and (g) criticizing, refining, and extending the newly acquired knowledge by imagining other uses of the information or counterexamples to the arguments. In short, reading is thinking, and thinking demands effort and skill (Brown, 1980). Our research question then became how to lead students who don't read critically in that direction.

FOSTERING READING COMPREHENSION VIA RECIPROCAL TEACHING

We have been involved in a program for promoting reading comprehension, termed reciprocal teaching (Brown and Palincsar, 1989), for almost a decade. Briefly, reciprocal teaching is a procedure that features guided practice in applying simple concrete strategies to the task of text comprehension. An adult teacher and a group of students take turns 'being the teacher', i.e., leading a discussion about material that they have either read silently or listened to the adult teacher reading. The learning leader (adult or child) begins the discussion by asking a question and ends by summarizing the gist of what has been learned. Questioning provides the impetus to get the discussion going. Summarizing at the end of a period of discussion helps students establish where they are in preparation for tackling a new segment of text. Attempts to clarify any comprehension problems that might arise occur opportunistically when someone misunderstands, or does not know the meaning of a concept, word, or phrase, etc. And, finally, the leader asks for predictions about future content if this is appropriate. . . .

The cooperative feature of the learning groups is an essential feature. The group is jointly responsible for understanding and evaluating the text. All members of the group, in turn, serve as learning leaders, the ones responsible for guiding the dialogue, and as learning listeners, those whose job is to encourage the discussion leader to explain the content and help resolve misunderstandings. The goal is joint construction of meaning. The reciprocal nature of the procedure forces student engagement. . . . Because the group's efforts are externalized in the form of a discussion, novices can learn from the contributions of those more expert than they. It is in this sense that reciprocal teaching sessions create a zone of proximal development (Vygotsky, 1978) for their participants; all may share in the co-construction of meaning to the extent that they are able. Collaboratively, the group, with its variety of goals, expertise, and engagement gets the job done; the text gets understood. What changes over time is who has the major responsibility for the learning activities.

The adult teacher plays many roles. She (1) models expert behavior; (2) monitors the group's understanding; (3) engages in on-line diagnosis of emerging competence; (4) pushes for deeper understanding; (5) scaffolds the weaker students' emerging competence; and (6) fades into the background whenever the students are able to take charge of their own learning.

The reciprocal teaching program has been used successfully as a reading and listening comprehension intervention by average classroom teachers with academically at-risk elementary and middle-school children. For example, between 1981 and 1987, 287 junior high-school and 366 early elementary-school children took part in reading and listening comprehension experiments. The teachers worked with small groups. (The ideal group size is six, but teachers have handled much larger groups.) Students enter the study with scores of approximately 30% correct on independent tests of text comprehension. Successful students achieve independent scores of 75–80% correct on five successive tests. Using this criterion, approximately 80% of students at both ages are successful. Furthermore, students maintain their independent mastery for up to a year after instruction ceases; the listening practice transfers to reading: students generalize to other classroom activities, notably science and social studies; and they improve approximately two years on standardized tests of reading comprehension. . . .

RECIPROCAL TEACHING IN THE CONTEXT OF AN INTENTIONAL LEARNING ENVIRONMENT

In our most recent extension of the comprehension fostering program, reciprocal teaching was only one feature of a radical restructuring of classroom activity. In fact, we took over total responsibility for the students' social studies program, three hours a week for the entire academic year. Students were 90 fifth and sixth graders (age 10–11) of a wide range of ability (approximately one-quarter were diagnosed as learning disabled).

What to teach: a biology curriculum

To take seriously the notion that critical thinking should be directed toward an acknowledged learning goal, we set out to invite children to learn about a topic in which they would be prepared to invest considerable time and effort. Because we wanted students to develop skills of plausible reasoning about probable cause, we selected the basic biological concept of interdependence in nature as the basis of the curriculum (after interviewing 10-year-old children about their interests). . . .

How to teach: the collaborative classroom

Students were involved in designing their own curriculum units. The basic idea was adapted from *The Jigsaw Classroom* (Aronson, 1978). Students formed research groups covering the five subunits of each topic. We provided suitable materials (texts, articles, magazines, videos, and access to a library, plus adult guidance upon request). They prepared a booklet on their research subtopic (using a simplified version of Hypercard on Macintosh IIs), and then regrouped into learning groups made up of one member from each of the research groups. The expert from each research group was responsible for teaching other members of the learning group about his or her topic of expertise. Thus, the choice of a learning leader was based on expertise rather than random selection, as in the original reciprocal teaching work.

All children in the learning group are experts on one-fifth of the material, teach it to others, and prepare questions for the test that all will take on the complete unit. The students are involved in (a) extensive reading in order to research their topic; (b) writing and revision to produce booklets from which to teach and to publish books covering the entire topic; and (c) computer use to publish, illustrate, and edit their booklets. In addition, a great deal of cognitive monitoring must take place in order for students to set priorities concerning what to include in their books, what to teach, what to test, how to explain, and so forth. They are reading, writing, and using computers in the service of learning.

In addition to improvement on standard tests of reading, writing, biological knowledge, and computer skill, dramatic qualitative improvement occurred in the thinking processes reflected in the discussions and in the writing samples. . . .

A CONTEXT BY ANY OTHER NAME

The original reciprocal teaching method achieved success at getting poorly performing students to strive for meaning. The simple extension of this work, asking students to read texts focused on recurrent themes led to significant increases in the use of analogy and cross reference. Having students generate their own learning materials led to activities that promote deeper understanding in the search for coherent causal explanations.

Students seeking an encompassing explanation to support facts create an active learning environment for themselves that is quite different from the passive reception of assigned knowledge that too often dominates classroom interactions. Involved students brought their own outside material to the classroom – books, newspaper articles, and reports from television news. Students felt a sense of ownership over the knowledge they were acquiring. They formed a culture of learning (Brown *et al.*, 1989), where reading, writing and thinking took place in the service of a recognized, reasonable goal – learning and helping others learn about a topic that deeply concerned them.

A COMMUNITY OF LEARNING

Within these communities of learning, students served as cognitive apprentices (Collins *et al.*, 1989) to the adults present and to each other. Expertise did not rest with a single authority figure, the teacher; it was distributed throughout the classroom. The teacher was not a domain-area specialist. Often she did not know the answer to questions and therefore provided useful modeling of 'how to find out'. The adults had varied computer skills, ranging from essentially none to M.A. level proficiency. Similarly, individual children 'majored' in various aspects of the curriculum. Some, like Tom, became computer graphics experts, some devoted considerable time to publishing, progressing from simple aspects of word processing to quite sophisticated control of PageMaker, a desktop publishing package. Others became expert in the predicaments of various endangered species. Children readily recognized expertise and sought help from others more expert than they in some aspect of the work.

But what were the students apprenticed to? Certainly not biology. Few if any of these students are likely to go on to be professional biologists, and the teachers and researchers were not biologists either. We argue that the students were *apprentice learners*, acquiring the skills of independent and collaborative research. The collaborative setting forced the students to engage in reasoning activities overtly, so that many role models of thinking emerged (Brown and Palincsar, 1989). We argue that with repeated experience explaining and arguing, justifying claims with evidence, etc., students will eventually come to adopt these critical thinking strategies as part of their personal repertoire of ways of knowing.

These collaborative learning classrooms diverge from traditional elementary school classes. In 'reading group', teachers assign the text and dole reading out in small pieces, and students have no right to put the task aside. This is in sharp contrast to how literate events evolved and are maintained in the real world. So too this practice is in contrast to our learning environment, where children write the texts, working at their own pace, with extended involvement in personally chosen projects. Another strange aspect of reading lessons is that students read in order to prove to the teacher that they have read and to answer questions posed by the teacher, who, clearly, already knows the answer. The teacher is also the primary consumer of any written products. But in our classroom, students answer their own questions and are accountable for the quality of the questions asked. Teachers do not always know the right answer.

Students read in order to communicate, teach, write, persuade, and understand. The goal is reading, writing, and thinking, in the service of learning about something. Teaching is on a need-to-know basis, with experts (be they children or adults) acting as facilitators. Student expertise is fostered and valued by the community. A community of discussion is created with distributed expertise. This change from traditional teaching and learning practices results in significant improvements both in the students' thinking skills and in the domain-specific knowledge about which they are reasoning.

NOTE

1   This chapter was first published in D. Kuhn (ed.) (1990) *Developmental Perspectives on Teaching and Learning Skills*, vol. 21 (pp. 108–26), Basel: Karger.

REFERENCES

Aronson, E. (1978). *The jigsaw classroom.* Beverly Hills: Sage.

Brown, A. L. (1980). Metacognitive development and reading. In R. J. Spiro, B. C. Bruce, and W. F. Brewer (Eds.), *Theoretical issues in reading comprehension* (pp. 453–481). Hillsdale NJ: Erlbaum.

Brown, A. L., Bransford, J. D., Ferrara, R. A., and Campione, J. C. (1983). Learning, remembering, and understanding. In P. H. Mussen (Series ed.), J. H. Flavell and E. M. Markman (Vol. eds.), *Handbook of child psychology: Vol. 3. Cognitive development* (pp. 515–529). (4th ed.). New York: Wiley.

Brown, A. L., and Palincsar, A. S. (1989). Guided cooperative learning and individual knowledge acquisition. In L. B. Resnick (Ed.), *Knowing, learning, and instruction: Essays in honor of Robert Glaser* (pp. 393–451). Hillsdale NJ: Erlbaum.

Brown, J. S., Collins, A., and Duguid, P. (1989). Situated cognition and the culture of learning. *Educational Researcher, 18,* 32–42.

Carey, S. (1985). *Conceptual change in childhood.* Cambridge MA: Bradford Books, MIT Press.

Collins, A., Brown, J. S., and Newman, S. (1989). Cognitive apprenticeship: Teaching the crafts of reading, writing and mathematics. In L. B. Resnick (Ed.), *Knowing, learning, and instruction: Essays in honor of Robert Glaser* (pp. 453–494). Hillsdale NJ: Erlbaum.

Glaser, R. (1984). Education and thinking: The role of knowledge. *American Psychologist, 39,* 93–104.

Resnick, L. B. (1987). *Education and learning to think.* Washington: National Academy Press.

Resnick, D. P., and Resnick, L. B. (1977). The nature of literacy: An historical exploration. *Harvard Educational Review, 48,* 370–385.

Vygotsky, L. S. (1978). *Mind in society: The development of higher psychological processes.* (M. Cole, V. John-Steiner, S. Scribner, and E. Souberman, Eds. and Trans.) Cambridge MA: Harvard University Press.

Chapter 10

Critical students: breakthroughs in learning[1]

Peter Woods

INTRODUCTION

So much pupil learning in schools is alienated in the sense that it consists of other people's knowledge purveyed in transmissional mode. Pupils have no share in the knowledge nor any control over the learning processes. In addition, it is difficult to see the relevance of such learning for their own interests.

There have been two broad lines of attempted antidote to alienated learning. The first involves the approaches associated with child-centred progressivism – learning by discovery, making teaching relevant to children's concerns, integrated knowledge, democratic decision-making, etc. – epitomized in the Plowden Report (1967). However, contrary to some assumptions, there seems to have been no widespread application of this kind of teaching (Galton and Simon 1980); indeed, in some areas, it is claimed, the ideas behind it have degenerated into an ideology that has little bearing on teachers' practice and operates as a constraining, rather than a liberating, culture (Alexander, 1984 and 1992). Even at its peak there were doubts about its efficacy. Atkinson and Delamont (1977), for example, revealed how conditional 'guided-discovery science' was upon prevailing knowledge and modes of learning. Edwards and Furlong (1978) concluded that 'resource-based teaching' was at heart a coping, rather than a teaching strategy. Sharp and Green (1975) argued that the progressivism of the schools of their research was operating in the interests of social control rather than the children's interests. The philosophical principles behind progressive pedagogies continue to guide many teachers, particularly at primary level (see Drummond 1991; David, Curtis and Siraj-Blatchford 1992); but their application is clearly not easy.

To the advocates of the second approach – critical pedagogy – this is not surprising, since progressivism is held to be a feature of the dominant liberal ideology which holds that educational practice is reformable from within. Critical pedagogues aim to empower students through emancipating them from ideologies and discriminatory practices. The persistence of these is to be explained, they argue, not by technical features of pedagogy, but by social structure and processes. These, therefore, have to be interrogated. Why is society structured as it is, whose interests does it serve, how is education part of that structure, how is knowledge socially constructed – are all necessary questions in confronting the issue. Critical explanations have included theories of correspondence (Bowles and Gintis 1976), reproduction theory (Althusser 1971), cultural reproduction (Bourdieu 1977), and resistance theory (Willis 1977; Giroux 1985). From resistance theory has developed the idea of a critical pedagogy, one that engages with these issues, but which emphasizes the strength of human agency, which recognizes the limits, but also the possibilities, of schooling, which does not simply react to oppression but actively constructs resistance which carries the seed of change. Schools thus become 'democratic sites dedicated to forms of self and social empowerment' (Giroux 1988: 194), and teachers assume the role of 'transformative intellectuals' in effecting an emancipatory pedagogy, in which the notions of 'struggle, student voice, and critical dialogue' feature prominently (ibid.: 195–7).

In asserting that education is inevitably political, critical pedagogues may themselves become open to charges of ideological dogmatism, and seeking to realize particular political interests (Hargreaves 1994: 40). Others have found other shortcomings. Ellsworth (1989) has wondered why critical pedagogy 'doesn't feel empowering'. Gibson (1986: 61) feels that critical theory is 'long on analysis and short on prescription'. Gore (1993: 4), similarly, concludes that the dualistic concerns of critical theory (for example attempts to connect macro and micro) 'do not reflect the empirical realities of pedagogy'. Wright (1993: 8) finds critical pedagogues strong and convincing advocates, but feels that 'there is a need for self-reflexivity, for specificity, for concrete classroom examples, for the enfleshment of the pedagogue, for actual student and/or teacher stories, for open-ended texts which invite response'.

This need appears even more stark when considering the demands of some of the advocacy. Giroux (1988: 195), for example, urges, that 'in order to function as intellectuals, teachers must struggle to create the ideology and structural conditions necessary for them to write, research, and work with each other in producing curricula and instructional power'. This vision, far enough away at the time, has become even more problematic with the intensification of teachers' work in recent years (Apple 1986). This involves increased pressures on teachers' time and energies, deprivation of freedom, skills and decision-making, routinization and de-professionalization. In England and Wales, the National Curriculum, in its fixation with measurable outcomes and its large measure of prescription, together with other measures for the organization of the system, has been seen as an illustration of this tendency (see Flude and Hammer 1990). Critical students require critical teachers, and intensification is not designed to produce them.

This paper starts from a different position from progressivism or critical pedagogy, though it is indebted in certain ways to both approaches. It has a looser set of principles that borrow from both of those, where appropriate, but also from other approaches, such as symbolic interactionism and social constructivism. This eclecticism is required by the study which employs a 'bottom-up' approach, seeking first of all to identify examples of student empowerment that have actually occurred, then drawing on a range of theories to explicate them. Thus some might seem to owe something to a 'progressive' teaching approach, some to critical pedagogy. The notion of empowerment used here also borrows from both. It involves ownership of knowledge, control of teaching or learning processes, having opportunities to be innovative and creative, and being relevant to students' needs within the values of a democratic society. These values lay emphasis on equality, social justice, democracy, care for others as well as self-achievement. This form of empowerment also entails a view of power as 'power with' as opposed to 'power over' (Kriesberg 1992), involving relationships of co-operation, mutual support and equity, which results in 'power to' advance one's interests together with one's fellows.

In this article I want to discuss one particular empowering feature which I term 'breakthroughs in learning'. They were identified in research projects focusing on 'creative teachers' (see Woods 1993a). My aim here is to establish that 'breakthroughs' can and do occur, and to give an indication of their empowering potential.

BREAKTHROUGHS IN LEARNING

Breakthroughs are potentially radicalizing moments when alienation is overcome, and structures superseded. Breakthroughs in themselves are not necessarily radicalizing. They need to be contextualized within appropriate value-sets and theories of learning. They are the spearheads of advance, susceptible to being cut off and isolated as tangential and irrelevant moments. However, given adequate support, they can bring a great leap forward. They will not in themselves counteract structure. But they will help bring it within view, a necessary stage in the path to change (Allport 1954). I have identified the following breakthroughs:

Moments or periods of profound insight

These lead to radical self-development and knowledge of the self. Among young persons, I noted such experiences in what I have called 'critical events' – critical in the sense of being highly significant, representing catalytic effect and uncommon advance, in the educational careers of those involved (Woods 1993a). One such event was the 'Rushavenn' project, which involved a group of primary pupils working with their teacher and a well-known children's author over a period of a year to produce a children's book (Whistler 1988). This won high praise from literary experts. It was also a considerable educational accomplishment. Thus the pupils involved all claimed considerable personal development, involving a great increase in confidence, a willingness to talk and to risk expression of ideas; heightened motivation; a growth in sense of self-worth and self-esteem; a feeling of control of the learning process; a sense of achievement, thrill and pride in a job well done, a record of which had been preserved for posterity. They also spoke of refinement of their learning skills – improved reading and writing, literary appreciation, the formulation and expression of ideas, insight into the artist's mind and the act of creation. These students had a remarkable ability to situate the event within their school career. It gave a perspective to things that had happened since, and provided a sharp awareness of alienative processes. The students themselves (now teenagers) attested to this. Stephen, for example, said it gave him

> confidence to write, whereas before confidence was like maths, was number crunching. You had to be given a task and you had to do it, and the teacher would look at the spelling, that sort of thing. . . . It taught me that's not what writing was about at all. There's no point in writing something down if you're not going to mean what you say. . . . You've got to feel inside that you're telling the truth.

The idea of the book, however, was more subtle than just to make you an author. Stephen thought

> It was to expand you as a person, as an individual, not just in areas of writing and illustrations and that sort of thing. If that's what it set out to do, then it's achieved its goal, because that set me off realising that there was more to life than just a teacher imparting knowledge upon you in terms of education.

Sarah found the project gave her

> a lot of confidence, speaking in a group and telling people my ideas, and it gave me probably confidence with the work I was doing. It made me feel that my pieces of paper weren't inferior to anybody else's. It made me feel it was worthwhile trying to do my best.

In another event, the production of the musical *Godspell* in a secondary school, the students spoke of the discovery of self, the fostering of their creative instincts, promoting spontaneity and intuitive powers of improvisation (Moreno 1972), and especially emotional development. There are many examples among the responses of the power of drama to bring people out, to give them voice and expression, and to 'achieve that absolute contradiction – the control of spontaneity' (Barrault 1972: 31). The participants were concerned with 'tapping their own reservoirs of emotional memories to find within themselves a sophistication, subtlety or depth of emotional engagement so that in concentrating on the character's actions, a wider, deeper range of emotions may be released' (Bolton 1984: 119). The play generated a range of profound emotions which induced chaos and despair at first, but eventually a new conception of truth as they came to understand their emotions, and, even more significantly, to stimulate similar emotional discoveries among their audiences which had a particular lucidity (Collingwood 1966).

Godspell was a multiple critical event with three distinct phases: 1) a school career, comprising the autumn term and culminating in the school performances at Christmas, as a result of which it was selected for the National Students' Drama Festival the following spring; 2) a national student career, leading to the Festival; 3) a public career, leading to a special performance for the general public in the autumn. At each phase, students spoke of 'going up a level', reaching 'more subtle and particular analyses', and 'new heights of feeling'. Extended evaluation through student and teacher voice of both projects is to be found in Woods 1993a. Students were feeling empowered through personal, emotional, aesthetic and spiritual development, aspects of education that are not at present of high currency in the National Curriculum.

The cultivation of marginality

'Marginality' is often represented as a negative state. Groups that are marginalized in a power situation are at a disadvantage, peripheral to the mainstream of events and its opportunities. However, it can be empowering in two senses. It can bring uncommon insights, leading to heightened achievement, and it can promote strong alliances within groups. Both of these applied to the young black women studied by Fuller (1980), Mac an Ghaill (1988) and Riley (1988). Middleton (1987) noticed similar effects among the group in her research, and concluded, 'Perhaps (finally), it is the experience of *marginality* – in terms of being working class, black, female, or a combination of these – which is radicalizing' (p. 87).

The nature of marginality and its educational possibilities were revealed to me in a life history of a teacher centrally involved with one of the critical events (Woods 1993b). The relevant part of his life history here is his childhood and his experiences of school. In general, he draws a sharp contrast between this constraining, directive, alienative world of school, and the autonomous, holistic, realistic, and totally absorbing world of nature. The latter was where Peter found meaning. It is what gave him his point of reference, his epistemological framework, for defining other situations. It gave him choices, where the world of school stamped them out. It was expansive, not restrictive; inspiring rather than deadening; educative rather than indoctrinating; co-operative rather than conflictual. School was also jealously bounded, in that the natural world was not allowed in. More than this, any attempts to import it were vigorously and painfully (for the perpetrator) resisted. Peter recounted several critical incidents where he was 'put in his place', including a caning, while he was a sixth former, from the headteacher for going out of school during the lunch hour to do some bird-spotting on the beach. This kind of escape was a necessary tonic for him to balance the alienative forces of school and to maintain the fine productive edge of marginality. But the school viewed marginality as deviant. Degradation ceremonies (Garfinkel 1956) were frequent.

Peter's recollections are of a painful divide between what he considered the real world of learning, and the alienated world of schooling. He managed this marginality (as a teacher) by contextualizing the school within the world at large, rather than contextualizing the world within the school. This gave him a comparative base. And both as pupil and teacher, his choice of significant others reflected his interests. Not many teachers figure here. But there was an agricultural labourer (from whom he learnt most of his Roman history) and a gamekeeper (who taught him nature study); a novelist (Leo Walmsley) and an occasional educationalist (for example, William Walsh). These have helped him experience the pleasures of marginality, as opposed to the more usual pains. As Berger (1971) comments, to move into the margins is to experience ecstasy, as well as terror. Turner (1969: 111) observes that 'in structured societies it is the marginal person who often comes to symbolise "the sentiment for humanity"'. Marginality clearly has considerable educational potential (see also Aoki 1983; Plummer 1983). I shall expand on this shortly.

Positive trauma

D. H. Hargreaves (1983) has argued that teachers' common-sense theories, which might be adequate for their own purposes, cannot account for the traumatic aspects of aesthetic learning, which can have a disturbing effect leading to radical change. Focusing on positive rather than negative trauma, and employing insights gained from his observations of adults' experience of art, Hargreaves identified four elements in such an experience:

1 A 'powerful concentration of attention'.
2 A sense of revelation of 'new and important reality'.
3 Inarticulateness, the feelings being so strong that they 'drown the words'.
4 The 'arousal of appetite' – the desire to continue or repeat the experience.

I drew from two of the critical events – the making of a book and the production of a play – to explore Hargreaves' ideas further, and to situate them within a theory of learning (Woods 1993c). This theory is based on a constructivist teaching style, charismatic personal qualities (of the teachers), naturalistic context, co-operation, appropriate content and grounded and open enquiry. These produce prior development conducive to experiencing trauma in an educationally productive way (such as confidence-building, sharpening sensitivities); and post-trauma development, both personal and social, and especially a coming-to-terms with the emotions aroused during the trauma. As for the four elements, they were all certainly there in some measure. These were wonderful, almost mystical events, which ranked top of people's academic and emotional experiences. There were counter-indications of inarticulateness in both events. Rushavenn, after all, was about developing articulacy, and *Godspell* about understanding new emotions. Some aspects of the 'magic' were difficult to explain, but they improvised with a range of expressions, body language, tone of voice and general demeanour which conveyed far more to me than the transcript. There was also another element which was to do with relationships, a kind of celebration of humanity, which I discuss below.

Positive conversive trauma is not limited to art, nor even to the arts. All subjects or areas of the curriculum have an aesthetic element to them, which can be exploited in this way, bringing unusual degrees of concentration, perceptions of a new and deeper reality or truth, and strong motivation to pursue the experience further and to seek others.

Similar features of aesthetic experience have been noticed by others (for example, Taylor 1992; Abbs 1994). Abbs (1994) feels that such measure of agreement suggests that

> We are on the trail leading to a defence of aesthetic response as primary and primordial engagement, as acts of revelation, as the tranced states of virtually inexplicable understanding, of modes of cognition 'free from concepts' to use Kant's formulation.

Abbs detects a 'modicum of hope' in the National Curriculum for the creative arts, since the orders allow for the 'interaction between the individual and the culture and recognize, to a considerable extent, the unique and irreducible value of aesthetic response'. But the aesthetic is still not given equality with other kinds of knowledge in the National Curriculum. While the aesthetic has been recognized, 'the broader struggle for aesthetic intelligence and aesthetic understanding has still . . . to be resolved'.

Communitas

So far, my examples of critical learning have all applied largely to individual development. My next two refer to social development. Turner (1969) has described the phenomenon of communitas. I referred earlier to the notion of 'power with', and this is well illustrated in communitas, which represents the social benefits of marginality. During the liminal (marginal) stage of status passages, 'among themselves, neophytes tend to develop an intense comradeship and egalitarianism. Secular distinctions of rank or status disappear, or are homogenized' (Turner 1969: 95). This state of 'unstructured, relatively undifferentiated comitatus . . . gives recognition to an essential and generic human bond, without which there could be no society' (p. 96). It has a 'spontaneous, immediate, concrete nature, as opposed to the norm-governed, institutionalized, abstract nature of social structure' (p. 127). It involves the whole person in relation to other whole persons, whereas structure has a cognitive quality. 'The notion that there is a generic bond between persons, and its related sentiment of "human kindness", are not epiphenomena of some kind of herd instinct but are products of "persons in their wholeness wholly attending"' (p. 128). Communitas has potential to create an 'open morality', breaking in through the 'interstices of structure'.

It is easy to see why sociologists should be interested in liminality and communitas (for example Berger 1963; Musgrove 1977; McLaren 1986). These are humanizing states to set against the alienating forces of social structure. In due proportion, they could mean control of, rather than control by, structure; an ability to recognize and rise above cultural norms; an amalgamation of persons and roles; a recognition of the virtues of equality; a restoration of 'humankindness'. Communitas was a prominent feature of critical events. It was most clearly evident in the *Godspell* production. A play might be regarded as a liminal feature of life. This one certainly stood outside the mainstream of school life. Though linked to it through the emphasis on creative arts in the school curriculum, all of its preparation and performances took place outside official time. And while there was no transition between official statuses as such, there was a distinct 'before' and 'after' as it applied to the individual's relationships with the official school structure and their part in it. As Turner (1969) notes 'The wisdom that is imparted during liminality . . . has ontological value, it refashions the very being of the neophyte' (p. 103). For many of the participants, teachers included, things had changed radically. Sally, the director, said, 'I shall never be quite the same person again.' It affected Sarah 'so much'. Matthew found 'more out about himself than he did about drama'. Josie felt 'you gained so much more from that experience than you ever could from sitting in a classroom' (see Woods 1993a for more detailed discussion).

These experiences fed directly into their understandings and activities in mainstream life. Thus, Martyn, a teacher in the cast, found his relationships with his students changed. Martyn mentioned one student with whom he was having particular difficulty before the play. Afterwards, their involvement in the drama 'really improved our working relationship in class'. Different rules did apply in the classroom, but the liminality found the interstices of structure even within a lesson. Thus

> They come into my classroom and they remember the relaxed atmosphere that we had on the Godspell set, and they know that they can talk to me like that – at the end of a lesson for example, or even when I'm walking

around the class helping in particular situations. But they know that they can't just suddenly, in the middle of a lesson, speak to me in that way. ... Having said that, it does facilitate relationships.

We see illustrated here Turner's (1969) point that 'social life is a dialectical process that involves successive experience of ... communitas and structure ... equality and inequality' (p. 97). People return to structure revitalized by their experience of communitas (p. 129). With too little communitas, life becomes over-structured, alienated and prone to conflict. With too much, social structure will become subverted. Anarchy will prevail until a new structure emerges or the old one is restored. As Turner writes,

> Spontaneous communitas has something magical about it. Subjectively there is in it the feeling of endless power. But this power untransformed cannot readily be applied to the organizational details of social existence. It is no substitute for lucid thought and sustained will. On the other hand, structural action swiftly becomes arid and mechanical if those involved in it are not periodically immersed in the regenerative abyss of communitas.

Unfortunately, this dialectic does not occur naturally. 'From the viewpoint of those concerned with the maintenance of structure, all sustained manifestations of communitas must appear as dangerous and anarchical' (Turner 1969: 109). As with Peter's elective individual marginality discussed earlier, group marginality is also generally discouraged. Certainly opportunities for communitas would appear to have been diminished by the National Curriculum. The compartmentalization of the curriculum, the differentiation of groups, the intensification of time and space, the emphasis on structural, formal, technicist aspects of the teacher role, the demise of extracurricular activities, the demotion of the humanities and the creative arts, the behaviourism of the assessment, the assault on Plowdenism and related approaches, all militate against communitas, and seek to establish a structure that closes off opportunities for it to occur.

Of course some schools specialize in liminality. It has become institutionalized in places, just as it has in the religious sphere in the monastic and mendicant states (Turner 1969: 107). Summerhill is an example, and to some extent, perhaps Stantonbury within the state system. William Tyndale is an example, perhaps, of a school that was too liminal and that became over-consumed with communitas (Dale 1979). 'Dick', the radical teacher, who sought to instigate a revolution in a conservative school on the brink of change itself, and failed (Woods 1981), is an example of an over-liminal teacher.

Social outrage

I refer here to the sense of anger, concern and human compassion that children can feel when they encounter social injustice. This is not to lose sight of the fact that children are often perpetrators of injustice (see, for example, Short and Carrington 1989; Troyna and Hatcher 1993). They do not stand outside the world of structure and prejudice. At the same time, they are not as fully socialized into this world as adults. While not 'innocents' (King 1978; Alexander 1984), they are more strangers to this world than adults. Sometimes they see things that adults have overlooked. In the 'Critical Events' research (Woods 1993a), a town planner told me of one of his experiences when he was giving a talk on rural issues to a group of sixth formers. They challenged him on his argument on the subject of the environment versus agricultural productivity:

> They said to me, 'You half hinted that you would really like to see some strong planning control over what the farmers do as they are damaging the environment, are you pressing for that?' and I said, 'I don't think it's realistic in this political situation', and they said, 'That's a cop out!' Now I remembered that, and that's actually coloured my approach to the whole subject ever since. What they said to me actually changed my attitude to wrestling with that issue. . . . So we get influenced. . . . And it is actually more refreshing than doing some of the other bits of consultation and participation.
>
> (p. 86)

Here is an example of how students, on occasions, can empower teachers and other professionals. By challenging some of the givens and taking people back to first principles they can be a catalyst in refining teachers' perspectives and strengthening their ability to bring about change.

Elsewhere I have witnessed children's concern at tragedy in the world – human and animal suffering, hunger and starvation, victims of natural disasters and of internecine warfare, child and animal abuse (on other occasions and with some students, these subjects can form a rich mine for adolescent sick humour – see Woods 1990). On a more mundane scale, I have seen primary school children observing assemblies or plays, and being called on to make moral judgements, which they occasionally do with some vehemence. For example, I once observed a group of primary children aged 8 to 10 watching a play about evacuation during the war, performed by an external company. There were times when they were called on to participate in the play. At other times they were asked to make judgements. I was impressed by their sense of outrage at some of the treatment meted out to evacuees. There was obviously some empathy here, which could easily be transferred to other minority groups. Short and Carrington (1987), for example, show an ability among primary children 'to view racism from the standpoint of the victim' (p. 231). But there was also an appreciation of the position of adults within the play, including a German prisoner. In this instance, I was again reminded of the strength of drama and role-play as tools in empowerment. It was the *strength* of feeling that came across.

We need to distinguish, however, between positive and negative outrage. Some children undoubtedly have experienced negative outrage. Short and Carrington (1987: 230), for example, show how some of the children of their research 'seem to have internalized the language and logic of racist discourse'. At its extreme, negative outrage can bring about 'flashpoints' and the breakdown of order, as in the Burnage case (for an analysis of this, and other instances of racial harassment, see Troyna and Hatcher 1993). The task is to mobilize outrage for positive purposes, through, for example, communitas, dialogic enquiry and critical pedagogy (Gitlin 1992; Burbules, 1993). Carrington and Short (1989) and Foster (1990) are optimistic about anti-racist innovations in schools, and Lee and Lee (1987) have shown children's ability to 'view things powerfully in class terms' (p. 213). We have had the monocultural, monolingual National Curriculum since, but it is still possible to raise these issues within the National Curriculum framework.

Troyna and Hatcher (1993) also have positive findings. While racism permeates primary schools more than some teachers might care to admit, their findings 'also reveal strong dynamics of racial egalitarianism within children's cultures', owing to 'a growing awareness of the significance of racial discrimination in society, and its injustice'; and the 'development of relationships among children on a basis of equality of treatment and an ability to take and value the viewpoints of others' (p. 198). Both racism and anti-racism seem to feature in children's cultures, and in individual perspectives. Troyna and Hatcher suggest that 'the existence in every class of children who have a clear anti-racist commitment is potentially the most powerful resource' (pp. 203–4). I discussed earlier how a number of researchers have found groups of 'marginalized' black girls doing well at school while boys from the same ethnic group do badly on the whole. There is a suggestion that, as the potential degree of disadvantage increases, so does the girls' political awareness and sensitivity to their structural position (see, for example, Riley 1988). These students would seem to be in a strong position for the kind of peer activity envisaged by Troyna and Hatcher.

I am suggesting that there is a way in, a potential breakthrough in children's social conscience and sense of morality, which can lead to feelings of outrage when they are presented with examples of unfairness and injustice. It is the feeling, the outrage that is the educational catalyst. As with the other categories, it is the emotional engagement that drives thought and development.

All of these forms of 'breakthroughs' (there are no doubt others) have certain elements in common. They have unusual power to provide insights and enlightenment. They cast a brilliant light on the here and now, and reveal startling new truths. There is a sense of ultimates and frontiers. There is new self-knowledge and self-development, significant advances in relationships with others. They are accompanied by profound feelings, great excitement, disturbed emotions, intense pleasure, sometimes pain. They liberate, endowing the learner with freedom from the chains of alienated ignorance and more freedom towards achieving one's goals. They provide resource, not only for oneself, but in one's relationships with others. In short, they are empowering both of the self, and through the self, of others.

ACHIEVING BREAKTHROUGHS

There are a number of favourable conditions for achieving breakthroughs. A form of democratic participation would appear to be the management structure most conducive to pupil empowerment (Carrington and Short 1989; Trafford 1993). Social constructivism, with its emphasis on pupil ownership of knowledge and control of learning processes, and social context, seems the most favourable learning theory (Pollard 1991; also Brown and Campione, and Murphy, this volume); though it needs to be 'strong' rather than 'weak' constructivism (Watts and Bentley 1991). The latter might suffer the fate of Plowdenism and transform to ideology (Alexander 1992). Pupil involvement in control of their own learning (Rowland 1987; Oldroyd and Tille 1987) and in the evaluation of their own work (Armstrong 1992; Towler and Broadfoot 1992; Quicke and Winter 1993; and see Murphy, Broadfoot, this volume) are indicated. In general, pupil 'voices' need to be heard. As Qvortrup (1990: 94) argues, 'If we seriously mean to improve life conditions for children we must, as a minimum precondition, establish reporting systems in which they are heard themselves as well as reported on by others' (see also Paley 1986).

We also need a curriculum where the central aim is the 'promotion of the student's well-being as a self-determining citizen' (O'Hear and White 1991: 6; also see White and O'Hear, this volume). Above all, perhaps, there can be no critical students without critical teachers. As noted earlier, such teachers have come under increasing attack in recent years. However, I have elsewhere (Woods 1995; see also Woods and Jeffrey, this volume) discussed how some teachers are involved in 'resistance' and 'appropriation'; how 'cultures of collaboration' (Nias, Southworth and Yeomans 1989) have been intensified, and self-determination generated; how potentially alienative forces have been 'recognized', and how teachers' own philosophies and goals have been more clearly 'identified'; how the changes have been 'engaged with', and 'alliances' formed. I argue that these schools manage to integrate the subject-based National Curriculum around their own distinctive relational ideas (Bernstein 1975; Maw 1993); and that they generate a form of power that is positive and productive in the realization of their aims (Foucault 1980). . . .

[*The original article continues with a case study of 'students as critical others'* – ed.]

CONCLUSION

The cases discussed here will not remove alienation, transform structures or empower in any grand sense. In general within the education system and in educational processes, structure still obtains over liminality. The central government currently enjoys unprecedented power. Teachers, particularly creative and critical teachers, have been besieged for some time (see Woods and Jeffrey, this volume). The management policies, teaching styles, educational philosophies and classroom climates conducive to the kinds of breakthroughs identified here do not currently meet official approval. Teaching is being de-charismatized. Some creative teachers in fact have felt compelled to leave teaching as an act of self-determination (for an example, see Woods 1995). This is not encouraging for the development of critical students. Yet most of the examples noted here took place within the National Curriculum. Breakthroughs in learning can and do still occur. They challenge the status quo, make the familiar strange, review conceptions of self that may have been unduly fashioned by structures, identify ideology and rhetoric, rise above and contextualize alienative forms. They are potentially empowering through what Freire (1970) calls 'conscientizacao', which 'enrols [people] in the search for self-affirmation' (p. 20), and which makes them subjects who know and act, rather than objects who are known and acted upon (Anderson 1989: 260).

Breakthroughs feature strong emotion, which engages the whole person in the learning activity, rouses passion and sensitizes the mind. There could be no more powerful motivation to learn, nor more intensive and extensive honing of the learning faculties. They free the learner from the grip of others' knowledge and restrictive assessments of their worth. They provide strength in new-found knowledge, newly discovered abilities and newly developed skills. They lead to self-enhancement and new appreciation of relationships with others. They provide a vantage point from which to survey other areas of learning of different types, and establish a marker to aspire to in future educational pursuits. While critical students remain on the agenda, breakthroughs, properly identified and contextualized, can aid in their development.

NOTE

1   This chapter was first published in *International Studies in Sociology of Education* 4 (2): 123–46, 1994.

REFERENCES

Abbs, P. (1994) *The Educational Imperative*, Lewes: Falmer Press.

Alexander, R. J. (1984) *Primary Teaching*, London: Holt, Rinehart and Winston.

Alexander, R. J. (1992) *Policy and Practice in Primary Education*, London: Routledge.

Allport, G. W. (1954) *The Nature of Prejudice*, Cambridge, Mass.: Addison-Wesley.

Althusser, L. (1971) 'Ideology and the state', in L. Althusser (ed.) *Lenin and Philosophy and Other Essays*, London: New Left Books.

Anderson, G. L. (1989) 'Critical ethnography in education: origins, current status and new directions', *Review of Educational Research* 59(3): 249–70.

Aoki, T. T. (1983) 'Experiencing ethnicity as a Japanese Canadian teacher: reflections on a personal curriculum', *Curriculum Inquiry* 13(3): 321–35.

Apple, M. W. (1986) *Teachers and Texts: A Political Economy of Class and Gender Relations in Education*, New York: Routledge and Kegan Paul.

Armstrong, M. (1992) 'Rendering an account', in T. Burgess (ed.) *Accountability in Schools*, London: Longman: 29–39.

Atkinson, P. and Delamont, S. (1977) 'Mock-ups and cock-ups: the stage-management of guided discovery instruction', in P. Woods and M. Hammersley (eds) *School Experience*, London: Croom Helm.

Barrault, J. L. (1972) 'Best and worst of professions', in J. Hodgson *The Uses of Drama*, London: Eyre Methuen.

Berger, P. L. (1963) *Invitation to Sociology*, Harmondsworth: Penguin.

Berger, P. L. (1971) *A Rumour of Angels*, Harmondsworth: Penguin.

Bernstein, B. (1975) *Class, Codes and Control. Vol. 3: Towards a Theory of Educational Transmissions*, London: Routledge and Kegan Paul.

Bolton, G. (1984) *Drama as Education*, London: Longman.

Bourdieu, P. (1977) 'Cultural reproduction and social reproduction', in J. Karabel and A. H. Halsey *Power and Ideology in Education*, New York: Oxford University Press.

Bowles, S. and Gintis, H. (1976) *Schooling in Capitalist America*, London: Routledge and Kegan Paul.

Burbules, N. C. (1993) *Dialogue in Teaching*, New York: Teachers' College Press.

Camsey, S. (1989) 'Evaluation of E-Mail Project', Barnehurst Junior School, Kent.

Carrington, B. and Short, G. (1989) *'Race' and the Primary School*, Slough: NFER-Nelson.

Collingwood, R. G. (1966) 'Expressing one's emotions', in E. W. Elsner and D. W. Ecker (eds) *Readings in Art Education*, Lexington, Mass.: Xerox College Publishing.

Dale, I. R. (1979) 'The politicization of school deviance: reactions to William Tyndale', in L. Barton and R. Meighan (eds) *Schools, Pupils and Deviance*, Driffield: Nafferton Books.

David, T., Curtis, A. and Siraj-Blatchford, I. (1992) *Effective Teaching in the Early Years: Fostering Children's Learning in Nurseries and in Infant Classes*, Stoke: Trentham Books.

Drummond, M. J. (1991) 'The child and the primary curriculum – from policy to practice', *The Curriculum Journal* 2(2): 115–24.

Edwards, A. D. and Furlong, V. J. (1978) *The Language of Teaching*, London: Heinemann.

Ellsworth, E. (1989) 'Why doesn't this feel empowering? Working through the repressive myths of critical pedagogy', *Harvard Educational Review* 59(3): 297–324.

Flude, M. and Hammer, M. (eds) (1990) *The Education Reform Act 1988: Its Origins and Implications*, Lewes: Falmer Press.

Foster, P. M. (1990) *Policy and Practice in Multicultural and Anti-Racist Education: A Case Study of a Multi-ethnic Comprehensive School*, Milton Keynes: Open University Press.

Foucault, M. (1980) *Power/Knowledge: Selected Interviews and Other Writings*, edited by C. Gordon, New York: Pantheon.

Freire, P. (1970) *Pegagogy of the Oppressed*, New York: Seabury.

Fuller, M. (1980) 'Black girls in a London comprehensive school', in R. Deem (ed.) *Schooling for Women's Work*, London: Routledge and Kegan Paul.

Galton, M. and Simon, B. (eds) (1980) *Progress and Performance in the Primary Classroom*, London: Routledge and Kegan Paul.

Garfinkel, H. (1956) 'Conditions of successful degradation ceremonies', *American Journal of Sociology* **61**: 420–4.

Gibson, R. (1986) *Critical Theory and Education*, London: Hodder and Stoughton.

Giroux, H. A. (1985) 'Critical pedagogy, cultural politics and the discourse of experience', *Journal of Education* **167**: 22–41.

Giroux, H. A. (1988) 'Critical theory and the politics of culture and voice: rethinking the discourse of educational research', in R. R. Sherman and R. B. Webb (eds) *Qualitative Research in Education: Focus and Methods*, London: Falmer Press.

Gitlin, A. (1992) *Teachers' Voices for School Change: An Introduction to Educative Research*, London: Routledge.

Gore, J. M. (1993) *The Struggle for Pedagogies: Critical and Feminist Discourses as Regimes of Truth*, London: Routledge.

Grugeon, E. and Woods, P. (1990) *Educating All: Multicultural Perspectives in the Primary School*, London: Routledge.

Hammersley, M. (1977) 'School learning: the cultural resources required by pupils to answer a teacher's question', in P. Woods and M. Hammersley (eds) *School Experience*, London: Croom Helm.

Hargreaves, A. (1978) 'Towards a theory of classroom strategies', in L. Barton and R. Meighan (eds) *Sociological Interpretations of Schooling and Classrooms*, Driffield: Nafferton Books.

Hargreaves, A. (1988) 'Teaching quality: a sociological analysis', *Journal of Curriculum Studies* **20**(3): 211–31.

Hargreaves, A. (1994) *Changing Teachers, Changing Times*, London: Cassell.

Hargreaves, D. H. (1983) 'The teaching of art and the art of teaching: towards an alternative view of aesthetic learning', in M. Hammersley, and A. Hargreaves (eds) *Curriculum Practice: Some Sociological Case Studies*, Lewes: Falmer Press.

Harvey, D. (1989) *The Condition of Postmodernity*, Oxford: Blackwell.

Holt, J. (1969) *How Children Fail*, Harmondsworth: Penguin.

King, R. A. (1978) *All Things Bright and Beautiful*, Chichester: Wiley.

Kozol, J. (1972) *Free Schools*, Boston: Houghton Mifflin.

Kriesberg, S. (1992), *Transforming Power: Domination, Empowerment and Education*, Albany: State University of New York Press.

Lee, V. and J. (1987) 'Stories children tell', in A. Pollard (ed.) *Children and Their Primary Schools*, Lewes: Falmer Press.

Mac an Ghaill, M. (1988) *Young, Gifted and Black*, Milton Keynes: Open University Press.

McLaren, P. (1986) *Schooling as a Ritual Performance*, London: Routledge and Kegan Paul.

Maw, J. (1993) 'The National Curriculum Council and the Whole Curriculum: reconstruction of a discourse?', *Curriculum Studies* **1**(1): 55–74.

Middleton, S. (1987) 'Streaming and the politics of female sexuality: case studies in the schooling of girls', in G. Weiner and M. Arnot (eds) *Gender under Scrutiny: New Inquiries in Education*, London: Hutchinson.

Moreno, J. L. (1972) 'Drama as therapy', in J. Hodgson (ed.) *The Uses of Drama*, London: Eyre Methuen.

Musgrove, F. (1977) *Margins of the Mind*, London: Methuen.

Nias, J., Southworth, G. and Yeomans, R. (1989) *Staff Relationships in the Primary School: A Study of Organizational Cultures*, London: Cassell.

O'Hear, P. and White, J. (1991) *A National Curriculum for All: Laying the foundations for success*, London: Institute for Public Policy Research.

Oldroyd, D. and Tiller, T. (1987) 'Change from within: an account of school-based collaborative action research in an English secondary school', *Journal of Education for Teaching* 12(3): 13–27.

Paley, V. G. (1986) 'On listening to what the children say', *Harvard Educational Review* 56(2): 122–31.

Plummer, K. (1983) *Documents of Life*, London: Allen and Unwin.

Pollard, A. (1991) *Learning in Primary Schools*, London: Cassell.

Quicke, J. and Winter, C. (1993) 'Teaching the language of learning: towards a metacognitive approach to pupil empowerment', paper presented at BERA Annual Conference, Liverpool.

Qvortrup, J. (1990) 'A voice for children in statistical and social accounting: a plea for children's right to be heard', in A. James and A. Prout (eds) *Constructing and Reconstructing Childhood*, London: Falmer Press.

Plowden Report (1967) *Children and their Primary Schools*, Report of the Central Advisory Council for Education in England, London: HMSO.

Riley, K. (1988) 'Black girls speak for themselves', in G. Weiner (ed.) *Just a Bunch of Girls*, Milton Keynes: Open University Press.

Rowland, S. (1987) 'Child in control: towards an interpretive model of teaching and learning', in A. Pollard (ed.) *Children and Their Primary Schools*, Lewes: Falmer Press.

Sharp, R. and Green, A. (1975) *Education and Social Control*, London: Routledge and Kegan Paul.

Short, G. and Carrington, B. (1987) 'Towards an anti-racist initiative in the all-white primary school: a case study', in A. Pollard (ed.) *Children and Their Primary Schools*, Lewes: Falmer Press.

Taylor, R. (1992) *The Visual Arts in Education: Completing the Circle*, Lewes: Falmer Press.

Towler, L. and Broadfoot, P. (1992) 'Self-assessment in the primary school', *Educational Review* 44(2): 137–51.

Trafford, B. (1993) *Sharing Power in Schools: Raising Standards*, Ticknall, Derbyshire: Education New Publishing Co-operative.

Troyna, B. and Hatcher, R. (1993) *Racism in Children's Lives*, London: Routledge.

Turner, V. W. (1969) *The Ritual Process*, London: Routledge and Kegan Paul.

Watts, M. and Bentley, D. (1991) 'Construction in the curriculum. Can we close the gap between the strong theoretical version and the week version of theory in practice?', *The Curriculum Journal* 2(2): 171–82.

Whistler, T. (1988) *Rushavenn Time*, Brixworth: Brixworth V.C. Primary School, Northamptonshire.

Willis, P. (1977) *Learning to Labour*, Farnborough: Saxon House.

Woods, P. (1981) 'Strategies, commitment and identity: making and breaking the teacher role', in L. Barton and S. Walker (eds) *Schools, Teachers and Teaching*, Lewes: Falmer Press.

Woods, P. (1990) *The Happiest Days? How Pupils Cope with School*, Lewes: Falmer Press.

Woods, P. (1993a) *Critical Events in Teaching and Learning*, London: Falmer Press.

Woods, P. (1993b) 'Managing marginality: teacher development through grounded life history', *British Educational Research Journal* **19**(5): 447–65.

Woods, P. (1993c) 'Towards a theory of aesthetic learning', *Educational Studies* **19**(3): 323–38.

Woods, P. (1993d) 'The charisma of the critical other: enhancing the role of the teacher', *Teaching and Teacher Education* **9**(5/6): 545–57.

Woods, P. (1995) *Creative Teachers in Primary Schools*, Milton Keynes: The Open University Press.

Wright, H. R. (1993) 'Transcendant possibility and abject failure: pedagogy as cultural praxis', paper presented at Symposium on Teaching, Curriculum and Educational Research, St Patrick's College, Dublin.

Chapter 11

Local student cultures of masculinity and sexuality

Máirtín Mac an Ghaill

[Editor's note: This article is an edited version of chapter 2 of the author's book The Making of Men: Masculinities, Sexualities and Schooling *(Buckingham: Open University Press, 1994, pp. 51–88).] The book reports an ethnographic study carried out in one secondary school (Parnell School) over a three-year period. The school was an inner-city comprehensive situated in the Midlands. Most of the students were from a working-class background, with about 10 per cent from a 'new middle-class' background. About 45 per cent of the students were Black, of Afro-Caribbean or Asian parentage, with roughly equal numbers of males and females. The research shows that boys do not all experience school in the same way, that various sub-cultures exist within the school, and that this helps promote different kinds of masculinities. In these extracts, the author explores connections with changes in the labour market, with changes in the structures of the family, and with ethnicity and racism.]*

The links between the male students' differing relations to schooling and their developing masculine identities were highlighted in their contrasting narratives. I have summarized these in the following terms: that of the Macho Lads' 'survival against authoritarianism', the Academic Achievers' 'ladders of social mobility', the New Enterprisers' 'making something of your life' and the Real Englishmen's 'looking for real experiences'. These links were further displayed by the students' differential participation in and celebration of formal and informal school rituals, through which masculine subjectivities are constructed and lived out, such as attendance at prize-giving and involvement in the playground smoking gang (Griffin 1993).

THE MACHO LADS: THE THREE FS – FIGHTING, FUCKING AND FOOTBALL

At Parnell School, a system of setting was in place. All of the Macho Lads were in the bottom two sets for all subjects. For some, this was a result of demotion, while others were placed there on their arrival at the school. Orientations towards school began to crystallize during year nine. The Macho

Lads came together as they found other male students with similar negative responses. Their shared view of the school was of a system of hostile authority and meaningless work demands (see Mac an Ghaill 1988b). They were seen by teachers and students as the most visible anti-school male sub-culture. 'Looking after your mates', 'acting tough', 'having a laugh', 'looking smart' and 'having a good time' were key social practices. As is indicated below, it was 'your [male] mates' who were the significant others in relation to evaluating what school is 'really about' and 'where you are going in the future'. Their vocabulary of masculinity stressed the physical ('sticking up for yourselves'), solidarity ('sticking together') and territorial control ('teachers think they own this place') (see Corrigan 1979; Cockburn 1983; Jenkins 1983).

> *John:*   The main way that we protect ourselves is by sticking together [as a gang]. From about the end of the third year a group of us got together and we now have a reputation. A lot of the teachers and the kids won't mess with us and we protect other kids.
>
> *Darren:*   I suppose a lot of kids here are able to defend themselves but it's the teachers that make the rules. It's them that decide that it's either them or us. So you are often put into a situation with teachers where you have to defend yourself. Sometimes it's direct in the classroom. But it's mainly the headcases that would hit a teacher. Most of the time it's all the little things in the place really.
>
> *M. M.:*   Like what?
>
> *Gilroy:*   Acting tough by truanting, coming late to lessons, not doing homework, acting cool by not answering teachers, pretending you didn't hear them; that gets them mad. Lots of different things.

Peer-group masculine identities were developed in response to the school's differentiated forms of authority. This was highly visible in relation to the Macho Lads' experience of the school's social relations of domination, alienation and infantilism that were mediated through their location in the lowest sets. These social relations were of central importance in the construction of their masculinity through 'conflict with the institutional authority of the school' (Connell 1989: 291; Johnson 1991). . . .

In relation to the Macho Lads, the primary [teacher] function was that of policing, which tended to make explicit the construction and moral regulation of teacher and student subjectivities (Walkerdine 1990). The school disciplinary regime operated in more overt authoritarian modes of interaction with this sector of students. The school's moral imperatives, which included a wide range of disciplinary instruments, were translated into the surveillance of the Macho Lads' symbolic display of working-class masculinity. The senior management, who were becoming experts at decoding the semiotic communication of contestation and resistance, legislated new control and surveillance mechanisms for these 'non-academic' students. At this time there was a vigilant policing, and subsequent banning, of the anti-school male students' clothes, footwear, hairstyles and earrings. This was accompanied by a high-profile surveillance of the students' bodies, with the constant demands of such teacher comments as: 'Look at me when I'm talking to you', 'sit up straight' and 'walk properly down the corridor' (Bourdieu 1986).

As Westwood (1990: 59) notes: 'Discourses as registers of masculinity are worked through a variety of spaces.' Spatially, Parnell School was geared to a set pattern of movement, which systematically discriminated against low-set students, who were viewed with suspicion if during breaks they were found in certain academic locations, such as the science laboratories or computer centre. These students frequently complained about the prefects' arbitrary power as they patrolled corridors and restricted their movement around the school.

> *Paul:*   We have different names for the teachers: big ears, big nose, big eyes and that sort of thing.
> *M. M.:*   What does it mean?
> *Jim:*   It's obvious. Teachers are always trying to catch you out. They're always trying to rule you. They use different means, some are really nosey, others try to catch you smoking and then others are always trying to get you to tell on your mates. . .

The Macho Lads rejected the official three Rs (reading, writing and arithmetic), and the unofficial three Rs (rules, routines and regulations). They explained why they opted for the three Fs – fighting, fucking and football (Jackson 1968). They interpreted their secondary school biographies as masculine apprenticeships in learning to be 'tough'. Like the 'anti-school' Asian male students, the 'Warriors', in *Young, Gifted and Black* (Mac an Ghaill 1988b), the Macho Lads objected to the *function* not the *style* of teachers, which they saw as primarily causal of school conflict. They refused to affirm the teachers' authority, claiming that it was illegitimate authoritarianism. Spending more time 'on the streets' than other students increased their visibility to the police. Hence, they linked teacher and police authoritarianism, seeing themselves as vulnerable to both state agencies of social control. In response to institutionalized surveillance and interrogation, they developed a specific version of masculinity, around collective strategies of counter-interrogation, contestation and survival (Mac an Ghaill 1988b: 136). . . .

> *Kevin:*   I'll tell you something, when we came to this dump we believed in the three Rs, we were right little piss artists, real plonkers. Well we learnt what schools were for, for keeping you down and bossing you about. Over the last couple of years we've been doing the three Fs.
> *Arshad:*   When kids come here in the first year, you can see that they're not tough. It's the main thing that you have to learn.
> *M.M.:*   Is it very important?

Arshad: In some ways, real ways, you know what I mean, you won't survive. You see the whole place is planned to boss you around. That's the main difference between here and posher schools. Somehow the kids in the posh schools accept it more.

Leon: The teachers think, I'm going to put this little sod down because he thinks he can rule the place. The kid isn't thinking that but the teachers think that he is.

M.M.:   Why do the teachers think that?

Leon: I don't know. Teachers have to win all the time, don't they? So, I don't know, maybe they think, I'll get him before he gets me, you know what I mean?

Noel: Teachers are always suspicious of us [the Macho Lads]. Just like the cops, trying to set you up.

Like Willis's Lads, the Macho Lads at Parnell School made a similar association of academic work with an inferior effeminacy, referring to those who conformed as 'dickhead achievers'. Consequently, they overtly rejected much school work as inappropriate for them as men. They were also a pivotal group within the school in creating a general ethos in which the academic/non-academic couplet was associated with a feminine/masculine division for a wider group of 'ordinary' male students, who were not overtly anti-school (Jenkins 1983).

Leon: The work you do here is girls' work. It's not real work. It's just for kids. They [the teachers] try to make you write down things about how you feel. It's none of their fucking business.

Kevin: We live in the real world. The world where we are going to end up in – no work, no money with the stupid, slave training schemes. We've gotta sort this out for ourselves, not teachers. They live in their little soft world. They wouldn't survive in our world for five minutes. Now I'm leaving I feel sorry for them. Well, for some of them, some were wicked bastards to the kids.

Arshad: They [the teachers] just look down on us. They think we're nothing because they say, 'you're like your brothers, they never got on to good training' [youth training schemes]. Some of them will do the caring bit. 'I come from Yorkshire lad, my dad was down the pit and I know what the real world is like.' Do they fuck. I wouldn't even ask them, what do you know about being a black man looking for work, when even the white kids round here haven't got work.

THE ACADEMIC ACHIEVERS

The Academic Achievers consisted of a small group of male friends who had a positive orientation to the academic curriculum. In contrast to the recent emergence of the New Enterprisers (discussed below), the Academic Achievers were reminiscent of grammar school 'scholarship boys', adopting the more traditional upwardly social mobile route via academic subject credentialism. There was a high proportion of Asian and white young men from a skilled working-class background represented in this group. However, they did not fit into a homogeneous pattern of being unambiguously pro-school. Rather, their appropriation of the curriculum involved complex social practices, informed by varied cultural investments. There was a range of shifting responses within a broadly positive relationship to the academic curriculum, that included criticism of the teacher practices of infantilism and disciplinary inconsistency (Hollands 1990: 69–73).

As was reported at Kilby School (Mac an Ghaill 1988b), the stages of the students' career at Parnell School were structured so that the teachers' main concern was the needs of the top stream. The Academic Achievers were among those students who had a number of material and social advantages, including permanent teaching locations, although there was a shortage of classrooms; access to specialist classrooms; provision of the most experienced teachers; the first choice of option subject choices in year nine; and preferential treatment in terms of timetabling, equipment and books. The hidden curriculum was of equal importance in terms of the teachers' high esteem and positive expectations of them. These cumulative material and social conditions helped to shape an institutionally confident student masculinity that was highly valued by the teachers.

I was particularly interested in how working-class male students developed a masculine identity within the context of the contradictions of their participation in the conventional 'feminine' curriculum sector of the arts. During year ten, the Academic Achievers, who spent much of their leisure time in the drama department, became publicly associated with 'feminine' arts subjects. This was made manifest on one occasion, when students severely ridiculed them for their involvement in a play, in which three of them took female roles. For them, this was a continuation of the bullying that they had experienced in their earlier years at the school (Gillborn 1993).

Ashwin: We were in the school band and they would really take the piss, saying we were girls because we carried round violins and that. And then we got into drama, the macho mob were really bad, everyday threatening and punishing us. But now, they still say things but we feel safer and most of the time we just ignore them and don't come in contact with them.

Tony: Me and Ashwin got the worst, picked on every day by the yobs and then the others would start. They'd be in their gangs. It sounds funny but I think it was little things like looking small, I was tiny then, and both of us wore glasses, things like that.

M.M.:   So those things would be picked up then?

Tony: Some kids got much worse. There was a kid who had a limp and they persecuted him for years. . .

A number of the teachers and the students positioned the Academic Achievers as 'effeminate'. The latter's self-representation and their stance on gender stereotyping was complex. On the one hand, by year eleven, as a result of being physically stronger, having a safe space in the drama department and one of the English teacher's protection, they responded creatively and innovatively to student and teacher heterosexist discursive resources that were employed against them. Their creativity involved parodying and subverting dominant institutional sex/gender meanings. At the same time, they strongly differentiated between masculine and feminine sensibilities within 'feminine' school subjects.

Tony: I think we're more confident now. You have to be in this school. It wasn't just the low-set kids but the men teachers would always be getting at you in little ways.

M.M.:   Like what?

Tony: Oh, stupid things, like put away your handbags or stuff about marrying us off because we stuck around together. I think it helped being in drama. We got more confident with language and how to respond with humour. Like in a school like this, a lot of the male teachers are very defensive, very macho and they've got a lot of power to put you down in front of everyone. So, we just started talking together about taking on the sexual jokes and camping it up. And they just couldn't cope with it. It was great.

M.M.:   Remember in class when Darren said that English literature and drama were girls' subjects? What would you say to that?

Edward: It's just typical. It's different for girls and blokes even if they are doing the same subjects. Girls like feminine writers and all the emotional stuff like they get in their magazines. It's completely different for a bloke. He's more into how to become more like expert, you know what I mean? Like if you look at a lot of the people who write about English Lit, they're nearly all men, like Andy's father lectures at the uni [university].

M.M.:   Why do you think that is the case?

Parminder: Because even if you're doing the same subjects, men and women have completely different things that they're interested in. I think that men would be more intellectual and women more emotional. They just feel different things.

The Academic Achievers illustrate the complexity of students' cultural investment in a specific masculinity. Despite successfully challenging heterosexist jibes, nevertheless they continued to operate within conventional gender essentialist categories. . . .

We need to consider not only gender *differences* but also *relations between* young men and women and *within* young men's peer groups. It is important to see masculinity not simply as complementary to femininity, which tends to reinforce perceived unitary conceptions and 'natural' binary differences. Masculinities are also developed in specific institutional contexts in relation to and against each other. . . .

Important to the Academic Achievers' masculine formation were the specific dynamics of the class continuities and discontinuities in relation to the Real Englishmen (discussed below) and the Macho Lads, both of whom ridiculed the Academic Achievers for their school work ethic. The Academic Achievers appeared to be developing a masculine identity in which they would not 'feel at home' either among the middle class or sectors of the working class (Walkerdine 1991).

> *Parminder:*   Sometimes you wonder if all the learning and study is worth it, you just get down in yourself. You lose mates and you can't really get on with the snobs. I mean you wouldn't want to, would you?
>
> *M.M.:*   So what keeps you going?
>
> *Parminder:*   I don't know. I like the work a lot of the time and I want to get on and that's what my family wants. I wouldn't like to be like the dossers here. My brother's like them. He's just wasting his life. . . .

Jenkins (1983: 42) reminds us that working-class academic success is not the same as middle-class success. The Academic Achievers may be in the process of equipping themselves for social mobility and a middle-class post-school destination, but 'it is largely on indigenous working-class principles and practices that they draw'. This was clearly illustrated in relation to the way in which the Academic Achievers were developing an academic identity that was informed by a strong working-class work ethic in contrast to the new middle-class Real Englishmen's 'effortless achievement' (this is explained below) (Aggleton 1987). For the Academic Achievers, their positive response to school was not reducible to a material utilitarian concern with the gaining of qualifications. Equally important was the symbolic significance of the latter, acting as a public sign of their own high cultural position. There was evidence of their ambiguous relationship to middle-class cultural capital that combined desire and fear. They spent long hours on homework assignments and revising for internal tests and examinations. However, in contrast to the Real Englishmen, they were reticent in class, lacking confidence to articulate what they knew, or question what they didn't. Their fear manifested itself in relation to the Real Englishmen, who embodied what the Academic Achievers desired. Whereas they could easily dismiss the Macho Lads' derisory comments, they were openly intimidated by the Real Englishmen's contempt, feeling unable publicly to match what appeared as sophisticated verbal exchanges.

Mark: You know the Heathfield crowd [new middle-class residential area] are full of bullshit. They're just wankers. But they still make you feel low. They know how to talk to teachers. They share more things, going to the theatre and art galleries and they all go round reading books. And with their background, it's easy for them to be clever. If I have kids, I'll give them the best education because that's what really matters. So they won't feel out of it. So no-one can look down on them.

Andy: A lot of the kids take the piss out of us. But it's different with different groups. With the low-set boys, they're more physical and say bad things you get used to. They're dickheads really. But with the middle-class ones, it's more difficult. They're real snides. When they're all together, they can put you down bad and what can you do? They've got all this alternative humour. I don't even understand it, using big words and all that business.

A central element of the Academic Achievers' masculine identity was their projected future of a professional career. They frequently spoke of their career aspirations as defining them as different from their working-class male peers. . . . An important aspect of the Academic Achievers' self-representation was the acceptance of the 'mental–manual' division of labour, and their identification with 'mental' production. This explicitly manifested itself in terms of distancing themselves from the Macho Lads, the embodiment of manual labour and 'low-life futures'.

Andy: I think the ones in the top sets can think for themselves more. We're more into the subjects, like history and English. But the nutters [Macho Lads], what are they interested in? They can't think for themselves, so they go round being hard and causing trouble all the time. They'll just end up on the dole.

NEW ENTERPRISERS

The vocationalization of the curriculum at Parnell School led to student restratification, with the development of new internal hierarchies between high- and low-status vocational spheres. In the resulting processes of student deskilling and upskilling, a new route of social mobility was created for the New Enterprisers. Working within the new vocationalist skilling regimes of high-status technological and commercial subject areas, the New Enterprise students were negotiating a new mode of school student masculinity with its values of rationality, instrumentalism, forward planning and careerism (see Hollands 1990). This was illustrated by their utilitarian involvement in mini-enterprise schemes, which were rejected by other sub-groups. They explained their enthusiasm for the schemes in pragmatic terms of their future value in the high-skilled sector of the labour market, which they were planning to enter.

> *Charles*: I picked my subjects carefully, knowing what I want from my future. Most of the academic stuff's a waste of time. I don't think that the teachers know that the real world has changed. One or two, like in business studies, Mr James will talk to you and push you in your ambitions. Like my dad says, you set goals and you work for them.
>
> *Wayne*: In class you just sit there in most lessons as the teacher just goes on and on, but in business studies and technology you learn a lot, you're really doing something, something that will be useful for your future.
>
> *Amerjit*: My dad really wished the CTC [City Technology College] was open when I started secondary school. My brother's got in and it's really good. . . . They do a lot of technology, so you have a lot of experience when you leave. . . .

At the student level, the New Enterprise students were most active in the gender appropriation of recent curriculum reforms. This included their 'colonizing' the computer club which . . . had been set up with the official aim of 'changing girls' negative views of technology'.

Among the New Enterprisers and Academic Achievers there were individual complaints against certain teachers for 'treating them like babies', but in principle they affirmed the legitimacy of the teachers' authority. From their different perspectives, they accepted the cultural exchange of student co-operation for qualifications. In developing their masculine identities against the Macho Lads, they were critical of the latter's 'childish' behaviour and the teachers' responses. . . . A major complaint of the New Enterprisers, aware of impression management, was that the teachers were too soft with the Macho Lads and that this would affect the school's reputation with future employers.

> *Parminder*: When you're younger, you mess about. But from about year ten you need to grow up a bit, you know what I mean. The nutters [the Macho Lads] will say they're not treated as grown-ups by the teachers but it's them. They'll always be babies and that's why they won't get anywhere. It's just horrible being here with them.
>
> *Stephen*: They [the Macho Lads] should just be thrown out. The teachers are trying to make this a good school, but the nutters just give us all a bad name.

THE REAL ENGLISHMEN: 'THE ARBITERS OF CULTURE'

. . . About ten per cent of the student population at Parnell School were from a non-commercial, middle-class background. Their parents' occupations included lecturing, teaching, public relations and work in the media and the arts. As with the working-class students, there was a range of middle-class masculinities, including an emerging group of Politicos, who were involved with environmental and animal rights issues (see Hollands 1990: 119). I chose a small group of male students who displayed an ambivalent response to the academic curriculum and who consequently were the most problematic middle-class peer group for many of the teachers. . . .

A central contradiction for the Real Englishmen was that unlike the Macho Lads' overt rejection of formal school knowledge and the potential exchange value it has in the labour market, the Real Englishmen had a more ambiguous relationship to it. They envisaged a future of higher education and a professional career. Like Aggleton's (1987) 'Spatown Rebels', they defined themselves as a younger generation of the cultural elite, who like modern-day high-priests positioned themselves as the arbiters of culture. From this self-appointed location, they evaluated both teachers and students in terms of their possession of high-status cultural capital (Bourdieu 1986). They were in the process of building a publicly confident school masculinity in which cultural capital was over-valorized.

> *Thomas*:   We're different to most of the people here. That's why we don't fit in. They're mostly boring people, no style, very conventional. I mean you couldn't have a real discussion with any of them.
>
> *Daniel*:   The teachers give you all the crap about having the right attitude to work and we shouldn't be going out at night and we shouldn't talk back to them. They have no idea there's some really interesting people out there that they'll never meet. I mean, who needs teachers' advice? What do they know about life?

Like the Macho Lads, the Real Englishmen, albeit on different grounds, refused to affirm the legitimacy of the teachers' authority, though their rebellion tended to take a more individualist and varied form. They brought with them into the school values that emphasized personal autonomy and gave high evaluation to communication strategies. They expected to be able to negotiate with teachers, particularly about compulsory aspects of the curriculum. Teacher–student interaction with this sub-group produced specific conflictual masculine social practices. Many of the teachers found these middle-class students' capacity for elaborated verbal self-justification much more difficult to respond to, than what appeared to them as the Macho Lads' more open contestation of their authority. The teachers were often confused by the Real Englishmen's highly competent communication skills, with their appeal to rationality and fairness, that enabled the latter discursively to invert classroom power relations, with teachers positioned as culturally subordinate.

> *Edward*:   Mark's the best when he starts arguing with the teachers. They never learn. They start off talking down to him and then realize that he can defend himself. They get wickedly mad with him when he quotes some European philosopher they've never heard of. Then they're really

shown up in front of everyone. And they hate that because that's their tactic with the kids.

The middle-class young men's name, the Real Englishmen, served as a triple signifier with reference to gender, sexuality and ethnicity, which were highly problematic inter-generational issues for them. The implications of this for their development of a specific mode of masculinity is discussed more fully below. Here I wish to concentrate on the development of their peer-group masculine identity in relation to working-class male peer groups. The Real Englishmen's own masculine values emphasized honesty, being different, individuality and autonomy, which they claimed were absent from middle-class culture. Against this background, the Real Englishmen were more ambivalent than the Academic Achievers towards the Macho Lads. At one level, this involved a fantasy of 'proletarian authenticity'. The Macho Lads were viewed as 'noble savages' for being unpretentious and unconscious of themselves. At another level, the Real Englishmen articulated excessive hostility towards the Macho Lads, who they referred to as 'trash', for their vulgarity and aggression, which was directed towards them. They were particularly resentful as they recalled how in earlier years the working-class lads had bullied them.

> *Adam*: You see it if you go down the arts centre, all the middle-class are totally aware of themselves, thinking that people are watching them all the time, as if they're always on show. And you see it in the kids, in their humour and everything, it's just not real. But the working-class are not so aware of their bodies. They are more straightforward, act more spontaneous.
>
> *Andy*: The Macho kids in this place are just wankers. When we first came here, they terrorized us. We hadn't mixed with them before. They're just very crude and loud. They'd beat you up for looking at them. It's their idea of being real men. The girls find them ugly.

The Real Englishmen were also critical of 'hard-working' students, including their middle-class peers and such groups as the working-class Academic Achievers and the New Enterprisers. The Real Englishmen's dismissive evaluation of these students as 'sloggers' had implications for their relationship to the academic curriculum. From their own self-appointed culturally superior position, they inverted the taken-for-granted relationship between academic success and a positive response to mental labour. Teachers working within discourses of individual under-achievement failed to acknowledge in the young men's response, their collective masculine investment and the links to family social practices. A key element of the students' peer group identity was a highly public display of a contradictory 'effortless achievement' to each other and outsiders (Aggleton 1987: 73). As members of a cultural elite, they rejected the school's dominant work ethic, assuming that intellectual talent was 'naturally' inscribed within their peer group.

> *Daniel:*   Teaching is a low-skill job. They're mostly technicists, not into ideas. They've no idea how patronizing they are to us. They don't like us because we're cleverer than them.
>
> *Robert:*   They're [the teachers] just guardians of mediocrity. They've this idea that you have to work all the time, slog, slog, slog to pass exams.
>
> *M. M.:*   Why do you think they feel that?
>
> *Robert:*   Because that's how they got through. When Ben asked Williams [science teacher], why do we have to do homework, you could see he had never thought of it. And we joined in. He just couldn't argue his case. So, it came down to the usual crap, because I'm telling you boy. And this is supposed to be funny, teacher humour! . . .

I now wish to examine the relationship between peer-group practices and their orientation to work, as another key feature of the complexity of the young men's identity formation (see Lee 1993).

REGENDERING WAGED LABOUR: A WHITE WORKING-CLASS CRISIS OF MASCULINITY

The students at Parnell School are part of a generation whose transition into adulthood is in the process of being reconstituted as a result of high rates of unemployment and punitive legislative changes that have led to the with-drawal of financial state support for young people. The cumulative effects of these social regulatory changes is to increase their dependency on parents or guardians. Harris (1992: 92) has suggested that: 'The end of youth culture . . . [is] . . . at hand. In real life, the youth of the 1980's in Britain ceased to be a metaphor for change and stylistic innovation and became victims of social and structural change instead.' Such a reading is not supported by this study. However, the immediate social class experience of students at Parnell School was one of social marginalization, involving widening regional poverty, diminishing local state services, increased police surveillance following the urban disturbances, and the long-term unemployment of family members and friends (Brindle 1993). . . .

Recently, young people – both collectively and individually – have been constructing masculine identities in a climate of rapid socio-economic change, which has led to a major fracturing in the process of coming-of-age in England in the early 1990s. For example, Willis (1985: 6) speaks of how the young unemployed now find themselves in a 'new social condition of suspended animation between school and work. Many of the old transitions into work, into cultures and organisations of work, into being consumers, into independent accommodation – have been frozen or broken.' These transitions are further shaped and differentiated by class, 'race', ethnicity, gender, sexuality and disability (see Brown 1989; Mac an Ghaill 1992). In short, we are witnessing highly disorganized and fractured post-compulsory school transitions, with large sectors of white and black young people 'learning not to labour' (Stafford 1981).

Brown (1989: 238) argues that the fundamental changes in the relationship between the reward structures of the school and the labour market may lead to great confusion among large sectors of working-class students concerning the purpose of school in preparing them for occupational and social destinies. At Parnell School, there was much evidence of this. But perhaps more surprising was the range of coping and survival strategies that were in the process of being established in the young men's transitions from school. In much of the school-to-work literature, there has been a concentration on gender differences rather than gender relations (Griffin 1993). In such work, there tends to be a certain unitariness and rigidity in working-class masculine forms, with little indication of their historical specificity. In other words, there is theoretical underdevelopment of the relational status of these sex/gender cultural forms or the possibility that under different conditions they might change. . . .

At Parnell School, the emerging diverse intra-class trajectories to employment were acted out in relation to such bridging mechanisms as 'work experience'. The students' responses might be read as a dress-rehearsal for the 'real thing'. Most of the Macho Lads dismissed work experience as an early version of the 'slave training schemes' that their older brothers and friends were on. Similarly, most of the Academic Achievers tended to evaluate their work placements in negative terms. However, their main objection was that it was an unnecessary distraction from examination preparation. Some of them explicitly indicated their aspirations for upward social mobility, distancing themselves from manual labour. This appeared to be particularly significant for those students whose fathers worked or had worked in manual jobs.

> *Edward:* They should just send the low-class kids. It's really for them. Me and my mates hated it. The job I had, it was just dirty and boring all the time. I suppose the only good thing to come out of it was that you would never end up doing that kind of job. But then again we knew that anyway 'coz most our dads are doing it. Could you think of doing that for all your life?

The New Enterprisers made individual complaints about their 'work experience' but overall they thought of it as highly worthwhile. This was in part a consequence of their own preparation, which included active negotiation of specific work placements. When I visited them at work, they tended to show more enthusiasm than the other student sub-groups, emphasizing the opportunities of 'experiencing the real world of proper work'. In contrast to the Macho Lads' defensive masculine stance, the New Enterprisers were in the process of building a positive, confident future work identity.

Bob: A lot of the kids here moaned about going out on work placements, the usual dossers. But it was good for some of us. Like most of
   our technology class, Mr James got special places for us. I had been in
   to mine before. My dad says it will be good. It will show that I'm keen
   to work. A lot of the kids around here are unemployable. So sometimes I think there's not much competition, but you have to keep
   pushing yourself to get on.

Graham: I really enjoyed getting up and going in. It's more real than a
   lot of boring school stuff here, with all the writing and it's more grown
   up. It was good experience. You go for a job and they're going to take
   the person with the experience. It's just as important as the qualifications, but you need to have them as well.

The Real Englishmen were also active in negotiating work placements.
However, in their case, they were not motivated by hoping to enhance future
work opportunities. Like Aggleton's (1987) 'Spatown Rebels', a primary
concern of the Real Englishmen – reflecting that of their parents – was the
gaining of personal control over the management of space, time and systems
of meanings. Hence, they were preoccupied with redefining public and private
spheres of experience. So, for example, they sought work places – as they did
in their part-time jobs outside school hours – that blurred the boundaries
between work and leisure, in which they could socialize with friends while
working.

The working-class student responses made an interesting contrast to those
of the middle-class Real Englishmen. The Academic Achievers' 'occupational
new realism' in relation to the new vocationalist curriculum must be located
within the broader terrain. For black and white working-class young men,
state schools remain a central ladder of social mobility, albeit for a minority,
in a racially and class-stratified society. This was not the case for the Real
Englishmen, who as the children of the agents of symbolic control, have alternative employment routes open to them other than those offered by schools
and training schemes. As Aggleton (1987: 135) has demonstrated for this
social class, qualifications are relatively insignificant in terms of predicting
employment destinies. This is particularly important at the present time, with
the expansion of the local service sector, which includes a large network of
middle-class parental contacts, who may act as sponsors through higher education and the labour markets.

The Real Englishmen were developing their masculine identity against a
background of collective self-confidence which, as a cultural elite, led them
to believe they would find employment. It was precisely on these grounds
that they were dismissed by the New Enterprisers and the Academic Achievers.
These working-class, socially mobile students were severely critical of the
privileged middle-class students for their pretentious lifestyle and lack of
work effort. They were particularly angry at the Real Englishmen's attempt

to appropriate proletarian and black cultural forms, imitating and exaggerating caricatured working-class representations (Jones 1988).

Having examined the young men's responses to work experience, I shall now explore their projected future work identities in relation to changing local labour markets. Willis developed Tolson's (1977) study of masculinity, arguing that work was central to working-class boys' masculine self-representation. By the early 1990s, much appears to have changed in relation to the school–waged labour couplet. The political-economic legacy of the 1980s for large sectors of working-class students, is that of a post-school anticipation of dependency, on low-skilled central government training schemes, as surplus youth labour in late industrial capitalism. Harrison (1993: 10) has described this rapid rise in local unemployment within the West Midlands: 'Last year the jobless figure leapt by more than 1,000 people every week (from 152,700 to 270,500), meaning more than one in ten of working people are on the scrapheap.' Of specific importance here was that following the post-war boom, the last twenty years have seen a major contraction in local manufacturing industries. This was in the order of 46 per cent, thus transforming a relatively prosperous area into one of the poorest in the country (Loftman and Nevin 1992).

At Parnell School, located within the West Midlands, the disruption and accompanying restructuring of the students' transitions from school to waged work, with the collapse of the local economy's manufacturing base, appeared to be creating a crisis in traditional white working-class forms of masculinity. This was of specific significance for the white Macho Lads, whose out-dated mode of masculinity continued to centre around traditional manual waged labour, at a time when their traditional manual work destiny has disappeared.

The current changing material conditions appeared to be less problematic in their effects for African Caribbean and Asian Macho Lads' masculine identity formation. This is not to suggest that mass unemployment, the resulting racialization of poverty and dominant state discourses of black pathology are not a major critical issue for African Caribbean and Asian young men. Nor is it to argue that these social changes go uncontested. However, black communities have a longer history of unemployment in racially structured local labour markets. During a decade of mass structural unemployment, black working-class men within the area have continued to be disproportionately affected by the rapidly contracting regional manufacturing base, as they have been concentrated in the declining metal industries (Brown 1992). A recent local union survey reported that 'black and Asian people are twice as likely to be jobless as white people' (*Evening Mail* 1993). Hence, the Asian and African Caribbean Macho Lads realistically appeared to have less emotional investment in future work in the local area. Further empirical work is required here.

A large number of working-class young men at Parnell School, and most emphatically the Macho Lads, were holding on to conventional views of domestic and waged labour arrangements and responsibilities in terms of a feminine–masculine bipolar split. However, this was against the background that for most of them there was no immediate prospect of finding a job. Hence, the Macho Lads could not appeal to a naturalized gender-divided world of 'breadwinners' and 'homemakers' (Finn 1987).

The Macho Lads constructed their masculinity within a perceived social world divided between the 'hard' and the 'soft'. The white Macho Lads' anti-authoritarianism was accompanied by the valorization of 'masculine' manual labour that informed the group's social practices (Willis 1977; Jenkins 1983). Inverting the institution's value system, the Macho Lads projected a tough masculine identity against male teachers' and students' involvement in academic feminized work. Like Hollands' (1990: 69–70) 'Manual Labour Lads', the Macho Lads drew on and asserted 'male experiences from the "real world"', ... continuing to mock [teachers] ... through humour and bravado'. Although their public display of highly ritualized forms of hyper-masculinity often appeared defensive, nevertheless they were deeply rooted in collective investments in wider working-class cultural forms and more concretely linked to their fathers' and older brothers' 'commonsense' gendered world views. They fantasized about an old England of full employment that their fathers occupied. Interestingly, with the exception of Paul, whose mother was active in the trade union movement, the students did not see trade unions as significant in relation to the creation of job opportunities.

> *Jim:*   The teachers try and advise us about training. I was telling my dad and he said, what would they know, they've never done a real day's work in their lives. He came up to the school when I was having my options because my mom was working that night. He said to the teachers, do you think you lot can get him a job? And they just kept talking and talking. He said, it made him think, nothing's changed.

The Macho Lads may be seen as inhabiting a descending mode of masculinity within the hierarchy of a working-class school's gender regime. In contrast, the New Enterprise students ... may be viewed as adopting an ascending modernized version of masculinity within an increasingly commercialized school arena. In contrast to the white Macho Lads' nostalgia for an imagined past, the New Enterprisers celebrated an imagined future of flexible work skills in managerial and self-employment positions.

> *Wayne:*   A lot of the kids in the low classes [in Parnell School] say that there's no jobs, but my dad has become self-employed. He says there's jobs for people but they have to get out and find them.
>
> *M.M.:*   And has the school helped you in this?
>
> *Wayne:*   I think it's a lot better now. If you show an interest, then teachers help you. Like the teachers say, you have to learn different skills, so if

things change you will look good to the employer because you can do different jobs. . . . And if you get a lot of experience, then you can become your own boss. That's what I'm aiming for. You don't want to be working for someone else all your life when you can make more money yourself.

In the local economy, the disappearing 'masculine' manufacturing base was being displaced by an increase in the traditional 'feminine' service sector. As Hutton (1993: 20) has recently pointed out:

A quiet revolution is going on which is transforming the lives of millions of workers in Britain. The world of full-time pensionable employment is retreating before their eyes; and in its stead is emerging an insecure world of contract work, part-time jobs and casualised labour.

A large proportion of this work is being carried out by white and black working-class women (Walby 1990). It was against this background that the regendering of youth waged labour was taking place. This was evident in male students' redefining of the sexual division of labour in their part-time work in the service sector. They were in the process of appropriating and redefining conventional female areas of work in supermarkets, video shops and fast food restaurants. Their explanations took different forms. Some of the male students differentiated between male and female spheres by associating the former with a more private world of 'hard physical labour' away from the public gaze of employers and customers. For other male students, the masculine sphere was defined in terms of their own superior gender expertise in relation to recent technological developments.

> *Graham:*   Where we work in the supermarket, the boys do all the harder work like filling shelves and dragging things around the warehouse. And you're freer there, away from the boss. And the girls are on the tills talking to the customers and that. Like you would prefer to talk to a girl in a shop wouldn't you?
>
> *William:*   Working in a sweet shop might be more girls' work. But in places like video and hi-fi shops, then it's mainly going to be men because they know about these things don't they?
>
> *M. M.:*   Why do you think that women don't?
>
> *William:*   Well you don't see women in these shops. Like where I work, the girls do the cleaning and making tea and that.
>
> *M. M.:*   Do you think that is because they choose to do that?
>
> *William:*   I don't know. But if you think of it, girls read all the girls' magazines with silly stories and that, but boys are always into video games and making things. So, they must be more interested in it, how things work and all that. Boys are just better at these things. So, they get those jobs that need technical experts more. . . .

FAMILY NETWORK–SCHOOL RELATIONS: AN 'ENGLISH' MIDDLE-CLASS CRISIS OF MASCULINITY

... One of the most surprising findings ... was how rapid social changes have helped to structure highly differentiated experiences of family life for young people. This included, as discussed above, changing work patterns in the local area, with mass male unemployment in manufacturing and changing patterns of women's work, with an increase in jobs, albeit low paid, in the local service sector. Another significant factor was the large number of lone-parent, mother-headed households and the accompanying feminization of poverty. Third, as made explicit in interviews with the Real Englishmen's mothers was the influence of modern feminism (see Arnot 1992; David 1993).

Working-class parental affirmation and legitimation of the school's authority was complex and diverse. In interviews with working-class students at Parnell School, parents were frequently mentioned as influencing their orientation to schooling. Nevertheless, there was no predictable mechanistic inter-generational links between parents' and their sons' evaluation of schooling. Parents who were actively supportive of the school sometimes produced Macho Lads, and parents who appeared indifferent or hostile to the school sometimes had as sons Academic Achievers or New Enterprisers (Willis 1977: 73).

> *Charles:* I really admire my dad. He came from nothing, now he's got his own business. He's worked hard and no-one's given him anything. He's pushing me to do well in school, so I can help him or start up my own business. A lot of the kids here are just wasters, just waiting to go on the dole and that.

Working-class male students also spoke of the different advice they receive from their mothers and fathers as significant in shaping their response to school and the development of sub-cultural practices.

> *Mark:* If I had listened to my dad, I would have ended up in a factory or on the dole like my brothers and his friends. It is really my mum who has pushed me, encouraged me to stay on at school. She sees education as important and thinks there are opportunities now that she never had. If she hadn't married my dad she could have really gone places and done things herself.

Against the background of recent educational reforms which are making a claim for legitimacy in terms of empowering parents, working-class parents' assessments of schools are informative. A main flaw of such legislation is the failure to acknowledge the differential positioning of parents to schooling and its discourses of social exclusion. Behind this 'apolitical' central government stance is hidden an appeal to 'parents' as a national homogeneous entity. Carby (1980: 2) has attacked the assumed nationalist consensus of official reports and documents, arguing that 'inherent contradictions and conflicting interests . . . within and between racial, sexual and class groupings are contained by and subsumed under an apparent unity of interests'. Parnell School was regarded by parents as having good relations with them and the wider local community. Nevertheless, some parents voiced a 'working-class suspicion of a formal institution and its mode of working' (Willis 1977: 73). Equally important in shaping their relations with Parnell School were memories of their own schooling. As Connell *et al.* (1982: 166) found: 'working-class people are often injured, insulted and disempowered by their experience with schools'. Such fractured school biographies informed some of the fathers' ambivalent and contradictory support for their sons' education, in 'pushing the kids to get on', while having severe doubts about the value of academic knowledge.

Hollands (1990: 10) suggests that 'the power position within the working-class household is crucial in forming masculine identities'. More specifically, he is critical of earlier academic representations of male youth cultures for failing to explore the significance of the domestic sphere in the transition of young men into adulthood. At Parnell School, male students tended to talk less than female students about their home lives. The domestic division of labour seemed to take more traditional gender forms among the working-class than the middle-class students, but there were significant intra-class variations, with the Academic Achievers and New Enterprisers more home-orientated than the Macho Lads. The latter spoke of spending much of their leisure time out of the house in peer-group activities and showed little awareness of, or concern for, domestic responsibilities. The Real Englishmen claimed that they shared housework jobs. However, . . . young men did not take responsibility for its organization and had little involvement in looking after younger siblings.

Nava (1984), writing of the different placement of girls and boys to their adulthood, captures the generational specificity of the problematic structure of young masculinities and their ambiguous relation to social power. She suggests that the implications of young men's identification of the temporary nature of their subordination as youth may inform their contentious transition into adulthood. She argues that the accentuated differentiation between manhood and boyhood is a recurring social phenomenon in many cultures. Nava (1984: 15) adds that: 'it echoes . . . the distinctive infantile rupture between boys and their mothers, the commonplace absence of fathers from the domestic domain, and may well signal a key aspect of masculinity as a problematic and ambivalent construct' (see also Chodorow 1978).

There was much evidence among the male students in this study to support these arguments. In interviews with the young men, they explained their contestation of the domestic domain and strained relations with parents, which were gender-specific in relation to mothers and fathers. However, no one pattern emerged, with some of the young men finding their fathers more problematic and others their mothers. Their explanations also tended to take class-specific cultural forms. I shall begin with the working-class students' views before examining those of the middle-class students.

Parminder: It's the same at home. My dad's really afraid of my mom. She rules our house.

Kevin: My mum used to always show me up when I was younger, especially when I was with my mates. My dad used to stick up for me, told her to leave me alone and stop nagging me. She used to get on my nerves. But now I think that she accepts me more as a man because I'm bigger than her.

M.M.: So what has changed?

Kevin: Well now she wouldn't make me do things around the house. My sister does it. And she gives me more freedom to come in late. She's just accepted that I'm grown up now. I'm more of a man.

Stephen: When my dad left I think my mom thought that she could boss me about more. So we were always fighting. She was trying to control me too much, treating me like a baby. So I left to live with my dad. But I got tired of looking after him, so I've come back home. Things are better. I think she missed me and she probably likes having a man around the place.

Connell *et al.* (1982: 98) have described the mutually supportive home–school relationship between a ruling-class boys' school and the production of masculinity, in terms of a sort of synchronization of family, school and student peer-group practices. In contrast, at Parnell School, which had a predominantly working-class student population, new middle-class mothers did not automatically affirm and legitimate the school's authority. They challenged dominant school gender practices, maintaining that recent socio-political changes were still absent from secondary schools' curriculum and pedagogy. They argued that schools were perpetuating the myth of a patriarchal British nuclear family. They contrasted local schools' unreconstructed gender regimes with their sons' participation in their own more democratic domestic arrangements. They were particularly critical of authoritarian male teachers, who acted as potentially damaging role models for their sons. However, they felt that new forms of young masculinities worked out within the home were strong enough to withstand the traditional patriarchal organization of schools.

Ms Bracey: Schools, I think particularly secondary schools, that are male-dominated anyway, are living in the dark ages. They transmit ideas of the nuclear family that have never actually existed. They have no idea of the broad changes taking place outside their gates.

Ms Fraser: They should be teaching them feminist ideas. Like how feminism has altered the rights of partners in marriage. Women are moving into whole areas of work that have been male preserves and that means that men will have to change. I think it's awful what Adam has to endure with some of those men, but he's surviving.

As pointed out above, the middle-class male students' name, the Real Englishmen, served as a triple signifier with reference to their parents' political position on issues of gender, sexuality and ethnicity. These were highly contentious issues that overtly underpinned the making of their masculine identity. . . . Here, the focus is on their critical and rather cynical views concerning their parents' involvement in the reformation of sex/gender relations.

M.M.:   Why do you call yourselves the Real Englishmen?. . .

Ben: Lots of meanings. We just call ourselves the REMs, rapid eye movement. Pretty cool, yeah? We're living in a fantasy world away from the heavy issues, away from having consciences about everything in the fucking world.

Thomas: I can't remember really. We were fooling about one night, talking about our parents and all the crap liberal stuff that they talk about all the time. And someone just said, they can believe what ever the fuck they want, we're real men.

Richard: It's all the crap about being new men and sensitive and caring. Okay sharing the housework and things like that are fair. But it's all the sexual stuff, all the stuff not making girls sex objects. It's ridiculous. What are you supposed to do? Become gay? And then there's a problem with that if you do.

M.M.:   And would you see yourselves as different to other guys?

Richard: Well that's the point. Our parents made a big principle of sending us to a comp [comprehensive school] and we've got to deal with all these ugly heavy macho types. They're really crude bastards with the girls and everything and we're forced to be with them. Our parents didn't have to go through this. They went to grammar school.

M.M.:   So the name [Real Englishmen] was directed towards other kids as well?

Thomas: Oh yeah. It was to the machos as well. They all go round thinking that they're real men, getting women and all that. It's all talk. They're just wankers. So, we started taking the piss out of them, saying we're the real men.

M.M.:   Would you say it to the macho crowd?

Ben: Do we fuck? They'd batter us. There's some really nasty kids here. And this is where we're supposed to become new men!

M.M.:   Why do so many of you say your parents are dishonest.

Adam: Because they are so screwed up about what they are supposed to believe or say, that they can't say or do what they really want to. Middle-class parents are definitely more dishonest than working-class parents, and the kids don't know what to believe now either.

Robert: We have been emasculated. Our feminist mothers have taken away our masculinity. When I was younger my mum would sit around with her friends and say bad things about men all the time. And then someone would say what about black men. And then they had to be anti-racist, so black men weren't included. And they'd hang around with these guys, who treated them like shit. The guys couldn't have respect for them, they had no respect for themselves. And at the same time I was an anti-racist by the age of four. It just does your head in.

Daniel: Like my dad he's anti-sexist and feminist and all this. You know he goes shopping and takes the baby out on his back, any fucking baby will do. And at the same time you hear him talking when they're drunk at parties to some of his mates about having sexual affairs with women at work.

Richard: And they say, you lucky bastard because they know he can use his power at work to get off with women.

Simon: It's true. And then they'll turn off Benny Hill and make a big deal about page three. They're just old hippy shits.

There is a danger of reading the young middle-class men's accounts presented here as confirming the idea that ' "progressive" child rearing produces ineffective, marginal, unproductive adults' (see Smart 1988: 233; Mac an Ghaill 1988a). Such a reading was prevalent among many of the male teaching staff at Parnell School, particularly the Professionals and the New Entrepreneurs. However, alternative readings are possible of a younger generational response to an inherited cultural legacy of gender reformation. These young people point out that such issues are far more complex than their parents 'rationally imagined'. Without wishing to generalize from this particular class fraction, they provide important criticisms – from the inside as it were – of a cultural world that progressive educators are attemping to construct. They illustrate the complexity of transforming male-dominated sex/gender systems in a wider social environment that appears to be threatened by such social change. At the same time, they point to the internal contradictions of the complex interrelationship of different forms of social divisions. More specifically, they graphically indicate the way in which the attempt to address one aspect of multi-oppressions has unintended consequences for other aspects (McCarthy 1990). . . .

WHITE ENGLISH ETHNICITY, RACISM AND SEXUALITY

. . . At Parnell School, a highly complex racialized map of student inter-ethnic relations was being constructed, from which individual racial behaviour could not simplistically be read or predicted. During the research, the white male students illustrated the generational and intra-class specificity of racist discourses, challenging conceptions of a unitary working-class inheritance.

Different sectors of male students, selectively drawing on racist constructs, offered diverse and inconsistent explanations (Gramsci 1971). Among the working-class students, the white Macho Lads tended to adopt a proletarian stance, showing more continuity with their parents than other peer groups, with particular references to their fathers' arguments that 'blacks had taken our jobs' and 'taken over our area'. The white Academic Achievers and New Enterprisers, adopting a more liberal perspective, challenged this interpretation, claiming that black people could not be held responsible for mass youth unemployment. A number of interrelated elements can be noted here. Black students' orientation to school and the accompanying masculine identities was of particular salience for the white English male students' responses to them. Also important, as John, a white Macho Lad indicates below, is that, unlike their fathers, these students have gone to the same schools as black students. This is not to imply that such contact necessarily leads to a decrease in white racist perceptions. However, the point to stress is that the institutional inter-ethnic relations played out among the young men has a historical contingency with its own set of social dynamics (Jones 1988).

John: I used to be a right little Nazi.

M. M.: How come?

John: Probably my dad the most. He just hates blacks and Asians. He always has. My mom is always telling him not to be so bad.

M. M.: So how did you change?

John: I don't know. You hang around with them all the time. Like the ones in our gang, they'd do anything for you. I mean we just stick together. We always get into trouble together. Like the teachers always pick on us, so we stick together more.

M. M.: What about the black and Asian kids you don't hang around with?

John: Well, they're all the same as the white pricks, sucking up to the teachers. You couldn't trust one of them. Our Asian mates say themselves that the Asians are the worst, the slyest. But they go their way and we go ours, en it?

Mark: Some of the bad nutters here are the Asian kids. But really they're just as bad as the white kids in the bottom classes and the blacks. They just stand around threatening people, especially the little kids. They have to be tough all the time causing trouble, you know. But probably a main difference is that there's always been more Asians in the top classes. So you hang around with them more. We've got more in common, to talk about and that. The bright ones have more in common. It's not really about colour. Like we're all friends in the top set and hang round together.

Much has been written by white middle-class social scientists about male working-class youth forms of racism. However, middle-class young men have remained invisible. At Parnell School, the latter group provided a most revealing perspective on institutional inter-ethnic relations. Like Aggleton's (1987) *Spatown Rebels*, the Real Englishmen differentiated themselves from other student sub-groups on the basis of what they were not. At the same time, the Real Englishmen were in the process of constructing a positive ethnic identity. At times, their talk of nationality appeared obsessive. They explained the significance of their name with reference to white English ethnicity. More specifically, they were developing a young masculine identity against their parents' denial and suppression of English nationality and nationalism. They pointed to the need for a local sense of ethnic belonging that notions of internationalism failed to provide.

> *Adam:*   It's like we can't be English, English men, be proud of being English. I argue about this with my dad all the time. He just dismisses it saying it's all constructed and we should all be internationalists.
>
> *M. M.:*   Why is it important to you?
>
> *Adam:*   Because it's unfair. All the Asian kids and the black kids, they can be Asian or black. They can be proud of their countries.
>
> *M. M.:*   Do you think of yourselves as racist?
>
> *Adam:*   No. No. That's what the teachers try and tell you, they try and force on you if you say anything, try to make you feel guilty like them. But we're not talking about colour. We're talking about culture.
>
> *Richard:*   English culture. And if you talk about the English flag or whatever, anything to do with Englishness, they call you a little Fascist.

In my discussions with the parents, they often appeared to either conflate 'race' and ethnicity or to subsume the latter under the former. They displayed a contradictory response to ethnic difference, acknowledging ethnic minorities but refusing to concede their own ethnic majority status. Some of the parents spoke of their sons going through a phase, as part of a broader adolescent search for an adult male identity.

> *Mr Stone:*   Adam reminds me of myself. Just trying out different things. He's very bright and the younger generation should challenge the older one. Adam and his friends at this age have very strong feelings. At times they try to shock us as parents. Quite healthy for young men. It's part of the process of their gaining their own independence.
>
> *Ms Taylor:*   You see them identifying with the Union Jack and talking a lot about English nationality. It's all tied up with the Falklands fiasco that ignited new forms of extreme nationalism in this country. Some of the parents wonder if we've produced little Fascists. But they'll come out of this surer of themselves. At other times, like when we visit Europe, Ben's very much at home as a European.

White students in all the peer groups were critical of their primary and secondary schools' anti-racist practices. Working-class male students appealed to varying forms of what Cohen (1988) refers to as the 'nationalism of the neighbourhood', with the white Macho Lads emphasizing 'defending our territory'. The Real Englishmen, in their defence of what they saw as a declining English masculine identity, nostalgically appealed to the demise of 'English culture'. White students often complained that the teachers responded to their complaints about what they perceived as black racism, with crude catechetical slogans such as 'whites are the problem' or 'all whites are racists'. The Real Englishmen were also critical of their teachers and parents for generalizing across generations about responsibility for the legacy of historical forms of white racism.

> *Thomas:*   It's the same as the anti-sexist stuff. Our parents are always on about anti-racism and all this. And it's the same here. I always remember when we first came here and we were doing paintings and we suddenly realized you got more marks if you did multicultural ones.
>
> *Ben:*   The teachers and our parents when they talk about racism always say white people mustn't be racist to blacks. That's fine. But they won't say anything when Asians and black kids are racist to each other.
>
> *Adam:*   And how come they keep on saying that racialism is really bad but we've had a load of hassle from black and Asian kids. The ones in the lowest sets the most, the nutters, and no-one says anything about that. Well why is that okay?
>
> *Adam:*   But no-one asks about us. The older generation don't ask what it's like for us who have to live with a lot of black kids who don't like us. No-one says to black kids, you have to like the whites. They'll tell them to fuck off.
>
> *M.M.:*   Do you think that it's the same thing for you and for black kids?
>
> *Richard:*   Well that's what the teachers come back with, only whites can be racist. It's crap, all the imperialist stuff. But the younger ones, we didn't cause that did we?

The Real Englishmen raise a critical issue that is often absent from anti-racist programmes – the question of how English ethnicity fits into the complex configuration of inter-ethnic interpersonal relations at school level. . . .

At Parnell School, inter-ethnic shifting tensions and alliances were present within a highly contingent and continually changing situation. For example, there was no fixed pattern of white or black inter-ethnic response in the different year groups. Rather, different student sub-groups assigned high status to particular individuals or peer groups in which different hierarchies of masculinity were competitively negotiated and acted out. During the research period, this was highlighted in relation to English-born Asian Macho Lads racially insulting year seven students who had recently arrived in the school from Pakistan.

Student inter-ethnic relations were a mixture of 'race'-specific elements and a broader range of social and psychic phenomena located within the school and linked to other social arenas. They involved specific emotional invest-ments and cultural attachments around popular cultural forms, such as music and sport. This is a long way from the fixed ethnic categories of much conven-tional equal opportunities discourse on the racialization of schools. Below, two black sixth-form students explain the inter-ethnic student complexity and ambiguity at Parnell School.

> *Carlton:* Like all the stuff we read on blacks in schools don't even begin to get at what is going on. They talk of blacks, Asians and whites and then ask them what they think of each other. It's crazy. Like here with black culture, the kids' language, cussing and that, their cool move-ment, the hairstyles, the music and the clothes, you see the Asians and the white kids really getting into it, deeply into it, right. But at the same time some of these Asians and whites will have racist views about blacks. And it's the same with the blacks about the others. It's really a mix up and difficult to work out, you know what I mean?
>
> *Rajinder:* You see there's a lot of sexuality in there. The African Carib-beans are seen as better at football and that's really important in this school for making a reputation. And it's the same with dancing, again the black kids are seen as the best. And the white kids and the Asians are jealous because they think that the girls will really prefer the black kids. So, the 'race' thing gets all mixed up with other things that are important to young kids. . . .

As Rajinder suggests, the complexity and contingency of the student inter-ethnic relations at Parnell School appeared most visible in relation to sexuality. This was made most explicit by the Macho Lads. The white Macho Lads adopted a range of contradictory racial and sexual discourses. At one level, there was a strong public masculine identification with the Asian and African Caribbean Macho Lads. The peer group constructed a hierarchy of sexual prowess in which they positioned themselves as the most successful with young women. This self-representation was worked out against white and black conformist students, who they publicly derided for their assumed sexual inexperience. At another level, individual white Macho Lads privately spoke to me – with more confidence outside of school – of the African Caribbean Macho Lads' perceived heterosexual success with young white women as ille-gitimate. At other times, white female students from Parnell School were labelled as 'slags' by white male students if they were seen with African Caribbeans or Asians from other schools, who were constructed as 'monstrous others' (Fanon 1967; Willis 1977).

> *Jim:* Some of the white girls at that school let themselves be treated like doormats by the black kids. And some of them even go off with the 'Pakis'.

Similar contradictions operated with the African Caribbean Macho Lads, who combined a public solidarity with the white Macho Lads and privately a general criticism of white men's sexuality. They positioned themselves as sexually superior both to white and Asian students and to conformist black students. More specifically, they spoke of themselves as the main producers of popular style, which they claimed made them attractive to young women. This could not be simply read in terms of youthful boasting. The African Caribbeans appropriated discursive themes from dominant ambivalent white student representations, in which black male students' behaviour was over-sexualized. As for some white male teachers, this consisted of contradictory cultural investments, of desire and jealousy in the highly exaggerated ascription to the black Macho Lads of stylish resistance, sporting skills and 'having a reputation with girls'.

In order to enhance and amplify their own masculinity, the black and white Macho Lads were overtly sexist to young women and female staff, and aggressive to male students who did not live up to their prescribed masculine norms. They adopted a number of collective social practices in their attempt to regulate and normalize sex/gender boundaries. The black Macho Lads were particularly vindictive to African Caribbean academic students, who overtly distanced themselves from their anti-school strategies. In response, the black Macho Lads labelled them 'botty men' (a homophobic comment). As Mercer and Julien (1988: 112) point out, a further contradiction in subordinated black masculinities occurs, 'when black men subjectively internalise and incorporate aspects of the dominant definitions of masculinity in order to contest the conditions of dependency and powerlessness which racism and racial oppression enforce'. Ironically, the black Macho Lads, in distancing themselves from the racist school structures, adopted survival strategies of hyper-masculine heterosexuality that threatened other African Caribbean students, adding further barriers to their gaining academic success. Consequently, this made it more difficult for academic black students to gain social mobility via a professional job and the accompanying middle-class mode of masculinity. At the same time, white teachers' typifications of 'black male aggression' were reinforced (Gillborn 1990).

REFERENCES

Aggleton, P. (1987) *Rebels Without a Cause? Middle Class Youth and the Transition from School to Work*. Lewes, Falmer Press.

Arnot, M. (1992) Feminism, education and the New Right. In M. Arnot and L. Barton (eds) *Voicing Concerns: Sociological Perspectives on Contemporary Education Reforms*. Oxford, Triangle Books.

Bourdieu, P. (1986) *Distinction: A Social Critique of Judgement and Taste*. London, Routledge and Kegan Paul.

Brindle, D. (1993) One in 6 live on safety net benefit, *Guardian*, 17 April, p. 8.

Brown, C. (1992) Same difference: The persistence of racial disadvantage in the

British employment market. In P. Braham, A. Rattansi and R. S. Kellington (eds) *Racism and Antiracism: Inequalities, Opportunities and Policies*. London, Sage/Open University.

Brown, P. (1989) Schooling for inequality? Ordinary kids in school and the labour market. In B. Cosin, M. Flude and M. Hales (eds) *School, Work and Equality*. London, Hodder and Stoughton.

Carby, H. V. (1980) *Multicultural Fictions*. Occasional Stencilled Paper. Race Series: SP No. 58. Birmingham, Centre for Contemporary Cultural Studies, University of Birmingham.

Carlen, P., Gleeson, D. and Wardhaugh, J. (1992) *Truancy: The Politics of Compulsory Schooling*. Milton Keynes, Open University Press.

Chodorow, N. (1978) *The Reproduction of Mothering: Psychoanalysis and the Sociology of Gender*. Berkeley, CA, University of California Press.

Cockburn, C.K. (1983) *Brothers: Male Dominance and Technological Change*. London, Pluto Press.

Cohen, P. (1988) The perversions of inheritance: Studies in the making of multi-racist Britain. In P. Cohen and H. Bains (eds) *Multi-racist Britain*. London, Macmillan.

Connell, R. W., Ashenden, D. J., Kessler, S. and Dowsett, G. W. (1982) *Making the Difference: Schools, Families and Social Division*. London, Allen and Unwin.

Corrigan, P. (1979) *Schooling the Smash Street Kids*. London, Macmillan.

Corrigan, P. and Frith, S. (1976) The politics of youth culture. In S. Hall and T. Jefferson (eds) *Resistance Through Rituals*. London, Hutchinson.

David, M. (1993) *Parents, Gender and Education Reform*. London, Polity Press.

Dean, M. (1993) Core problems on the periphery, *Guardian*, 9 January, p. 22.

Evening Mail (1993) Ethnic jobs famine shock, 9 March, p. 7.

Fanon, F. (1967) *Black Skins, White Masks*. London, Paladin.

Finn, D. (1987) *Training Without Jobs*. London, Macmillan.

Gillborn, D. (1990) *'Race', Ethnicity and Education: Teaching and Learning in Multi-ethnic Schools*. London, Unwin Hyman.

Gillborn, D. (1993) Racial violence and harassment. In D. Tattum (ed.) *Understanding and Managing Bullying*, London, Heinemann.

Gramsci, A. (1971) *Selections from the Prison Notebooks*. London, Lawrence and Wishart.

Griffin, C. (1993) *Representations of Youth: The Study of Youth and Adolescence in Britain and America*. Cambridge, Polity Press.

Harris (1992) *From Class Struggle to the Politics of Pleasure: The Effects of Gramscianism on Cultural Studies*. London, Routledge.

Harrison, K. (1993) Don't hold your breadth, *Sunday Mercury*, 2 May, p. 10.

Heward, C. (1991) Public school masculinities: an essay in gender and power. In G. Walford (ed.) *Private Schooling: Tradition, Change and Diversity*. London, Paul Chapman Publishing.

Hollands, R. G. (1990) *The Long Transition: Class, Culture and Youth Training*. London, Macmillan.

Hutton, W. (1993) A country of casuals, *Guardian*, 30 March, p. 20.

Jackson, P. W. (1968) *Life in Classrooms*. New York, Holt, Rinehart and Winson.

Jenkins, R. (1983) *Lads, Citizens and Ordinary Kids: Working-class Youth Life Styles in Belfast*. London, Routledge and Kegan Paul.

Johnson, R. (1991) My New Right education. In Cultural Studies (ed.) *Education Limited: Schooling, Training and the New Right Since 1979*. London, Unwin Hyman/University of Birmingham.

Jones, S. (1988) *Black Culture, White Youth: The Reggae Tradition from JA to UK*. London, Macmillan.

Lee, C. (1993) *Talking Tough: The Fight for Masculinity*. London, Arrow.

Loftman, P. and Nevin, B. (1992) Urban regeneration and social equity: A case study of Birmingham 1986–1992, *Research Papers 8*, Birmingham, University of Central England.

Mac an Ghaill, M. (1988a) Review of 'Rebels Without a Cause', *British Journal of Sociology of Education*, 9(2), 226–31.

Mac an Ghaill, M. (1988b) *Young, Gifted and Black: Student–Teacher Relations in the Schooling of Black Youth*. Milton Keynes, Open University Press.

Mac an Ghaill, M. (1992) Student perspectives on curriculum innovation and change in an English secondary school: An empirical study, *British Educational Research Journal*, 18(3), 221–34.

McCarthy, C. (1990) *Race and Curriculum*. Lewes, Falmer Press.

Mercer, K. and Julien, I. (1988) Race, sexual politics and black masculinity: A dossier. In R. Chapman and J. Rutherford (eds) *Male Order: Unwrapping Masculinities*. London, Lawrence and Wishart.

Morris, J. (1991) *Pride against Prejudice: Transforming Attitudes to Disability*. London, Women's Press.

Nava, M. (1984) Youth service provision, social order and the question of girls. In A. McRobbie and M. Nava (eds) *Gender and Generation*. London, Macmillan.

Smart, C. (1988) Review of 'Rebels Without A Cause', *British Journal of Sociology of Education*, 9(2), 231–3.

Stafford, A. (1981) Learning not to labour, *Capital and Labour*, 51, 55–77.

Tolson, A. (1977) *The Limits of Masculinity*. London, Tavistock.

Walby, S. (1990) *Theorizing Patriarchy*. London, Basil Blackwell.

Walkerdine, V. (1990) *Schoolgirl Fictions*. London, Verso.

Walkerdine, V. (1991) *Feminism and Youth Culture: From 'Jackie' to 'Just Seventeen'*. London, Macmillan.

Westwood, S. (1990) Racism, black masculinity and the politics of space. In J. Hearn and D. Morgan (eds) *Men, Masculinities and Social Theory*. London, Unwin Hyman.

Willis, P. (1977) *Learning to Labour: How Working Class Kids Get Working Class Jobs*. Aldershot, Saxon House.

Willis, P. (1985) *Youth Unemployment and the New Poverty: A Summary of Local Authority Review and Framework for Policy Department on Youth and Youth Unemployment*. Wolverhampton, Wolverhampton Local Authority.

Chapter 12

Integrating learning and assessment – the role of learning theories?

Patricia Murphy

INTRODUCTION

Assessment has come to the fore in education as a mechanism for changing and controlling the curriculum. The National Curriculum assessment programme (DES 1988a) was introduced in 1989, piloted in primary schools in 1990 and the first national testing of 7 year olds conducted in the summer of 1991. Continuous assessment of pupils' achievements by teachers was a critical feature of this programme. Thus, in the space of a few years views of assessment, its nature and purpose were revolutionized.

The model of assessment proposed in the national programme was a formative one. In this model assessment is viewed as a tool to facilitate curriculum planning and teaching. A central aim of the national programme was to integrate learning and assessment by ensuring that all pupils' achievements and needs were identified and taken into account in teachers' planning. This perception of the role of assessment reflects what has been labelled as a paradigm shift away from traditional psychometric approaches to the measurement of achievement towards an educational assessment culture (Gipps 1994).

A constructivist view of learning characterized much of educational research throughout the 1980s. It is also evident that the national assessment programme for England and Wales is at least loosely based on the constructivist rhetoric of the pupil as agent in the learning process. Yet educational assessment is in its infancy and the articulation of the learning-assessment relationship has barely been addressed in practice. To integrate assessment and learning it is essential that assessment practice corresponds to teaching practice. This correspondence has to be in terms both of how knowledge is considered to develop in pupils and how that knowledge is believed to be organized and accessed. Both aspects of learning need to be taken into account when selecting assessment methods and interpreting pupils' responses to them.

This paper examines some of the implications for assessment of current views about the nature of learning and of achievement. In so doing it highlights the intimate relationship that exists between assessment and learning;

a relationship that is much heralded in policy statements about assessment but which is little understood in practice. Evidence from assessment helps to illuminate some of the characteristic ways learners make sense of situations. These insights need to be available to teachers if they are to better understand how to promote individual learning. In providing evidence about pupils' perceptions and ways of knowing assessment information also provides insights to challenge current assessment practice. The paper explores some of these challenges and offers strategies for addressing them.

BACKGROUND

Assessment reform

Educational assessment developed primarily to play a 'constructive' role in the educational process. As part of that role it had to provide valid information about educational achievement. Valid achievement was described by Murphy and Torrance as not that which is 'easily measurable but that which is desirable in terms of the broad aims of those concerned with what children gain from the process of education' (Murphy and Torrance 1988: 100).

Educational assessment stands in opposition to traditional psychometric approaches to assessment. Psychometric tests developed for selection purposes assume that individuals possess a fixed, measurable level of intelligence that determines intellectual development and so can substitute for, and predict, achievement. The tests also assume that general intelligence is represented in the population normally. For these reasons items in psychometric tests must discriminate between the sample assessed in order to spread scores along a normal distribution. A failure to exhibit high discrimination would lead to an item being rejected.

Educational assessment is based on a quite different conception of intellectual development. It presumes that many achievements are attainable by all pupils but how and when they attain them will vary from individual to individual. Such assessment is criterion-referenced to provide the 'users' of the education system with a detailed breakdown of pupil competencies which more fairly represents all pupils' achievements. In criterion-referenced assessment pupils' achievements are judged against explicit criteria. For criterion-referenced tasks the important factor is not discrimination but how adequately the tasks represent the criterion being assessed. Criterion-referenced assessment can, unlike traditional psychometric testing, serve both summative and formative purposes. It provides information about the nature of pupils' progress and difficulties which can be used to facilitate curriculum planning and to improve pupils' learning.

A wide range of assessment initiatives were developed in the UK during the 1970s and 1980s based on an educational view of assessment (Murphy and Torrance 1988). One of the most influential of these, both in the UK and world-wide, was the Assessment of Performance Unit monitoring programme funded by the Department of Education and Science. A key contribution of the APU project was the development of an educational assessment framework for subjects with associated assessment tasks and methods that exemplified what to assess and how to assess it for the whole population. The APU project foreshadowed the national assessment programme. The results of the project form the main source of evidence drawn on by this paper.

The Assessment of Performance Unit (APU)

The Assessment of Performance Unit (APU) was established in response to a perceived need to evaluate the curriculum. The Unit conducted a series of annual surveys in England, Wales and Northern Ireland to monitor the performance of populations of 11-, 13- and 15-year-old pupils in maths, language, science and design and technology from 1978–89. A sample representative of the population was used at each age. Individual pupils and schools could not be reported on in contrast to the current national assessment programme. A principal part of the Unit's remit was to develop new assessment methods to enhance the validity of assessment by broadening the *range of achievements* assessed and ensuring that the methods used reflected 'fitness for purpose'. That is that they allowed valid assessment of the criterion under consideration. For example if the criterion to be assessed was the ability to use measuring instruments then a practical assessment involving pupils in deciding when and how to use a range of measuring instruments would be more 'fitting' than a paper and pencil test that required them to read pre-set values from drawings of scales. Prior to the APU monitoring assessments, in the UK were typically for the purpose of selection and restricted to sub-samples of the population. Examples of these include the 11 plus exam which was used to select pupils for grammar schools, and the GCE and CSE exams at 16 plus which certified pupils' achievements at the end of compulsory schooling.

Particular reference is made in the paper to the APU science results (DES 1988b, DES 1988c, DES 1989). The APU science results were based on a broad, criterion-referenced definition of scientific achievement using tasks involving an extensive range of methods of presentation, operation and response. The data collected ranged from generalized population scores on test categories to detailed diagnoses of pupils' errors on individual tasks. In addition, questionnaires were used to collect data on issues thought to influence science performance such as out-of-school activities and interests. A characteristic of the science results was the variability in individual performance both across the subject as a whole and within fairly narrow components of it such as interpreting and using different data forms. This variability in performance was due to sub-effects related to the tasks and/or their administration and pupils' interaction with them. Assessment attempts to establish what pupils know and understand *intellectually*, i.e. their *cognitive* achievements. However, how pupils feel about themselves, their beliefs about what they know and can do and their understanding of how others see them also affects how they respond to situations both in school and outside of it. These characteristics of individuals are referred to as *affective* characteristics. Whilst it is helpful to distinguish between affective and cognitive characteristics of pupils they are nevertheless interdependent attributes of human responses.

The collection of background information in the APU surveys concerning pupils' interests, attitudes and experience – both outside and inside school – made it clear that the sub-effects in performance results arose in part from the affective responses of pupils. The APU data provided influential evidence of the interdependence of pupils' affective and cognitive responses.

VIEWS OF LEARNING AND ASSESSMENT

The educational aims of the UK national assessment programme were to integrate assessment with learning to inform teachers' planning and evaluation and to serve pupils' needs to reflect on their learning. The Task Group's report on assessment (DES 1988a) said very little about the view of learning and teaching that the assessment practice was to be integrated with. In keeping with general educational assessment practice the Task Group recommended using a wide range of modes of presentation, operation and response in assessment tasks. This was 'in order to widen the range of pupils' abilities that they reflect and so to enhance educational validity' (VII, 49). It was also argued that observed responses must be shown to be 'typical'. This recommendation alluded directly to the way pupils' affective responses mediated their cognitive responses but only in general terms. Thus it was stated that 'pupils perform differently on different days and in different circumstances (IX, 60). What these different circumstances might be or their consequences was not, however, discussed.

Within the national curriculum guidance for England and Wales there is no explicit rationale for learning given. It is possible to discern elements of a constructivist approach, particularly in the science national curriculum guidance (DES/WO, 1988). Constructivism has been the dominant view of learning within the science and mathematics education communities over the last few decades. Constructivism is an umbrella term which covers a range of perspectives. Constructivism is essentially a theory of knowledge which involves conceptions of the learner, of knowledge and of the relationship between them. Key constructivist principles include the view that knowledge is not passively received by pupils but actively built up by them. It is also widely held by constructivists that personal knowledge rather than informing us about the world tells us about our experiences and how they are best organized. Taken to its extreme this means that people can never compare their understanding of their experiences with an independent objective reality. There is no reality outside an individual's mental construction so there can be no certainty about our mental representations of the world. This view of knowledge has important implications for teaching and assessment. A teacher rather than knowing what goes on in pupils' heads can only construct models of what she *believes* to be going on. Such models are based on teachers' experiences of and beliefs about pupils. In other words teachers *give* meaning to pupils' actions and responses. The same is true of pupils who similarly give meaning to teachers' actions and words and to the activities they face in learning and assessment situations. The meanings pupils give will depend to an extent on their understanding of school and assessment practices.

Critiques of constructivism have increased in recent years reflecting a growth in alternative perspectives on knowledge and learning. Sociocultural approaches to the process of coming to know are increasingly being applied by educationalists trying to understand how to promote effective teaching and learning. In constructivist theories thought is analysed in terms of conceptual processes located in the mind. Sociocultural theorists argue that such a view of thinking is inadequate because it fails to take account of the socially constituted nature of individuals. Individuals cannot be considered in isolation from their social and historical context. Furthermore in this perspective individuals' engagement with activities has to take account of the context of the activity, i.e. the larger social, historical, political, and economic influences that shape the activity. Wertsch (1991: 6) describes a sociocultural approach in the following way.

> The basic goal of a sociocultural approach to mind is to create an account of human mental processes that recognises the essential relationship between these processes and their cultural, historical and institutional settings.

Sociocultural theorists consider concepts to be socially determined and socially acquired. The acquisition of understanding from a sociocultural perspective is achieved by individuals coming to share in meaning through negotiation and discussion. Bruner considers the shared use of language as the key which unlocks others' minds to us. For Bruner culture is the 'implicit, semi-connected knowledge of the world from which through negotiation people arrive at satisfactory ways of acting in given contexts (Bruner 1986: 65).

Both constructivist and sociocultural theories are currently exerting considerable influence in educational practice. For some researchers both perspectives provide useful and necessary ways of looking at learning (Cobb 1994). What is common to both perspectives is the view that the process of coming to know is constructive. This means that pupils are *actively* engaged in thinking and that the ideas and experiences they bring to situations matter. Whereas constructivists argue that pupils' interpretations and meanings are private and individual and to an extent unknowable, socioculturists consider that meaning derived in interactions is not exclusively a product of the person acting. Rather we should think of the individual acting in a setting engaged in *relational* activities with others (Lave 1988). Therefore when pupils engage in school activities they do so with some shared understanding. However, how this shared understanding is used will reflect the pupils' understanding of and involvement in the activity. Consequently sociocultural theorists stress the *homogeneity* of people in established communities and look for patterns in social and cultural practices. In stressing the significance of the activity and the context in which individual learning takes place socioculturists argue that there is an intimate connection between knowing and doing. Human knowledge from this perspective is therefore *situated* in that the activity, 'is not separable or ancillary to learning and cognition. Nor is it neutral. Rather it is an integral part of what is learned. Situations might be said to co-produce knowledge through activity' (Brown, Collins and Duguid 1989: 32).

Taking some of the key ideas from these theories it is possible to identify some fundamental problems for assessment as it is typically practised. For instance if pupils are 'active meaning-makers who continually give contextually based meaning to . . . others' words and actions' (Cobb 1988: 88) then more attention has to be paid to pupils' interpretations of assessment tasks. Assessors cannot assume that tasks can be given ready-made to pupils, rather it is they who determine what is problematic. One of the main findings of the APU science project was that pupils failed to gain marks not because of a lack of knowledge but because they tended to answer alternative tasks to those intended by the assessors. The message here for assessment is that assessors, be they teachers or others, interpret pupils' meanings on their behalf.

However, if we think of pupils as situated in a number of communities we can consider the potential social and cultural bases of their experiences and try and identify patterns in the meanings they derive. Lerman (1993) provides a useful description of this that can be applied to assessment

> since any pupil will be situated in many contexts, depending on his or her socio-cultural experience, the teacher [or the assessor] may not always be able to predict what will be called up by the activities [tasks] s/he offers. Consequently teachers [and assessors] need to find ways of enabling pupils to find, create and negotiate their meanings.
>
> (Lerman 1993: 8)

Such views of learning suggest that assessors need to establish pupils' various understandings in order to first consider the tasks they may perceive given apparently the same set of circumstances; and second to interpret their responses to the tasks perceived. Valid interpretations will depend on assessors understanding the significant characteristics of pupils and of assessment tasks and how these interrelate.

Another key idea that follows from sociocultural theories of learning is that knowledge is not separable from the activity in which it is acquired. Hence if assessment practice is to be fair to pupils attention needs to be paid to the context and activities used to develop the achievements being assessed as these will define in part the achievements of the pupils. Such a view of knowledge as situated also raises a question mark about the validity of generalizing about achievement, or indeed lack of achievement, from a small number of assessment instances. Good assessment practice has to recognize the tentative nature of judgements made about pupils' achievements.

PUPIL–TASK INTERACTIONS

Evidence from the research of the Assessment of Performance Unit (DES 1988d, DES 1989, Kimbell *et al.* 1991) and more recently research into public exams in England (Stobart *et al.* 1992) and Australia (ESSA 1993) has shown that sub-effects related to tasks and/or their administration affect pupils' performance. The features of tasks identified as significant influences include the following:

- The *content*, i.e. what the task is about.
- The *context*, i.e. the setting of the task.
- *Task cues*, i.e. the help given to pupils to make sense of the task.
- The *mode of presentation*, i.e. practical etc.
- The *mode of operation*, i.e. interaction with objects, with other pupils, in writing, etc.
- *Mode of response*, i.e. the form of written response, direct observation, dialogue, etc.
- The *openness* of the task, i.e. the extent to which the solution is determined by the pupil.

These features of tasks have been found to influence pupils in a range of ways. The effects depend in part on pupils' *cognitive characteristics*, i.e.

- Pupils' actual and potential achievements.
- Pupils' experience of how and when to apply those achievements.
- Pupils' learnt approaches to tasks and preferred styles of expression.

These in turn are mediated by pupils' affective characteristics, i.e.

- Pupils' expectations of themselves, of others, and of the subject being assessed.
- Pupils' experience both inside and outside of school.
- Pupils' self-image and values.
- Pupils' confidence in themselves and their abilities.

The evidence from the research suggests that a complex web of potential interactions will be brought to bear when groups of pupils attempt assessments. Whilst the complexity may at first glance seem daunting it never-theless only mirrors what is understood to happen when teachers attempt to teach groups of pupils. In this latter regard, though, we expect teachers to have access to a repertoire of pedagogic strategies for handling diversity both within a pupil and between pupils. Unfortunately the same cannot be said of assessment practice.

A problem for assessment practice is the assumption of rigour and precision we attach to interpretations of outcomes. This assumption relates to psycho-metric views about the nature of human ability and is no longer tenable when we adopt either constructivist or sociocultural perspectives of learning. There are messages emerging from research which provide insights into the processes underlying task performance which indicate ways that the validity of assessment can be enhanced. These messages reinforce the sociocultural view of how individuals act in settings as they reveal uniformities in responses by groups of pupils to particular assessment situations. These characteristic responses provide useful illumination of the way pupils make sense which enable interpretations and generalizations about outcomes to be made with more authority. Some of these characteristic responses are described next.

PUPIL–TASK EFFECTS

Content effects

Validity in assessment is concerned with the justice of the interpretations placed on performance outcomes. Performance outcomes are typically inter-preted in terms of whether the knowledge, skills and understanding taught in schools have been achieved. There is, however, an increasing amount of evidence that differences between sub-groups arise because of their different experiences both in school and outside of it.

The content of an assessment task is essentially what the task is about. For example whether one has to write a description of a holiday experience or a shopping trip. The content in the former is the holiday, in the latter the shopping trip. The task, to describe the episode in writing, is the same. Clearly how well a pupil is able to respond to such a task depends in part on his or her experience of the content. Yet typically assessors fail to consider differences in pupils' out of school experiences when setting assessment tasks. For example in one of the standard assessment tasks used in the national assessment of 14 year olds in England (SEAC 1994) the task was to distin-guish between living and non-living things. One item to be classified was a crab (see Figure 12.1). However, from the simple drawing and photograph provided it was difficult to distinguish whether it was a crab shell or a living or dead crab. Children's experiences on beaches etc. are far more likely to have been of crab shells looking very similar to the drawing, hence a response that it was dead may well have been tempered by this. Such a response would

Name of pupil _____

item seen at the seaside		is it living?	
		yes	**no**
plant			
seagulls			
deck chair			
horse			
crab			
boat			

Figure 12.1 Standard assessment task – science

be quite correct in relation to the pupils' understanding of the content. The assessor, without access to the pupils' thinking, however, would interpret such a response as a lack of knowledge. For other children the problem may not be to do with the nature of their experience on beaches but rather an absence of any experience of them. Assessment tasks commonly assume shared experiences that are often not justified. To enhance the validity of assessments it is necessary to reconsider the content in terms of the task being addressed. The question then is, is it a viable content for the task?

In the APU science results boys' and girls' performance on tests of reading and using measuring instruments at ages 11 and 13 was the same overall. There were, however, specific instruments where girls as a group were doing significantly less well than boys, e.g. stop clocks and hand lenses at age 11, microscopes, ammeters, voltmeters and forcemeters in addition at ages 13 and 15. Pupils were asked in a questionnaire what experience they had out of school of the various measuring instruments used. It was found that boys' performance is better than girls' on those instruments that they report to have more experience of outside of school.

In learning situations it is assumed that pupils' total experience matters and the same should obtain in assessment situations but rarely does. The different experiences of pupils does not just effect the skills they develop but also their understanding of the circumstances and problems where their skills can be used. In the APU example pupils' different experiences outside school affected their actual achievements. At other times content effects in tasks also reveal differences in experience but the effect is not directly related to differences in achievement of what is being assessed. A lack of experience will also affect how pupils interact with tasks, i.e. their *affective responses*.

When the results for the whole of the APU science question banks were reviewed it was apparent that irrespective of what criterion was being assessed questions which involved content concerned with human functions and concerns like health, reproduction, nutrition and domestic situations were generally answered by more girls than boys across the three ages surveyed. The girls also tended to achieve higher scores on these questions. In questions with a 'masculine' content such as cars, submarines and industrial sites the converse was true. For example, girls and boys at ages 11 and 13 were equally well able to use and interpret pie charts. Yet if the chart was about the different composition of textiles used to make school blouses some boys did not respond whereas girls tackled the question with confidence and so, as a whole, obtained a higher score. If on the other hand the data represented was about spare parts for a workshop the reverse happened. For some pupils the questions were not about skills of using data representations but about their experience of the content. These performance effects arise from the combination of avoidance by some pupils and the heightened confidence of others. The questions therefore measure those pupils' affective rather than cognitive responses and would need to be avoided for summative assessment

School car parking

The school has four car parking areas. The entrance to all of them is through the school gate.

There are different ways of getting to each car parking area.

All the roads are one-way.

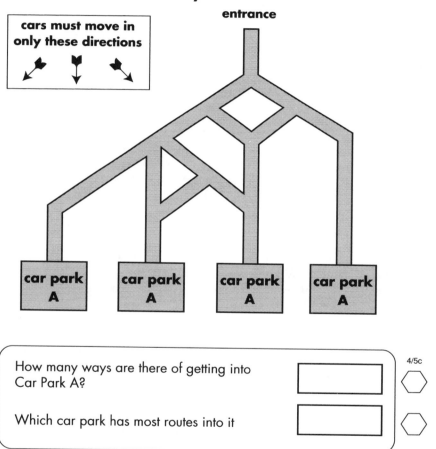

Figure 12.2 Pilot assessment task – maths

Source: Leeds University, 1993

purposes of reporting and evaluating. On the other hand they provide the teacher with valuable insights to aid curriculum planning.

Without information about the different ways pupils perceive themselves and their capabilities teachers cannot develop effective strategies to help them. It was suggested that the questions to an extent measured pupils' *alienation* from areas of experience rather than their *achievements*. Alienation may ultimately lead to underachievement, however, as pupils fail to engage with certain learning opportunities. It is therefore essential that content effects are considered when selecting tasks for both summative and formative assessments. Content effects should also be brought to pupils' attention by providing them with different situations to react to and discuss together. In this way assessment does become integral to learning both in monitoring it, and importantly, in promoting it.

Context effects

Evidence that pupils' responses to assessments were context dependent came largely from the research of the APU science project (see Murphy 1990 for example). This finding corresponds to the view that knowledge is situated (Brown, Collins and Duguid 1989). To enable pupils to access their knowledge appropriately and to use it, they have to see the link between what they know and its relevance to the task in hand. Consequently context is not separable from the task but rather an integral part of it. Assessors differ in the value they accord context and in the role that they see it plays in pupils' construction of meaning. These differences between assessors reveal differences in how learning and learners are viewed. An example of a pilot standard assessment task for pupils at age 11 reveals one particular interpretation of context (see Figure 12.2).

The setting or context is ostensibly a real life situation within children's everyday experience, that of a school car park. Contexts such as these are used to give validity and purpose to assessment tasks. It therefore reinforces the view that pupils are active meaning-makers, or does it? Note that in this car park you can get in but there is no way you can get out. So what does the thoughtful pupil do? Reject the task because it is a foolish one or treat it as the ritual it is and provide the right answer, irrespective? The answer of course depends on the pupils' understanding of the wider context, i.e. the school culture and assessment practices. Pupils will vary in the extent to which they understand, and can distinguish between, the practices of school and the practices outside of it. Pupils will also vary in the extent to which they are prepared to behave in testwise ways. Those children who do may not necessarily be those who have made the most progress. Consequently a misuse of context can serve as a further source of assessment invalidity.

Context we have argued is an integral part of a task so any attempt by assessors to manipulate it will alter the task perceived by some pupils. The

APU science tests, for example, included two versions of the same practical investigation: to find out how fast a solid dissolves in different conditions. In one version the solid was labelled a chemical and the apparatus was typically scientific. In the other version the solid was labelled a sweet and the equipment was everyday, e.g. measuring jugs, teaspoons, plastic cups, etc. More pupils attempted the everyday version and were able to make sense of the task. However, the everyday context cued an everyday solution so that pupils did not attempt to control variables or to take measurements. The context altered the task perceived by the pupils hence their solution was quite different and in scientific terms less adequate (DES 1989).

Context is a problematic concept from an assessment perspective. It is not an abstract variable that can be manipulated by assessors. Rather it is something that is, or is not, perceived by pupils as they attempt to create meaning in the tasks they are faced with.

The APU science surveys have shown that more girls than boys tend to value the circumstances that activities are presented in and consider they give meaning to the task. Contextual features are therefore as significant for girls in the process of meaning-making as the information provided to convey the assessor's task. This was not found to be the case for boys generally. In the example in Figure 12.3 taken from the APU (Murphy 1991a) the circumstances of survival on a mountainside were provided for motivational reasons only, they did not alter the assessment task which is in the small box. The task could have been set in a number of contexts, not least the laboratory.

However, many girls gave value to these contextual issues which meant that their task involved looking at thermal conductivity in dry and wet conditions and windy and calm conditions. Assessors observed girls dipping the test materials in water, blowing air through them, cutting out prototype jackets and lagging cans with the wet test materials and then determining the rate of cooling. These behaviours were observed for some girls in all sorts

SURVIVAL

Imagine you are stranded on a mountain side in cold, dry, windy weather. You can choose a jacket made from one of the fabrics in front of you.

This is what you have to find out:

Which fabric would keep you warmer?

Figure 12.3 Survival

of schools but not for boys. The girls were concerned to find out if the effectiveness of the materials was affected by their porosity and waterproofness and whether indeed the materials were suitable for making the proposed jacket, hence the prototype jackets. This was not the task the assessor intended and indeed was a much more difficult one. Depending on the subject being assessed, girls' attention to circumstantial variables will either be valued or rejected as evidence of poor understanding.

What is of concern for assessors is to consider how contextual variables are being treated. Are they central to the task? Are they given credit in marking schemes? For example, in contrast to research findings in science and design and technology where questions set in social contexts were found to advantage girls, research into maths assessment has reported that girls are disadvantaged by contextualized tasks (Foxman *et al.* 1991). Cooper (1992) examined this finding looking at tasks used in the UK national curriculum assessment in maths. The lift task is an example of what is referred to as a contextualized mathematics task (see Figure 12.4).

It is, however, crucial in such a task *not* to pay attention to the context as though it relates to real life in any significant way. The single point to

---

This is the sign in a lift at an office block:

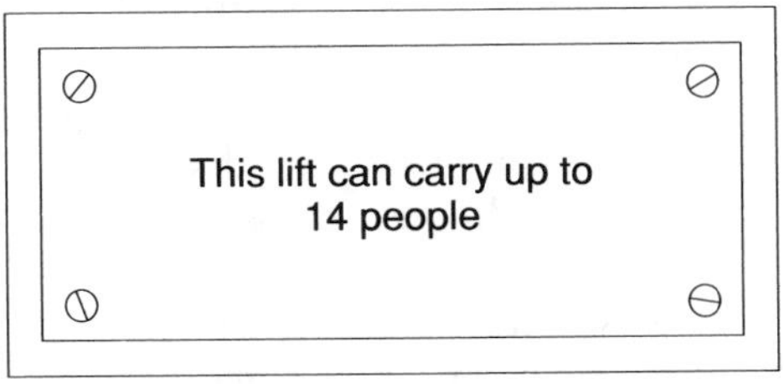

This lift can carry up to
14 people

In the morning rush, 269 people want to go up in this lift.

How many times must it go up?

Reproduced from: National Pilot Mathematics Test Summer 1992, Band 1–4, Paper 1.
Calculator allowed

Figure 12.4 The lift problem
Source: Cooper 1992: 234

remember is that cutting people up is not acceptable. However, it is not acceptable to imagine quite reasonably that not all people are of homogeneous size or indeed temperament. Some people late for a meeting, for example, might decide to use the stairs and reject the lift. Yet others who may not be obese may be carrying files, or a bulky computer or even pushing a buggy on the way to the office crèche, hence taking up different amounts of space. The finding that girls are disadvantaged by such questions has been substantiated by similar research reported by Boaler (1994). She comments that the inclusion of such contextual variables provides a source of assessment invalidity if no account is to be taken of them in the assessor's view of the task and the marking of responses. If we want pupils to transfer their understanding and make use of it in novel situations then context matters in planning learning activities. To assess whether pupils can transfer their understanding, and have indeed acquired useful 'robust' knowledge similarly requires assessors to set questions where the context is *integral* to the task. If this is the case then mark schemes will reflect this and give value to contextual variables appropriately.

One strategy that can be used if assessment practice is to take account of pupils' ways of knowing and making sense is to set very open-ended activities that enable pupils to reveal their initial reactions to activities. An example used by the APU asked pupils aged 8–15 to design a new vehicle. The pupils' designs covered a wide range but there were striking differences between those of boys and girls. Many boys chose army-type vehicles, secret agent transport or sports cars. The girls mainly chose family cars for travelling, agricultural machines or children's play vehicles. The detail the pupils focused on was also different. Where boys and girls chose the same type of vehicle they still differed in their main design function. For example, the group of girls designing a pram dealt with improving its efficiency and safety. The boys' pram design was computerized to allow infants to be transported without an accompanying adult! Similar differences in the solutions pupils judge to be appropriate and relevant have been noted across problem-solving situations in science, maths and design technology.

Assessment activities such as these serve several functions. They allow teachers to appreciate pupils' different world-views and how these might influence the way they perceive tasks. The activities also act as useful self-assessment strategies. Pupils can be encouraged to take note of the similarities and differences in their responses and to consider the value in all of them. Such activities serve to open pupils' minds to the way previous experiences influence future ones. If differences in pupils' awareness of the relevance and use of their knowledge are not made explicit it can limit their future learning opportunities. Teacher assessors have been found to be quite reluctant to disrupt learning situations with tasks they consider to be for the purpose of assessment only. Yet such activities do serve as a tool for learning as well as assessment and are very similar to the types of tasks often used to elicit pupils'

Lindsey 6

When he swallows it, it goes into the tummy. It moves about in your tummy. It goes down in your legs or arm.

Figure 12.5 The response of a 6 year old to the question 'What happens to food and drink inside you?'
Source: Wadsworth 1992

conceptual ideas in science. Figure 12.5 is an example of an annotated diagram used to establish a child's view about nutrition. This is typically regarded as a learning activity and, of course, it is if used in discussion with pupils. However, it is also a valuable assessment task.

Questions to consider when interpreting assessment outcomes to help check on potential context effects include 1) is the performance a reflection of a lack of achievement of what was assessed? 2) could the performance reflect differences in experience, i.e. the opportunities to learn available to pupils; 3) could the performance reflect an affective response related to pupils' differing expectations of themselves? of assessment? of the subject?

Cues and their effects

Cues differ from context and content in that rather than being essential attributes of the task they serve as supports to tasks. They do this either by providing pupils with clues to the meaning of the task or by facilitating their decision making about what is an appropriate solution to it. Assessment cues can take many forms, they can include written instructions, drawings and physical resources for example.

The role of cues takes on greater significance in sociocultural approaches to assessment. In sociocultural approaches assessors need to consider not only pupils' actual achievements but also their potential achievements. Vygotsky (1978) coined the term the 'zone of proximal development'. This describes the gap between a pupil's unaided achievement and his or her potential achievement with the help of a more informed adult. To plan pupils' learning teachers need therefore to assess the 'dynamic development state' of pupils. This perspective on assessment has important implications for practice as it suggests that radically different assessment circumstances can and should be adopted. Assessment practice hitherto has made little effort to help pupils' reveal their achievements. Traditionally pupils have had to accept extremely alienating test situations. It is therefore quite difficult for assessors first to accept that helping pupils is a valid thing to do, and then to develop ways of supporting pupils. Some examples of cues are described next.

An APU science investigation was set to pupils aged 13 to find out the effect of the height of water in a container on the rate of flow from it. When this task was trialed most 13 year olds could not understand what to investigate. They could not identify or relate the variables of height and rate of flow. A further version of the task was then prepared which included a cartoon of a tea urn gradually emptying and a queue of irritated people simultaneously growing (see Figure 12.6).

Provided with this analogous experience pupils had no problem understanding the task and over 90 per cent happily engaged with it. Many pupils have demonstrated difficulty understanding various 'rate' measures. Yet most 11 year olds in primary schools can handle rates of cooling or dissolving

Figure 12.6

because they can draw on common everyday experiences of these effects. These findings emphasize the need for assessors to look at the ways in which pupils know things which may bear little relationship to traditional subject-definitions of knowledge. Analogies have a crucial role to play in assessment in helping pupils access their knowledge and apply it. Which analogies function in this way will vary between pupils.

Teacher assessors have to provide opportunities that enable all pupils to reveal what they know and can do. Yet there is very little advice available to teachers about how to achieve this. Investigative situations can be ideal for providing differentiated outcomes as pupils define their own hypotheses and plan their own investigations. However, the activities have to be resourced in such a way to enable differences between pupils' achievements to be revealed. One example of this (Murphy 1991b) involved 9-year-old pupils exploring patterns in buildings as part of their ongoing work in class. A couple of groups were exploring why walls were constructed in particular ways.

To do this the pupils constructed walls, initially using real bricks then using cardboard boxes in various ways. The pupils tested out different patterns. These varied in the degree of overlap between the 'bricks'. The decisions about what to make the walls from and which patterns to test were made by the pupils. No instructions were provided. The measurement strategy for one group was to roll balls at the different patterns of bricks. They wanted to test to see which was 'stronger'. The group controlled variables such as the distance of the balls from the test walls but were content to alter the force by judging it for themselves, i.e. rolling the ball at different speeds and using different sized balls. For another group who started with this strategy this was not satisfactory. They evolved a strategy using different numbers of bricks with a plank acting as a slope to alter the height at which the ball was delivered. Hence in their words 'altering the force fairly'. In their table of results they recorded the number of bricks needed in the slope before the test wall collapsed.

The teacher had arranged to have various resources available, including the bricks and specific measuring instruments in anticipation of a range of possible needs and understandings. Her resourcing of the task allowed the group to move from a qualitative to a quantitative strategy using non-standard measures. The resources acted as cues to support the pupils. They did not provide 'answers' which many assessors assume. The APU results showed that it made no difference if pupils were provided with a range of measuring instruments if they did not see the point of taking measurements or, indeed, see how to take them (DES 1989).

Other children involved in the same activity spent time constructing different patterns of bricks but were not ready to formulate a testable question linking variables. To plan for pupil progress effectively teachers need to know the detail of pupils' present achievements and their most likely next steps forward.

Tasks such as the one described differentiate between children by outcome. The tasks are sufficiently open and accessible to a range of pupils to enable them to develop solutions which reflect their various and different achievements. There are problems for teachers in using the strategy of differentiation by outcome as it is difficult to plan for assessments in advance. Furthermore only certain aspects of the curriculum will be covered by some pupils. Consequently teachers' records become a critical element of the assessment cycle. An alternative approach is to use differentiated tasks. These are assessment tasks that are structured to produce a specific response indicative of a particular achievement. Using differentiated tasks has, however, been found to have even more drawbacks as teachers have to make judgements about pupils' expected level of achievement in order to assign them to appropriate tasks. Recent research shows that teachers prejudge pupils' achievements often on the basis of beliefs about their *affective* rather than *cognitive* traits (Stobart *et al.* 1992).

SUMMARY AND IMPLICATIONS

The evidence presented in this paper makes one conclusion self-evident: that there is much that we do not yet understand about how to carry out assessment that is consistent with current constructivist and sociocultural perspectives of learning. The need to integrate assessment with learning actually derives from a view of the pupil as agent in the learning process. It is the information from formative assessment that provides the teachers with the insights they need to begin to understand pupils' various ways of knowing. Without these insights teachers cannot effectively plan individual's learning. The ideal scenario would therefore be to develop teaching and assessment strategies side by side. As knowledge about one grows this would then feed the development of the other and so on.

Another clear message that emerges is that assessment strategies are needed that not only elicit pupils' ideas but also their interests, concerns and views of what is relevant. There are useful methods already developed that will help with this. For example the SPACE project (1990–91) in the UK made much use of drawings either with or without annotation (an idea we have discussed in this paper). Creative writing is another useful tool, for example asking pupils to write three things you know about; imagine you are, etc. Pupil diaries are also valuable assessment devices both for informing teachers and supporting pupils' self-assessment. The use of concept maps is also growing in teachers' practice but their use both as assesment devices and as learning tools for pupils themselves is less evident.

Other strategies we have referred to involve pupils in talking together about their learning, yet others rely on simple observations of pupils as they carry out activities. In selecting activities it is important to establish the circumstances that reveal pupils' 'best' performance, and to consider the content, context and mode of response and operation used in tasks and their effect on pupils' performance.

In any assessment that claims to reflect a view of the pupil as the active meaning-maker it is essential to be tentative about the generalizations made about pupils' achievements. It is therefore necessary to present generalizations in the context of the assessment tasks used and the demands within those tasks. A central idea in educational assessment is that individual rates of progress differ. It is also the case that progress is not linear. This means that assessors need to be alert to apparent disruptions in progression which signal that development of a different kind might be happening. For example the more pupils become aware of issues related to scale and measurement error the more tentative and often the less adequate their measurement strategies become. The APU carried out a longitudinal study in science (SEAC 1991) which found that pupils' 'newly acquired knowledge appeared to disrupt existing knowledge'. In other words as pupils progress their overt performance can show an apparent decline as they struggle to integrate new understanding with old.

The development of assessment consistent with current thinking about learning has barely begun and it is without doubt a demanding enterprise. It is, however, extremely beneficial. The evidence emerging from the UK about the influence of good teacher assessment is that it dramatically alters both teachers' and learners' understandings rendering both more effective. Whilst our understanding about the process of coming to know remains uncertain and changing we must expect assessment practice to evolve. What is essential is to ensure that there is greater consistency between assessment and teaching practice. One important step towards this is to make explicit what view of knowledge and learning underpins them.

REFERENCES

Boaler, J. (1994) 'When do girls prefer football to fashion?', *British Educational Research Journal* **20**(5): 551–64.

Brown, J. S., Collins, A. and Duguid, P. (1989) 'Situated cognition and the culture of learning', *Educational Researcher* **18**(1): 32–41.

Bruner, J. (1986) *Actual Minds, Possible Worlds*, Cambridge, Mass.: Harvard University Press.

Cobb, P. (1988) 'The tension between theories of learning and construction in mathematics education', *Educational Psychologist* **23**(2): 87, 103.

Cobb, P. (1994) 'Where is the mind? Constructivist and sociocultural perspectives on mathematical development', *Educational Researcher* **22**(7): 13–20.

Cooper, B. (1992) 'Testing National Curriculum mathematics; some critical comments on the treatment of "real" contexts for mathematics', *The Curriculum Journal* **3**(3): 231–43.

Department of Education and Science (1988a) *Task Group on Assessment and Testing – A Report*, London: DES.

Department of Education and Science (1988b) *Science at Age 15 – A Review of APU Survey Findings*, London: HMSO.

Department of Education and Science (1988c) *Science at Age 11 – A Review of APU Survey Findings*, London: HMSO.

Department of Education and Science (1988d) *Language Performance in Schools, A Review of APU Language Monitoring 1973–1983*, London: HMSO.

Department of Education and Science (1989) *Science at Age 13 – A Review of APU Survey Findings*, London: HMSO.

Department of Education and Science/Welsh Office (1988) *Science for Ages 5–16*, London: DES.

Essa (1993) *Gender Equality in Senior Secondary School Assessment (ESSA) Project*, Department of Employment, Education and Training, Australia.

Foxman, D., Hutchinson, D. and Bloomfield, B. (1991) *The APU Experience 1977–1990*, London: SEAC.

Gipps, C. (1994) *Beyond Testing: Towards a Theory of Educational Assessment*, London: Falmer Press.

Kimbell, R., Stables, K., Wheeler, T., Wosniak, A. Kelly, V. (1991) *The Assessment of Performance in Design and Technology*, York: Schools Examination and Assessment Council.

Lave, J. (1988) *Cognition in Practice: Mind, Mathematics and Culture in Everyday Life*, Cambridge: Cambridge University Press.

Leeds University (1993) *Maths Book B Main Booklet Levels 3–5*, Commissioned by the Schools Examination and Assessment Council.

Lerman, S. (1993) 'The problem of intersubjectivity in mathematics learning: extension or rejection of the constructivist paradigm', London South Bank University Technical Report SBU-CISM-93-3.

Murphy, P. (1990) 'National Curriculum assessment: has anything been learned from the experience of the APU?', *The Curriculum Journal* 1(2): 185–97.

Murphy, P. (1991a) 'Gender differences in pupils' reactions to practical work', in B. Woolnough, (ed.) *Practical Science*, Milton Keynes: Open University Press.

Murphy, P. (1991b) *Assessment and the Primary Curriculum*, Milton Keynes: Open University.

Murphy, R. and Torrance, H. (1988) *The Changing Face of Educational Assessment*, Milton Keynes: Open University Press.

Schools Examination and Assessment Council (1994) *Assessment Matters No 5, Profiles and Progression in Science Exploration*, London: HMSO.

Schools Examination and Assessment Council (1994) Key Stage 3 Science 1/2 Seaside Task/Activity A/Pupil Sheet, London: SCAA.

Space *Research Reports 1990–1991*, Liverpool: Liverpool University Press.

Stobart, G., White J., Elwood, Hayden M. and Mason, K. (1992) *Differential Performance in Examinations at 16 plus: English and Mathematics*, UCLEAC/NFER.

Vygotsky, L. S. (1978) *Mind in Society: the Development of Higher Psychological Processes*, Cambridge, Mass.: Harvard University Press.

Wadsworth, P. (1992) 'Children's ideas in science', in P. Murphy, *Science in the Primary Curriculum*, Milton Keynes: Open University Press.

Wertsch, J. V. (1991) *Voices of the Mind: A Sociocultural Approach to Mediated Action*, Cambridge, Mass.: Harvard University Press.

Chapter 13

Learning from Jason[1]

Mary Jane Drummond

In February 1985, a class of seven and eight year olds, in their first year of junior schooling, were taken into the school hall where they sat at individual tables to take a mathematics test (NFER 1984). The headteacher read out the questions, and the pupils wrote the answers in their individual test booklets. One of those children was Jason, aged seven years, six months, who had spent two and a half years in the infant department. There are 36 questions in the test and Jason answered them all. One of the answers was correct, giving Jason a raw score of two, and a standardised score of 81, a 'moderately low score', according to the teacher's guide to the test.

A teacher in Jason's school showed me his test booklet, and I date my interest in assessment from that day. In the analysis of Jason's test performance that follows, we will be able to see some obvious inadequacies in the

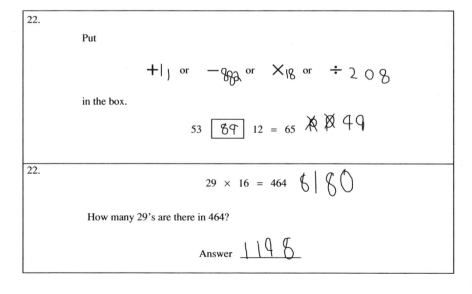

Figure 13.1

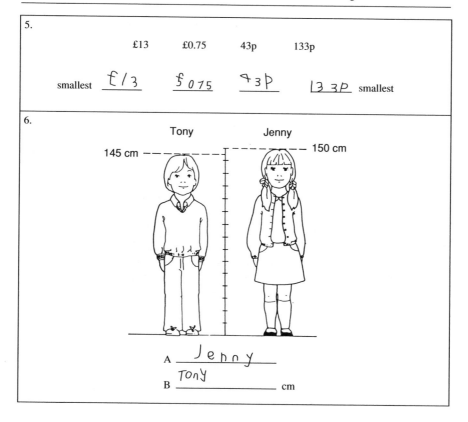

Figure 13.2

use of formal group testing as a way of assessing individual children's learning. But I will also argue that the test booklet does tell us some very important things about Jason's learning, and about other children's learning, that must be taken into account in a full understanding of the process of assessment.

Jason's test responses show us, first of all, what he has failed to learn about mathematics. More significantly, they give us an indication of the gap that yawns between what his teachers have taught him and what he has learned. In other words, the test booklet forces us to look critically at the relationship between teaching and learning. Furthermore, Jason's case-study invites us to explore the interplay of the rights and responsibilities of teachers and learners.

But first, what has Jason learned during his eight terms in school? He has learned how to take a test. His answers are written neatly, with the sharpest of pencils. When he reverses a digit and sees his mistake, he crosses it out tidily. He places his answers on the line or in the box as instructed, though he often adds some more digits in other empty spaces, as if he interpreted a space as an invitation to write (see questions 19 and 22 in Figure 13.1.) He has learned to copy numbers and letters neatly and accurately, even though this is not what is being asked of him (see questions 5 and 6 shown in Figure 13.2.)

In question 5, Jason has been asked to rank the four amounts of money in order, from the smallest to the largest. In question 6, he has been asked (A) who is the shorter of the two children, and (B) by how many centimetres. Jason has simply copied the print from the question into the space provided for the answer.

He has learned to listen and to follow instructions carefully, as closely as he can, though his short-term memory does sometimes let him down. In question 1, for example, he was asked to write in numerals the number two hundred and fifty two. As we can see (Figure 13.3), he has almost done so, writing two, a hundred, and forty two. He has learned to stay with a task and complete it. Other pupils in the same class answered only a few of the test questions, leaving many items blank. Others scrawled and smudged their responses: Jason's presentation is exemplary.

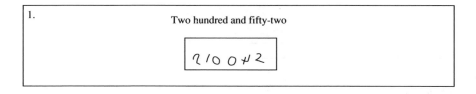

1.

Two hundred and fifty-two

Figure 13.3

He has not, it is apparent, learned very much mathematics. He has learned that in a mathematics test, he is required to write numbers, which he does, with one exception (see question 14 below, in Figure 13.11).

There is no evidence that he has learned the value of the numbers that he writes. So, for example, in question 4, he is asked to calculate the weight of the parcel on the left, if the scales balance (Figure 13.4). He has responded by writing four digits in the space provided. I am certain that he has not calculated or miscalculated – that 9182g + 50g = 500g, or that 500g – 50g = 9182g. He has simply written some numbers in the appropriate place for an answer. He uses the same approach in question 7, question 9, and question 17 (Figure 13.5).

Question 7 is a simple division problem; question 9 asks how much more money is needed to buy the football, and in question 17, the pupils are

4.

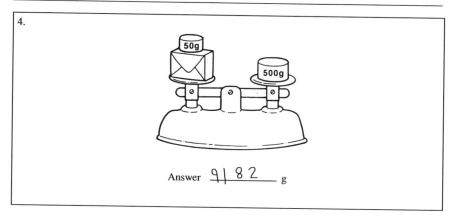

Answer ___9 8 2___ g

Figure 13.4

7.

484 grams shared by 4

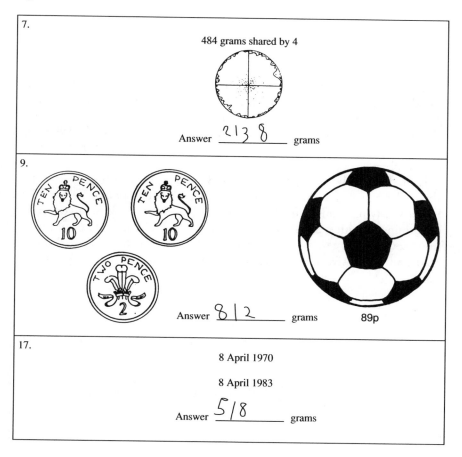

Answer ___2 3 8___ grams

9.

Answer ___8 2___ grams   89p

17.

8 April 1970

8 April 1983

Answer ___5 8___ grams

Figure 13.5

21.

Put a ring round each even number.

82   8   11   56   44   8 8

23.

What number is 3 less than 200?

Answer   8 | 8

Figure 13.6

required to give the age of a child born on 8 April 1970 on 8 April 1983. Another child in Jason's class interpreted this question as a subtraction problem; working from left to right he seems to have thought to himself: '8 from 8 is 0, put down 0; April from April is 0, put down 0; 1983 from 1970' – here the answer trails away as the pupil realises he cannot complete the problem.

Jason frequently writes the number 8, and it is tempting to speculate about the reason for this (see questions 21, 23 for example, Figure 13.6). Is it a satisfying number for him to write? Has he recently mastered the art of forming it with a single stroke? Or is it possible that he has noticed the front cover of his test booklet (Figure 13.7), and that he has seized on this bold and impressive numeral as a possible clue to what is being asked of him?

National Foundaion for Educational Research in England and Wales

MATHEMATICS 8

Figure 13.7

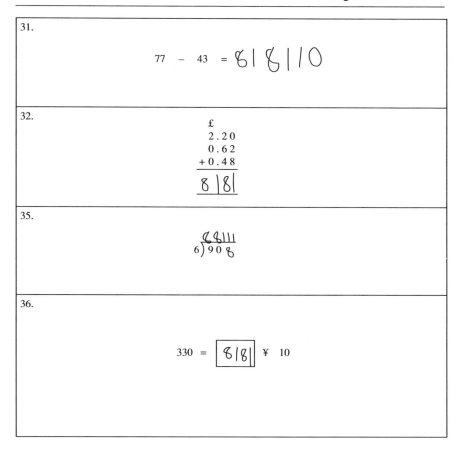

Figure 13.8

He uses the same configurations of numbers several times, suggesting that he is not attending to or discriminating between the meaning of the context of the different questions (Figure 13.8).

But sometimes, it seems, there may be other reasons for responses; in question 28, for example (Figure 13.9). It seems just possible here that Jason has read off the length of the rod on the ruler as nearly 8, and interpreted the half-centimetre mark on the rule as figure 1. How long is the rod? It could be that Jason said to himself '8, and back a bit to this 1 here. 8. Eight. One.' Why has he written it twice? To fill the allocated space?

More convincing evidence that Jason attends to at least part of the content of the question, as he sees it (not as the tester sees it), can be seen in question 34, Figure 13.10. What time does this clock show? Did Jason reflect 'There is the 9, there is the 1; perhaps an 8 for good measure. . .'? It is at least a possibility.

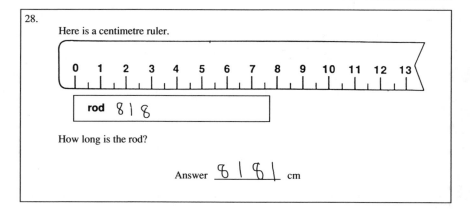

Figure 13.9

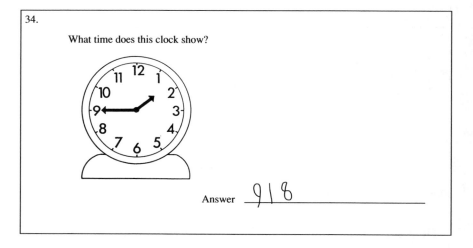

Figure 13.10

Question 14 is more complex (see Figure 13.11). The instruction is 'Draw this shape as it will look when it has been rotated one right-angle clockwise.' Here I believe Jason makes his first real error, and writes a letter (lower case 'e') before remembering that this is a mathematics test. It is not, at any rate, an impossible or improbable interpretation of what he has done – he will, after all, have seen the capital and lower case letters presented together in just this way in many contexts during his school career. The rest of his response is more interesting; I suggest that Jason heard the word 'clock' as a significant instruction and remembering previous class-work on clocks, responded with a sketch of a clock, on which he then duly marked the 8.

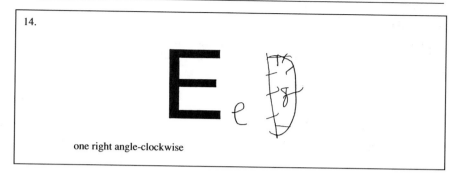

14.

one right angle-clockwise

Figure 13.11

In these last two examples, I believe there is substantial evidence that, against what must be, for him, inconceivable odds, Jason is struggling to make sense of the test, and what his headteacher is asking him to do. His mathematical understanding is still too scanty to be of much use to him, but he uses all the other clues he can get. This is, I think, a remarkable achievement, and a tribute to Jason's persistence, to his longing for meaning.

It is also possible to recognise Jason's self-restraint, and his passivity, during what was presumably an uncomfortable experience. He cannot have been feeling relaxed, confident, sure of himself and certain of success, during the test. Or does he not even know what it is he does not know? It seems more reasonable to assume that he does know, very well, that mathematics, and the mathematical tasks his teacher gives him, make no kind of sense at all. And yet he is prepared to sit and comply, as far as he is able, with a string of incomprehensible instructions.

Jason may not have learned much mathematics but he has learned some important rules about being a pupil. Mary Willes' study (1983) of children entering a reception class charts the inexorable process by which children – spontaneous, curious, independent – are transformed into pupils, who know the rules. Her pessimistic summary of the task of the pupil seems to describe Jason's condition all too accurately:

> . . . finding out what the teacher wants, and doing it, constitutes the primary duty of a pupil.
>
> (Willes 1983, p. 138)

NOTE

1   This chapter was first published as part of chapter 1 in M. J. Drummond, *Assessing Children's Learning*, London: David Fulton, pp. 1–8.

REFERENCES

NFER (1984) *Mathematics 8*, Windsor: NFER-Nelson.
Willes, M. (1983) *Children into Pupils*, London: Routledge & Kegan Paul.

Chapter 14

Educational assessment: the myth of measurement[1]

Patricia Broadfoot

Every day in the Autumn, in the pre-dawn chill, 45-year-old Lee Soon-rye walked to a Buddhist temple to pray for her daughter. Clad in traditional white Buddhist prayer robes, she appealed to the higher powers to give her daughter the strength to endure the baptism-by-fire of every young Korean – passing the country's intensively competitive university entrance exam.

On the day of the exam, the entire nation is mobilised. This year, office workers in Seoul started an hour later so that the 250,000 students sitting the exam would not be caught in the traffic jams. Police are on hand to ferry students to exam sites. After 12 years of middle and high school, success or failure comes down to a fateful eight hours on one December day.

Out of the 662,000 students who took the exam in December 1990, about 146,346 will enter the 115 universities and colleges in March. The failures will either cut their losses and look for a job or return to their books, join the ranks of the army of 'repeaters' who comprise almost 50% of examinees each year.

(Michael Brean 'A Plea to Buddha for Exam Success',
Times Educational Supplement 15.1.91)

The international scourge of the so-called 'diploma disease' which has transformed so many educational systems into the kind of dispiriting and wasteful rat race described here for Korea is a malady, which has now infected every country of the world. Thanks to the 'diploma disease', education systems in virtually every country are to a greater or lesser extent being deflected from their true purpose of promoting education and developing the skills, abilities and potential of young people to meet the needs of their society into a punishing and more or less irrelevant paper chase in which few will win and many must fail. Education is frequently reduced to drilling in test-preparation and students' horizons defined by what is in the test.

Where the stakes are so high and the currency in such short supply, this reaction is not surprising. Nor is it surprising that in the examinations of many countries cheating and corruption is endemic. Despite tight security, in some countries exam papers are 'sold' in advance, candidates are impersonated, and invigilators bribed to turn a blind eye to portable telephones and pocket computers. Indeed, so normal have such practices become that in Bangladesh, for example, students too poor to give bribes recently mounted a major street demonstration for 'the right to cheat'! (Heynemann 1993).

These examples provide some insights into both the pervasiveness and the significance of the phenomenon of the 'myth of measurement'. They illustrate the way in which educational assessment has become established as the key mechanism for the allocation of individual life-chances in modern societies, the central role it plays in determining opportunities for future social status and earning potential. In every country of the world, the assumption is now made that the techniques available to measure students' educational achievements are sufficiently accurate that their use provides the most rational, the most just and hence the most acceptable method of allocating educational opportunity. Typically countries are willing to pay the price of having curriculum goals distorted by the need for syllabuses to concentrate on what is readily measurable on a mass scale. The spectre of the 'Rhonin' in Japan who spend hours at their juku (cram) schools as they seek to absorb the endless quantity of facts they will be judged on in the all-important, multiple-choice examinations which will determine their future, may be among the more extreme manifestations of what Collins (1979) has called, 'The Credential Society'; but it is not atypical. Private tuition to help children to do well in highly competitive selective examinations is currently a growth industry in many developing countries.

In his classic book *The Diploma Disease* (Dore 1976) Ronald Dore describes how education systems around the world have become distorted by irresistible parental pressure for their children to have access to high status academic examination courses despite the overwhelming need to develop vocational and entrepreneurial skills.

The price of our commitment to 'the credential society' is very high. As I have suggested, it leads to distortion of the curriculum. Even more serious, however, is the effect of existing educational practices on the process of learning itself. 'Trading for grades' is an expression that encompasses the kind of instrumental attitude and the sort of extrinsic motivation to which the race for credentials leads. As educationists we are likely to deplore the corresponding loss of spontaneous enthusiasm for learning which this produces at all levels of the education system. But the problem is much more serious than this. The price of our continued commitment to the myth of measurement I shall argue is the fundamental incapacity of education systems to meet the economic and social needs of contemporary society.

THE MYTH OF MEASUREMENT: A NECESSARY EVIL?

But if the price of our commitment to 'the credential society' is very high, it may be, nevertheless, that that price is justified, even inevitable, if the only alternatives are nepotism or the arbitrary operation of a lottery. If educational measurement does indeed provide for fair and rational selection, we must perhaps put up with its undesirable side-effects. But if it does not, if it could be shown that those measurement techniques, the existence of which constitute the central justification for a system of educational and social selection, are actually deeply flawed, there would appear to be little justification for the continuation of practices which have such undesirable 'wash-back' effects on the process of education. The perceived legitimacy of educational assessment is based on the assumption that the measures generated are true. If it can be shown that such measures are in practice open to a good deal of error, that the widespread trust in them is largely due to their mythological power rather than to their practical efficiency, this might provoke the beginnings of a challenge to the hegemony of the assessment edifice that I have described, and with it, a fundamental re-consideration of what our educational priorities ought to be.

The force of this argument is further strengthened if we bear in mind that the pathology of the 'diploma disease' is not confined to individuals. In a world increasingly concerned with international competition and apparently falling standards the currency of certificates and diplomas is increasingly being used as a performance indicator of the quality of the education process itself. Governments, teachers, parents and students around the world have learned to define *educational quality* in terms of the results of public examinations and of other kinds of standardized tests. But is this the best way of judging the quality of institutional functioning and systemic output? What price do we pay for accepting at face value both the accuracy, and the relevance, of such measurement data as an index of quality?

It is the purpose of this paper to explore some answers to these questions, to consider the justification for those practices of educational measurement that, internationally, we currently rely on. My argument will have three strands. First, I shall attempt to establish, historically and sociologically, where 'the myth of measurement' came from. Second, I shall attempt to establish why it is indeed a *myth*. Third, and most important, I shall explore the significance of the continued persistence of this myth. In particular I shall argue that it is in large part the perpetuation of the myth of measurement that stands between contemporary educational practice and the achievement of genuine quality.

But first, some definitions are necessary. The *Oxford English Dictionary* defines 'myth' as 'a purely fictitious narrative, usually involving supernatural persons, actions or events, and embodying some popular idea concerning natural or historical phenomena . . . a tale devoid of truth'. In his *Myths and*

Dreams, published in 1885, Clodd defines 'myth' as a fictitious or imaginary person or object; 'myth was the product of man's *emotion* and *imagination* acted upon by his surroundings' (cited in the *Shorter Oxford English Dictionary*). In his exploration of 'mythologies', the French semiologist Roland Barthes (1973) draws attention to the role of myth in making arbitrary things seem normal. 'Myth', he writes, 'has the task of giving an historical intention a natural justification . . . and making contingency appear eternal' (p. 142) . . . of making things 'falsely obvious' (p. 11) . . . 'myth is depoliticised speech', it is a language that makes things innocent; that 'purifies them . . . and gives them a clarity which is not that of an explanation but that of a statement of fact' (p. 143). Interestingly, 'myth' is also another word for measurement!

In this paper I argue that a great deal of the edifice of educational measurement is actually rooted in myth, and that, like other myths, it is not a neutral or accidental creation, but rather a manifestation of the culture and power structures of our contemporary society. Partly this is because a technology that evolved to meet a particular purpose has, like so many other technologies, a large number of unanticipated effects. As Winner has suggested, this is because once the process of technological development has been set in motion, it proceeds largely by its own momentum irrespective of the intentions of its originators (Winner 1986: 40, cited in Madaus 1993). But perhaps the main reason for the incredible pervasiveness of this particular myth is because the particular technology of educational assessment is inevitably political, its potency rooted in its capacity to project meaning and define values. The way we measure reflects broader social and political characteristics in our society. The notion of 'measurement' is particularly powerful rooted as it is in post-Enlightenment scientific culture and in a world-view in which phenomena are assumed to be amenable to objective, systematic description. Measurement is inevitably a political, as well as a technical device, in that it gives power to those who control it. Even the language that we use, words like measurement and scores, marks and grades, is an extension of the way in which we conceive assessment and serves further to define what is actually thinkable in this respect.

RELATIVES AND ABSOLUTES

While measurement may appear to be based on absolutes, it is in fact a more or less arbitrary, socially-relative creation. Ball (1992) gives an illustration of this in his description of the measurement of time. He describes how primitive peoples hit upon the idea of 'days' by observing the motion of the sun and the alternation of dark and light. They invented the idea of 'months' by observing the behaviour of the moon. They discovered the year by noting the coming of the snows or harvest or springtime. While their precise boundaries are not immediately obvious, days, months and years are (to a very large extent) natural divisions of time. Yet the Maya and Aztec calendars have 18 months. The Chinese and Sumerian calendars intercalated seven extra months into the normal 12 month cycle: they independently discovered that you need seven extra months over a period of 19 years to keep things straight.

By contrast, weeks are arbitrary. Our seven-day week was probably also a market-week in origin, but it was given a powerful religious authority by what for many is another myth – the creation story in the first two chapters of the Book of Genesis. The measurement of length offers some 'natural' units, such as the hand-span and the foot, but there are also many arbitrary units, e.g. the chain and furlong: a chain, like a piece of string, has no natural or predetermined length.

Thus both the concept of educational measurement and the particular forms of its expression in any particular culture are rooted in, and reflect, a particular world-view. The ability to define the nature of the technology of educational measurement or to control its use is associated with the power that comes from the ability to set norms and standards. A second source of power comes from the ability to control how the results of educational measurement are used.

And yet the core of this technology is in fact very simple. As far as educational assessment is concerned, there are only three generic ways to judge performance: first, as Madaus (1993) describes it, you can ask the person to supply a product. This may be an oral or written answer to a series of questions. It may be in the form of an essay or short answer questions. Another variation is the oral disputation, such as the Ph.D. viva. Alternatively the product may be a portfolio of work, a research paper, a chair or a piece of cut glass. Second, you can require the person to perform an act to be evaluated against certain criteria. They may be required to conduct a chemistry experiment, to read aloud from a book, or to repair a carburettor. Third, you can have an examinee select an answer to a question or a problem from among several options. This is the multiple choice or true/false item. 'Strip away the linguistic veneer,' writes Madaus,

> and whatever noun you choose, assessment, exhibitions, examinations, portfolios, or just plain test, they all rest on the same basic technology, that is, you elicit a small sample of behaviour from a larger domain of interest, such as algebra or aptitude, to make inferences about the person's probable performance relative to the domain, and on the basis of the inference, you classify, describe, or make decisions about individuals or institutions.
>
> (Madaus 1992: 5)

Indeed, it is worth noting at this point that it is this necessity to make inferences from the small particular to the larger whole that lies at the heart of the 'myth' of measurement.

Over the last century or so this sort of generic activity has developed into a highly specialized professional domain complete with its own jargon and arcane knowledge. The now highly esoteric nature of professional testing is of considerable significance in helping to uphold the myth of measurement since it acts as a distancing mechanism. Typically the public accepts the scientific credentials of the enterprise in the same kind of way as it would accept the scientific credentials of the technology that produces the video recorder or satellite television.

Historically, however, educational assessment has been neither technical nor a specialized preserve, functioning for the most part as non-competitive tests of knowledge or skill set, administered and marked by adults who know the candidates. Such tests have probably existed since the earliest 'rites of passage' were instituted in tribal societies.

THE EVOLUTION OF ASSESSMENT

The pedigree of our modern examination systems can be traced rather more precisely, however, back to a mixture of ideas that originated in ancient Egypt, Babylon, and China in the third century BC, in Rome in the first century BC and AD, and in western Europe in the early medieval period (Frey 1992). Although modified by time and place, these attempts at assessment were rooted in the need to attest to personal competence and by association, to the quality of work or goods or skills of a given crafts-man. Gradually, however, a second purpose for such assessment, that of selection, became established. This reflected the need to regulate entry to the ranks of particular professions or trades in terms of *numbers* as well as of competency.

Perhaps the most famous historical example of the use of examinations which embodied both these purposes, was the exam system of ancient China which originated some time in the twelfth century BC when the Chinese Chou dynasty implemented school admissions exams. The system endured for over three thousand years. The mythological status of such measurement is attested to by the fact that ancient Chinese mythology includes a god of examinations 'Chung-Kuei'. Having been denied first place in the examinations which he had won, Chung committed suicide and so became 'Kuei' (Christie 1968). This was followed by the implementation of written exams for the selection of Civil Servants under the Han dynasty in the third century BC. In the tenth century AD during the Sung dynasty, began the creation of specialized subject exams, in letters, law, rituals and sophics. In the eleventh century, copyists were employed to ensure candidate anonymity and papers were marked twice. The need to avoid any possibility of cheating or favouritism which these provisions implied, is a reflection of what were to become the three central purposes of all examinations. First, to assess as reli-ably as possible, the level of a given competence; second, to rank candidates

Stage 1: District Level
- Content: Confucian classics (recall and interpretation)
- Duration: 1 day and 1 night
- Marking: content; penmanship
- Failure rate: 93–97%

Stage 2: Province Level
- Content: prose and verse composition
(Two copyists to disguise handwriting)
- Failure rate: 90–99%

Stage 3: National Level
- Content: write about what you know
- Duration: 3 days and 3 nights

Figure 14.1 The selection of Chinese civil servants AD 1300

in terms of their relative achievement and so provide for fair competition; third, for control – to convince the unsuccessful of the fairness of the procedures used so that they will accept the result.

Figure 14.1 describes what candidates had to undergo in order to be selected for the Chinese Civil Service in AD 1300. It will be clear from these procedures that all three of the above purposes were involved for the stakes were very high indeed. There is an appealing historical irony in the fact that at the very time when the use of this kind of examination began to grow rapidly in the west as a way of providing for fairer competition, the Chinese Manchu dynasty decided in 1905 to abandon its ancient testing system because it had become so corrupt, in particular by the practice of paying someone else to take the test for you.

However, most of the early examples of formal assessment were much less elitist than this. They consisted, typically, of groups of skilled workers who set up the standards which had to be demonstrated by those aspiring to join a particular craft guild. Indeed, it was these traditional mechanisms for ensuring standards of competence in different trade skills which were used as the model for the subsequent use of examinations in Europe. For example, the assessment stages which marked the progression from apprentice to journeyman and from journeyman to Master craftsman in the medieval craft guilds, were incorporated into both the names of different levels of qualification – such as 'Baccalauréat' and 'Brevet' – and the more academic examinations which came later in the Napoleonic Université of nineteenth-century France. The Baccalauréat examination which marked the first grade of the Université was a direct legacy from the orders of chivalry of feudal times when it marked the stage of apprenticeship before the attainment of a particular social role.

By the same token, the influence of feudal bases for social organization on the emerging structure of the exam-based qualifications which were to replace them in the new social order of an industrial society were also manifest in France in the widespread use of the term 'brevet' for lower and more applied qualifications. For example, from 1816 prospective French elementary school teachers had to sit for the 'brevet' examination. Traditionally a royally given right to an apprenticeship, the word 'brevet' incorporates the same feudal idea of apprenticeship and the attestation of a particular level of competence as is clear from the following description.

> an act taken before a lawyer by which an apprentice and a master make a mutual commitment, the apprentice to learn an art or a craft, the master to teach him during a certain period of time and under certain agreed conditions.
>
> (Cherval 1874: 5)

The ideology implicit in the frequent choice of feudal terms, to label the different rungs of the new hierarchy of educational qualifications, points to the way in which, during the nineteenth century in particular, social status became increasingly bound up with educational qualifications and thus to the newly powerful role of the technology of measurement.

By contrast, in the centuries before the industrial revolution, schooling was largely irrelevant to the process of occupational selection. Educational assessment, if it existed at all, was largely a formality which confirmed the differential socialization experiences which served as a preparation for the very different future lifestyles of the various social strata. Writing in 1778, for example, Vicessimus Knox provides graphic testimony to the mainly social nature of education at this time and to the consequent insignificance of formal assessment in his disgusted description of finals examinations at Oxford University.

> As neither the officer nor any one else usually enters for the room for it is considered very ungenteel, the examiners (usually three M.A.s of the candidate's own choice) and the candidates, often converse on the last drinking bout, on horses, or read the newspaper or a novel, or divert themselves as well as they can in any manner, until the clock strikes 11 when all parties descend and the testimonium 'is signed by the Masters'.
>
> (Lawson and Silver 1973)

In effect four years residence was the only qualification for a degree – not an inappropriate training for an elite for which the qualifications were

---

EXAMINATION FOR A DIRECTORSHIP
(From "The City Man's Vade Mecum.")

Promoter. Are you a gentleman of blameless reputation?

Candidate. Certainly, and I share that reputation with a dozen generations of ancestors.

Promoter. And no doubt you are the soul of honour?

Candidate. That is my belief – a belief shared by all my friends and acquaintances.

Promoter. And I think, before taking up finance, you have devoted a long life to the service of your country?

Candidate. That is so. My career has been rewarded by all kinds of honours.

Promoter. And there is no particular reason why you should dabble in Stock Exchange matters?

Candidate. None that I know of – save, perhaps, to serve a friend.

Promoter. Now, be very careful. Do you know anything whatever about the business it is proposed you should superintend?

Candidate. Nothing whatever. I know nothing absolutely about the business.

Promoter. Then I have much pleasure in informing you that you have been unanimously elected a member of the Board of Management!

[Scene closes in until the Public demands further information.

Figure 14.2 *Punch, or the London Charivari,* 16 January 1901

almost entirely social. A similar picture is depicted in Figure 14.2 which is a reproduction from *Punch* at the turn of the last century.

Radical economic changes in the mode of production during the nineteenth century made the expansion of educational provision a necessity. The post-Enlightenment belief in the power of science and rational forms of organization also created pressure on all the various rungs of the educational ladder so that assessment procedures had to *seem* more fair and become more rigorous. As Morley wrote in his life of Gladstone: gradually, 'the lazy doctrine that men are much of a muchness gave way to a higher respect for merit and for more effectual standards of competence' (quoted in the Beloe Report).

But if the principal reason for introducing the use of formal examinations was to replace the existing system of patronage and nepotism, it was also bound up with the search for a new form of power. Thus, for example, in 1748, Frederick the Great of Prussia set up a two-stage examination, partly written and partly oral to control recruitment to the German Civil Service. Although this was ostensibly an initiative aimed at curbing nepotism and corruption, arguably the real motive behind it was that of power – Frederick's desire to reduce the power of the landed aristocracy and to centralize power in his own person (Eckstein and Noah 1993). Napoleon's somewhat later, but rather similar initiatives in France concerning the Baccalauréat examination had very similar motives.

ASSESSMENT AND MASS EDUCATIONAL PROVISION

Nevertheless the idea of the meritocracy continues to have a broad appeal. Like the colossus of Rhodes, the twin principles of equity and freedom dominate the western liberal tradition. They provide the justification for a society in which the allocation of privilege and opportunity is based on performance rather than privilege, competitition rather than corruption (contumacy). The nineteenth century was a time of belief in self-improvement through effort in education and success in examinations.

> Herbert Spencer's thesis that social growth was promoted by survival of the fittest . . . meant that examination systems came to be regarded as a natural complement to belief in individual autonomy and responsibility and to faith in the justice of a society that rewarded each individual according to his or her measured deserts.
>
> (Eckstein and Noah 1993: 17)

To many, the mass provision of formal education which is typically a feature of industrialization and the contemporaneous growth of formal procedures of educational assessment are almost synonymous. Like the honeysuckle and the bindweed, they may now be so inseparable that any attempt to release the education system from the constrictions of assessment procedures could result in the collapse of the system itself. Whether the concern was to make the maximum use of the 'pool of ability' using what Beatrice and Sydney Webb termed a 'capacity catching machine', or whether it was to produce social justice or social order, the effects were the same: a search for an accurate and thus fair way of identifying talent and of discriminating among pupils on apparently educational, rather than, as had previously been the case, social grounds. From these ideological and pragmatic pressures the concept of the meritocracy was born and with it, the important social role of educational measurement.

But if the rapid development of educational measurement in the nineteenth century was in keeping with the spirit of the age and with the twin principles of uniformity and standardization that began to be applied to industrial production at that time, it was essentially a development in the *way* in which privilege was justified rather than a genuinely open competition. When examinations were introduced in Japan, for example, following the Meiji restoration of 1868, Samurai families who had long monopolized the elite social positions conserved much of their traditional status via the new exam-based system. Although only 6 per cent of the population, they constituted overwhelmingly the candidates for Tokyo University, and the other elite government training institutions (Amano 1990). Bourdieu describes a similar pattern for France in his book *Homo Academicus* in which the elite are able to manipulate the ostensibly meritocratic examination system to reproduce their own power positions in society.

At least part of the reason why privilege was able to reproduce itself, despite the introduction of examinations based on merit, may be, as Foden (1989) has pointed out, that the principles regarding methods, motivation and the effect of examinations which were embodied in the examination movement of the nineteenth century, were almost wholly untested and unvalidated. At the time there was little substantial critique of examinations as a technique or as a process and there was no serious questioning of the utilitarian values of the examination reformers.

Although many such critiques have subsequently emerged, both technical and sociological, they have made remarkably little impact. To understand why this is and hence an important strand in the explanation of the 'myth of measurement' we must look to the next stage of development in educational assessment practice, a stage which embodied the move from the assessment of some kind of *achievement* to that of *innate ability*.

Enter the 'science' of measurement

Ostensibly, the development of psychometrics – the measurement of the mind – was simply a further stage in the search for some means of implementing a meritocracy, of the search for ever-more objective means of measuring merit. In fact, the growing interest in the measurement of individual achievement that led many nineteenth-century psychologists to study the determinants of various personal characteristics, gradually developed into a conviction among psychologists that the determining factor in an individual's scholastic achievement was their innate ability or intelligence, a quality that was regarded by some at least as both fixed and measurable. Work by Binet, Galton, Spearman and others quickly convinced academics and laymen alike that not only was it possible to *measure* intellectual ability objectively, but also that from these measurements, future academic and occupational performance could be accurately predicted.

> To the scholars and men of science of the Victorian era imbued as this era was with the spirit of the physical sciences, the thought that qualities as intangible and insensible as intelligence could be accurately measured, was revolutionary indeed.
>
> (Williams 1974)

Revolutionary or not, by 1933, Sir Cyril Burt was able to write

> by intelligence, the psychologist understands inborn all-round intellectual ability, it is inherited or at least innate, not due to teaching or training, it is intellectual, not emotional or moral, and remains uninfluenced by industry or zeal. It is general, not specific, i.e. it is not limited to any particular kind of work but enters into all we do, or say or think. Of all our mental qualities, it is the most far-reaching. Fortunately it can be measured with accuracy and ease.

It is not hard to account for the rapid establishment of intelligence testing. Despite the understandable caveats and scientific caution of the academics involved, to policy-makers it must indeed have seemed an answer to prayer, that by means of a simple test, children could be readily and justly identified as 'bright' or 'dull', their future predicted, and on this basis categorized into different channels of the education system. Furthermore, that the scientific, superficially objective nature of such tests, their apparently proven predictive power (Kamin 1974) and their measurement of a characteristic believed to be as inborn as eye colour, meant it was almost impossible for individuals not to accept the results of such a test. As a mechanism of social control intelligence testing was unsurpassed in teaching the doomed majority that their failure was indeed the result of their own genetic inadequacy.

So, if before the nineteenth century educational assessment had been about the measurement of achievement, psychometrics represented a revolution in its concern henceforth to measure not *learning* but *ability to learn*. Without question, the scholars who pioneered the testing revolution were individuals of good faith, their efforts to change assessment technology in keeping with the spirit of the age, being geared to increasing both efficiency and social justice in making the assessment system more manageable, standardized, easily administered, objective, reliable, comparable and inexpensive as the number of examinees increased (Madaus 1993: 20). It is very true, however, as Eric Hoffer has pointed out, 'they who are engrossed in the rapid realisation of an extravagant hope, tend to view facts as something base and unclean. Facts are counter-revolutionary' (Auden and Kronenberger 1962: 326). Or, in the more trenchant words of Thomas Huxley, 'Science commits suicide when it adopts a creed' (Auden and Kronenberger 1962: 330). The mistake that was made by the scientists involved in developing educational measurement techniques was not that of promoting the widespread use of testing and examinations. Rather their mistake was not to recognize the power dimension inherent in what they were doing; that tests are products of power and their use is the exercise of power (Berlak *et al.* 1992: 185). Early test constructors appeared not to recognize the impossibility of a measurement that is not overlaid by the socially-derived norms and values which are inevitably embodied in it. One good example of the way in which such power operates to elevate particular values is the manner in which the increasing university domination of the emerging examination systems of the nineteenth century shaped both the form and content of what was measured and, hence, ultimately, of what was learned.

So, while it may well be argued that the strenuous efforts to find a scientific approach to the measurement of human capacity in the nineteenth and twentieth centuries were informed by a long-standing desire which has been characteristic of human history for the 'just measure', such quests always ended in failure because the society in which they were to operate was not itself just. Thus, Kula (1986) argues, objective attempts at measurement were essentially only a veneer. But how far do such apparently objective measures merit the description of myth?

The measurement myth exposed

To establish this part of my argument, I shall make three general points. First, educational assessment can never be scientific; and thus, second, so-called psychometric tests can never be totally objective in the way that is claimed for them. Rather, I shall argue, the explanation for the widespread acceptability of educational measurement as a model for such tests and hence, of its significance, lies not in their scientific worth, nor in the capacity of techniques developed to measure accurately what they purport to measure, but quite simply because we believe in them.

Writing in the 1950s, Werner Heisenberg, the Nobel prize-winning physicist, described the inseparability of the observer and the observed, the inappropriateness of a belief in the truly real.

> Because we observe using instruments which we construct, we interpret what we observe using what we already know and describe what we observe using the language we have available. Making knowledge is a constructive, interpretive process. A process of using instruments to observe changes the very nature of what is observed.
>
> (cited in Johnson 1991)

If Heisenberg recognized this in the 1950s. Plato recognized it as far back as the fifth century BC when he wrote in his *Theaetetus*, 'man is the measure of all things' (*OED*, Protagoras 481–411 BC). If this relativity applies to scientific observation, to the overlay of culture and values in our interpretation of the *natural* world, how much more must it apply to attempts to measure human beings and their achievement. In 1943, the American scholar

Skates addressed this issue in his distinction between the kind of measurement used in the field of physical science as manifested in the then emerging use of standardized objective testing, and that used by teachers in the classroom.

> Any notion of science which stems from a background of engineering concepts in which all significant variables can be readily identified, isolated, measured and controlled, is both inadequate and misleading. Education in both its theory and its practice requires a new perspective, a science which will enable it to deal with composite phenomena where physical science normally deals with highly specific single factors.
>
> (cited in Stiggins 1993)

Given that all kinds of educational measurement are ultimately interpersonal in character, it is not surprising that a huge volume of research evidence has now accumulated which testifies to its inevitable inaccuracies. Sir Philip Hartog's classic *An Examination of Examinations* in 1935 cited the vagaries of pupil performance, the effects of exam stress, of differences between markers and in the difficulty of questions as some of the more significant causes of inaccuracy in examinations which would seem to be largely unavoidable. Subsequent writers have produced even longer lists, such as that of the American scholar Mary Lee Smith (1991). She suggests, among a host of reasons, the following:

The teacher may not have covered what is tested in the examination; the test may be too long for students to concentrate on it; students may guess if the format is a multiple-choice one; the test may be incorrectly normed for a given population of students; perhaps one summative grade is offered which conceals substantial differences in the quality of performance in underlying contributory aspects of achievement; the test may measure performance on a given day which has no connection with long-term retention by the student; students may be bored and disaffected and not engage to the best of their ability with the test or examination; they may find the questions confusing or ambiguous; they may not be able to apply their knowledge because of the limitations of handwriting or other mechanical abilities; many achievement tests merely measure endurance or persistence rather than performance; some students who are divergent thinkers may read too much into the test items; some students become frightened and 'freeze up' in the testing situation, especially those who have no self-confidence or some kind of emotional or family disturbance.

Research in the psychology of assessment has consistently demonstrated that small changes in task presentation, in response mode, in the conditions under which assessment takes place, in the relations between assessor and assessed and within students on different occasions – all have an effect on the performance. This finding has led some psychologists to extend their understanding of learning by changing their focus from the cognitive processes assumed to underlie performance to the study of 'forms of social engagement' in which the performance is situated (Lave and Wenger 1991).

The scale of variability and hence errors of judgement that can be involved, is well illustrated by Black (1993). He describes a study of one hundred students on a first-year university physics course. The students took two parallel exam papers covering the same syllabus, containing the same mix of types of questions, set by the same teachers and marked by the same people. Thirteen students failed both papers but significantly, thirteen failed the first and passed the second and thirteen failed the second and passed the first. Thirty-two students had scores which were either 10 per cent more or 10 per cent less than the average on the other paper and six students had scores which were either 20 per cent more or less than on the other paper.

> The unreliability of exams is a problem well-understood by the creators of tests but not by the public at large. . . . It is very difficult in a written test to get the information on which you can, with confidence, make a decision about the future of a student.
>
> (Black 1993)

In 1970, the German scholar Karlheinz Ingenkamp was able to write

> traditional oral and written school examinations have been shown to be neither objective nor reliable; their validity jeopardised by subjective influence, their predictive power low.
>
> (p. 14)

> We have not yet been able to produce research findings to refute the suspicion that we are continually selecting the wrong people with the wrong methods.
>
> (p. 62)

Even the invention of so-called 'objective' multiple-choice format testing in the USA in 1914, and the later invention of the optical mark reader in 1955, could not overcome these problems. For though it helped to overcome some of the more obvious subjectivities in marking, it could not remove the bias inherent in cultural differences between students; nor could it eliminate the effect of the test situation on students' performance. Furthermore, as Nuttall suggests (1987: 116), 'the utility of such tests is questionable since not only are they as unlike real life as you can get, they also fail to represent pretty well every other context in which what has been learned can be demonstrated or applied.

However, none of this evidence seems to have affected public and policy-makers' belief in the myth of measurement. Not only does the diploma disease continue to spread unchecked in the developing world, even in the western world where problems of finding ways to *exclude* students are rapidly being overtaken by the need to find ways of *retaining* students in education, the myth persists. One clear example of this was the British Government's decision in 1990 drastically to reduce the amount of coursework permissible in GCSE examinations on the grounds that external examinations are 'known' to be more rigorous, despite protests from researchers, schools, industrialists and inspectors that the inclusion of coursework assessment had typically led to an increase in standards.

In the light of such evidence, it is necessary to explore further why the myth of measurement was so readily established and continues to persist so powerfully. Part at least of the answer lies in the larger myth of the belief in technology itself, which is a reflection of the commitment to rationality and scientific progress which has been so much a feature of the post-Enlightenment industrial era and hence of modern society (Habermas 1968).

This point is perhaps most clearly set out in the popular classic *Zen and the Art of Motorcycle Maintenance*, in which the author, Pirsig (1974), distinguishes between the technological, rational, scientific 'classical' mode and the imaginative emotional, aesthetic, intuitive, 'romantic' mode. Notions of good and bad are replaced by facts, and the organization of reality itself is an arbitrary, but significant, carving up of perception. Belief in the possibility of educational measurement is part of the more general culture in which the salience of the interpersonal and of individual idiosyncracies is excluded. By the same token it may be that as the significance of chaos theory and of 'fuzzy logic' in particular becomes increasingly influential in scientific thinking, so the inevitably 'fuzzy' character of assessment will also be both recognized and accepted. Meanwhile, it is important to realize, as Hughes (1989) suggests, that Americans, like members of other advanced technological societies:

> need to realise that not only their remarkable achievements but many of their deep and persistent problems arise in the name of order, system and control, from the mechanisation and systematisation of life and from the sacrifice of the organic and spontaneous.
>
> (quoted by Madaus 1993: 21)

The French philosopher Michel Foucault also explores the significance of this commitment to technology which is characteristic of the emergence of industrial and post-industrial society. Foucault attributes particular importance to educational assessment as one of the new disciplinary technologies in the contemporary era. Education, he suggests, ceases to be an essentially personal quest. Just as traditional, descriptive forms of accounting had been transformed in the eleventh century by the introduction of double-entry book-keeping using numerical notation (Hoskin and McVe 1988), so the recording of individual achievement began to involve not words but numbers which provided for measurement, classification and ranking (Hoskin and McVe 1988). With the use of numbers to express achievement came the idea of normalizing judgement and the notion of a pre-defined hierarchy of performance. Intelligence tests which rank individuals on the basis of a particular test are a classic example of this kind of device.

In short then, the continually increasing significance of educational assessment at all levels of the education system may be traced to a belief in the possibility of applying a scientific technology to the measurement of human achievement and even of underlying ability. Yet, I have argued, such measures can never be objective since they are inevitably limited by the social nature of the assessment situation and the values and culture which overlay the interpretation of the quality of a given performance. If this is so, then the concept of educational measurement is a myth. But it is none the less a very significant myth. Because of its apparently scientific character, it legitimates a whole variety of evaluative practices, which, far from being neutral, operate as a powerful structuring force in society. Sociologically these assessment practices are enormously significant since they lead to considerable social inequality in terms of who gets what in society.

But such practices are arguably even more significant in terms of their *psychological* effect since they exert a strong influence in defining both the way in which students engage in education and what they perceive to be its rewards. This is one of the most significant consequences of the continued persistence of the myth of measurement and constitutes the core argument of this paper. The 'myth of measurement' is significant above all because of the way in which educational assessment is currently used – the characteristics attributed to it and hence the faith put in its operation obscures its inability properly to fulfil the purposes for which we currently use it. At the same time, such beliefs, such misplaced trust, work against the possibility of seeing the purposes for which educational assessment can and should be used. In short the myth of measurement has inhibited the positive and creative use of assessment to *promote*, rather than to *measure* learning.

MISSED OPPORTUNITIES

This argument may usefully be developed a little further. One of the main effects of the 'diploma disease' and hence of the 'myth of measurement' has been to marginalize more fundamental discussion concerning educational goals. Means have become elevated into ends. Testing as a solution has become 'a continually improved means to carelessly examined ends' (Merton 1964: vi). As Edmund Holmes pointed out so eloquently in 1911, in what has become a frequently-quoted passage:

> a school that is ridden by the examination incubus is charged with deceit. All who become acclimatised to the influence of the system, pupils, teachers, examiners, employers of labour, parents, M.P.s and the rest, fall victims and are content to see themselves with outward and visible signs, class lists, orders of merit, as being of quasi-divine authority.

In many countries, the overriding policy imperative for education is to help maintain a competitive edge such that the raising of standards has been elevated to become *the* national objective. This point is trenchantly put by Muller (1977): 'we are turning out highly skilled people who are literally barbarians' (cited in Frey 1992). Tomlinson (1992) argues that if the forces of market competition remain dominant along with the language of marks and grades, performance indicators and league tables that sustain it, then 'teachers and their collaborators will have to keep the spirit of human kindness and vision of nobility alive in the catacombs while rendering unto Caesar the things that are Caesar's.'

Furthermore, despite the growing international obsession with raising standards, it is arguable that the assessment procedures in use have not kept pace even with current educational priorities. One reason for this is undoubtedly the traditionally Cinderella status of assessment as a professional concern such that educators at all levels of the system in the majority of countries are still almost completely illiterate concerning the development and use of sound assessment strategies in educational contexts, especially those that can promote learning. So great has the preoccupation with measuring become in order to provide data on which league tables of performance indicators can be published, that scant regard has often been paid either to the quality of these data or whether there might be rather more effective ways both of raising standards and of providing for accountability.

A recent report from the US National Council on Educational Standards and Testing (1992), for example, asserts that 'standards, and assessments linked to the standards, can become the cornerstone of the fundamental systemic reform necessary to improve schools', a belief in the power of examinations to lead to some kind of educational golden age that Winner (cited in Madaus and Kellaghan 1991: 23), describes as equivalent to the 'optimistic technophilia' of the last two centuries. There is no evidence to support either this belief in the power of examinations *by themselves* to raise standards or the associated belief in market forces as a way of raising standards through the provision of assessment information. Such evidence as is available suggests that it is the quality of teaching itself and the learning climate created in the classroom which are of critical importance in raising the standard of learning outcomes (Mortimore *et al.* 1988). Strategies which have as their core strengthening the accountability of individual teachers and schools through various forms of assessment of performance do not necessarily offer teachers any insight about what to do in terms of changing their practice to *achieve* the higher standards sought (Corbett and Wilson 1988).

If, historically, the practice of educational assessment has been largely driven by a perceived need to *measure* individual capacity, it now needs to be driven by the need to *promote* that capacity – and to create new kinds of capacities. Problem-solving ability, personal effectiveness, thinking skills and willingness to accept change are typical of the general competences straddling cognitive and affective domains that are now being sought in young people. Clark (1994), referring to the examination-driven system in Hong Kong, sets out the following list of factors which lie behind the need for new priorities in learning goals:

- The knowledge explosion and the growing mass of information to which it has given rise, together with the advances in technology to store and communicate it.
- The change in the nature of employment away from manufacturing towards information-based and service industries requiring higher-order thinking and problem-solving skills.
- The growth of a global economy and global interdependence and the increase in the numbers of those who live and work in multicultural and multilingual environments.
- The move towards greater equity and towards greater participation in decision making.
- The demand for greater accountability and transparency.

(Clark 1994: 36)

It is becoming increasingly apparent, however, that until we develop new kinds of assessment procedures that can relate to this wide range of skills and attitudes, not only will it be impossible to produce valid judgements about the success of the *educational enterprise as a whole* in terms of its goals, it will also help to guarantee that certain desired educational outcomes will be neglected in the classroom.

This is a lesson which, ironically, is rapidly being learned with regard to the assessment of institutional quality. Certainly there is the widespread use of league tables based on performance indicators. This is yet another manifestation of the measurement 'myth' that the encouragement of competition – in this case between institutions – will *in itself,* lead to raised levels of performance. Indeed, there are indications that when you manage by results, in fact quality goes down. Nevertheless, a great deal of the activity associated with the relatively new concern with quality assurance also involves self-referenced, descriptive assessment procedures designed with the primary goal of *improving* performance rather than simply *measuring* it.

ASSESSMENT AND LEARNING

Neither an institution nor a student is the same after the assessment event. For better or worse, assessment is a very special part of the learning process. Both students, and now increasingly institutions, use assessment information to make important decisions about themselves – what they are capable of achieving; whether to make an effort to learn, what targets to pursue, how and when; assessment conditions the relationship of individuals to institutions of learning and of such institutions to the education system and its clients. It frames the goals of the institution and hence embodies what students perceive as the institution's true values.

Samuel Butler once wrote that 'there is no such source of error as the pursuit of absolute truth'. In the preoccupation with *measuring*, too often *learning* itself and how it may be achieved has been overlooked as a focus of concern. This situation is well illustrated by findings from research on learning, which reveal that the assumptions underlying most forms of educational measurement are at odds with the insights now emerging from educational psychology. Constructivist learning theory in particular argues that

> Learners become more competent, not simply by learning more facts and skills but by re-configuring their knowledge. By chunking information to reduce memory loads and by developing strategies and models that help them discern when and how facts and skills are important.
>
> (Mislevy *et al.* 1991)

Rote learning, by contrast, is difficult to retain in the longer term.

But even more important for today's society is the need to support the development of learners' metacognitive skills – to give them the understanding of themselves as learners which will give them the confidence to impose their own meaning on the task and enable them to self-regulate the thinking process. Those who lack such effective metacognitive strategies are unlikely to be able to participate fully in the 'learning society' of the future. Yet there is plenty of research evidence which testifies to the possibility of teaching even very young children – 5 and 6 year olds – the skills of monitoring and managing their own learning. In one experiment, primary-school children had to record what they had done and when they started and finished (Merrett and Merrett 1992). The pupils assessed their work themselves and the teacher commented on it too. The children were asked to set targets for each hour concerning what they wanted to do and to review at the end of the period – if necessary working out what had not been achieved. A bell was rung every ten minutes and the children were asked to monitor themselves to see if they were on task and working well. The children recorded the results of this monitoring without the teacher seeing it. It was found at the end of the period of the experiment that in comparison with a control group the children had greater self-awareness concerning their use of time, the importance of planning and in their ability to be self-critical. An independent teacher who 'blind marked' the work from before and after this initiative found a significant improvement in the children's work. These studies show what can be achieved by deliberate incorporation of opportunities for students to assess their own learning strategies during the process of teaching and learning.

Assessment also exerts a powerful effect on students' motivation. For every student who is extrinsically motivated by the 'carrot' of good results, there

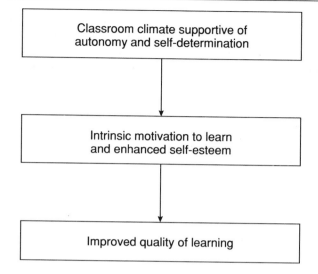

Figure 14.3 Motivation to learn

Source: McMeniman 1989

are many more that learn not to try for fear of failure. Students whose self-esteem is progressively eroded by negative assessment results frequently acquire 'learned helplessness'. Their negative view of themselves as learners makes them anxious and less willing to try hard with a task, for research by Bandura (1977) and others shows that the amount of persistence exhibited by students is to a considerable extent a function of how successful they expect to be. Previous experience of success or failure is acknowledged to be the prime source of student motivation.

But perhaps most significant of all in this respect is the degree of control students feel they have over their own learning. Students who are given greater responsibility for their own learning demonstrate both improved motivation and actually learn better, a relationship which is illustrated in Figure 14.3.

All of these crucial ingredients which contribute to the quality of student learning are linked to the way assessment is used. Crooks' (1988) review of the short-, medium- and long-term effects of assessment on learning provides powerful research evidence to testify that assessment shapes an individual's learning aspirations, confidence, strategies and effectiveness; it underpins their priorities and ultimately plays a key role in the formation of social identity.

It is widely assumed that students need competition and hence the threat of measurement to motivate them. Yet, learning research suggests this too is not necessarily so. Indeed history testifies to this as Durkheim recognized in his account of education in Europe in the early middle ages. He writes

> We are so accustomed to believing that emulation is the essential moti-
> vating force in academic life that we cannot easily imagine how a school
> could exist which did not have a carefully worked out system of gradu-
> ated awards in order to keep the enthusiasm of pupils perpetually alive.
> Good marks, solemn statements of satisfactory performance, distinctions,
> competitions, essays, prize giving, all these seem to us in differing degrees
> the necessary accompaniment to any sound educational system. The system
> that operated in France and indeed in Europe until the 16th century was
> characterised by the surprising fact that there were no rewards at all from
> success in examinations. What is more any candidate who had assiduously
> and conscientiously followed the course of studies was certain of success.
>
> (Durkheim 1947: 159)

Many teachers today in a number of different countries also have the experience to testify that this is so. In Britain, for example, over the last twenty
years, teachers have been experimenting with new ways of recording achievement. The movement started with the idea that by broadening the *range* of
achievements that could be formally acknowledged in a school-leaving document, it would improve the motivation of those students who could not hope
to succeed in public examinations which were explicitly designed so that only
a small proportion of the age group could pass.

Gradually, however, teachers came to realize that what was really making
a difference in students' motivation and the quality of their learning was not
the provision of a new form of certificate. It was the changes they were introducing actually in the classroom. These changes included

- Sharing and discussing curriculum goals with students.
- Encouraging students to set their own learning targets and to draw up
  more general 'action plans'.
- Involving students in assessing their own work so that they were both
  more willing and more able to monitor their own learning.
- Reviewing progress together.

The opportunity for one-to-one discussion in particular made an enormous
impact on many students who had never before had the chance of a sustained,
individual conversation with their teacher about their learning.

Thus, both experience and research evidence provide clear testimony to
the importance of assessment in its potential either to promote, or to inhibit,
the quality of learning. To insist on traditional forms of educational measurement over which students have no control and which rely essentially on
extrinsic motivation to induce high levels of achievement, must be to recognize that substantial numbers of students will not perform to their best
advantage.

By contrast, research provides us with a blueprint for improving learning
standards in which assessment is employed to *empower* students as respon-

sible partners in the learning process. The following are two examples which illustrate how assessment that is designed to promote learning can work in practice. The first is from Edward, 9-year-old pupil in a primary school who has been asked to 'review' his Autumn term's work.

Autumn Term Evaluation: Edward aged 9

I think that I need to concentrate more on my work, and not go around saying and thinking I can do this straight off when i know I cant. I have enjoyed the Art work this term, and I think I have done well on it. It has always been my best subject. I never had to mount my work and make my topic books in Mr. Ashley's class. i think I am managing quite well, but I often make slipups when i try to go to fast. The writing this term I think has got my brain thinking more than last. I would like to do some assemblies like plays about what we have been learning about during the term.

The second is from a student on a Master's course offering his own critique of an assignment he has written.

Assignment for Course H000

Self-assessment by Paul Jones

I have worked very hard on this essay as I found the topic of assessment in nurse education both absorbing and important. Although I had some difficulty locating relevant books and articles, I think I have succeeded in linking the central issues of this initiative to the literature.

I found your comments on my first draft very useful in helping me to construct a clear argument since I know I always try to put in everything I've read, ie too much!

I still feel the essay is a bit long but I couldn't decide what to leave out. I think it succeeds well as an account of recent developments but I feel I still need to strengthen my ability to be critical.

Thanks for a stimulating course – I enjoyed it!

signed . . . *Paul*

In both cases, there is a strong sense of the way in which being involved in assessment of their work is making the learner engage more with it and think about its strengths and weaknesses. They are getting to know themselves as learners.

Testimony to the growing international popularity of learning-centred assessment because of its power to enhance students' learning are the efforts currently being made around the world to train and motivate teachers to use such strategies (see for example Bachor and Anderson 1994; Klenowski 1995; Shephard *et al.* 1994). This is not an easy task, however. Not only does it require a transformation in assessment thinking and practice, it actually requires a new approach to teaching itself – one that recognizes that the learner must be an active participant in the learning process if real understanding is to be achieved. This means resources – time and money – need to be invested in training – resources which are inevitably at a premium. Yet without such a significant change in assessment perspectives and practices, aspirations to implement constructivist learning theories which emphasize providing each learner with the support appropriate to their unique learning needs cannot be fulfilled. Too much of the 'black box' of how and why learning takes place for a given individual will remain hidden. Without the active involvement of learners themselves in the assessment process so that together with the teacher they can learn to recognize their own unique combination of learning skills, aspirations and needs, effective diagnosis and remediation will be inhibited by a lack of vital insights concerning each learner's unique pattern of development.

The biggest single obstacle to achieving such a change is the myth of measurement. The recent history of Standard Assessment Tasks (SATs) in England provides a good example of this tension. Having been designed to match as closely as possible the full range of knowledge and skills in the curriculum for each subject, the SATs proved incapable of providing data that was sufficiently reliable to provide the basis for meaningful league tables of school performance. Evidence from an ESRC-funded national study of the SATs for 7 year olds (Pollard *et al.* 1994) suggests that it is impossible accurately to 'measure' children's achievements at this age. Yet the evidence also shows that teachers have derived great benefit from the opportunity to develop their professional skills with regard to assessment, and that where such practice is in evidence children's learning is improving (HMI 1992, Pollard *et al.* 1994).

THE SCALE OF THE CHALLENGE

Thus a review of educational, and especially assessment, priorities is urgent, not least because the UK government's own learning targets for the future represent a formidable challenge for the contemporary education systems (see Figure 14.4). This challenge will not be met while large numbers of young people continue to see education as irrelevant to their needs. Many young people do not wish to continue their education when it ceases to be compulsory. Selection is no longer the assessment imperative it was in the nineteenth century. While developing countries need still to ration educational provision severely, the industrialized and post-industrial countries do not. On the contrary, they need to expand the take-up of education. But the myth of measurement stands in the way of achieving this goal. As Alexis de Tocqueville so trenchantly put it

> There is no philosopher in the world so great but he believes a million things on the faith of other people and accepts a great many more truths than he demonstrates.

We have been taken in by the myth of measurement for too long. 'A knowl-

---

THE SCALE OF THE CHALLENGE

Foundation Learning Targets:

Foundation Target 1
  By 1997, 80% of young people to reach NVQ2 or equivalent
  (4 GCSEs, Grades A–C)

  Starting Point: 51% in 1991
  Progress Required: 5% points per year

Foundation Target 2
  Education and training to NVQ3 or equivalent to be available to all
  young people who can benefit

Foundation Target 3
  By 2000, 50% of young people to reach NVQ3 or equivalent
  (2 A levels)

  Starting Point: 30% in 1991
  Progress Required: 2% points per year

Figure 14.4 The scale of the challenge
Source: The National Training Task Force, 1995

edge of the past should arm [people] against surrendering to the panaceas peddled by too many myth-makers' writes Elton (cited in Madaus 1992). That so far it has not done so is only to be expected given the power of myth to make alternatives almost literally unthinkable.

Thus, there is an urgent need to challenge the *myth* of measurement and to look at the *facts* of measurement instead. If the goal of education is truly to be that of enhancing quality, this means looking at fitness for purpose. Churchill suggested that 'the farther backward you can look, the farther forward you are likely to see' (quoted in Bray 1979: 178) It might therefore be appropriate to enquire why it was that for nearly two thousand years the Chinese examination system never caught on anywhere else despite several attempts. One explanation is that the 'myth of measurement' like those other myths peopled by the gods and heroes of ancient civilisations, served its purpose for a given time and place. The 'myth of measurement' provided for the transition to a more open society and kept in check the aspirations of the many for whom there could be no outlet. That time has now gone, however, and the perpetuation of the myth now serves only to cloud our vision and to inhibit the implementation of those assessment strategies that are desperately needed if an education is to be provided that both sustains economic growth and develops people with a vision of the good life – an education that is capable of providing a viable foundation for life in the third millennium.

Meanwhile, in a world obsessed by qualifications, credentials and diplomas, it is important to remember that assessment and reporting have in the past been allowed to become one of the biggest barriers to learning for many young people. It has been the argument of this paper that it is time to challenge the legacy of the past so that assessment can instead become the key to more effective learning for many more people.

NOTE

1. This article is dedicated to the late Professor Desmond Nuttall who did so much for the cause of promoting quality in assessment and who died 24.10.1993. It formed an inaugural lecture given at the University of Bristol, 25.10.1993.

REFERENCES

Amano, Ikuo (1990) *Education and Examination in Modern Japan*, translated by W. K. Cummings and F. Cummings, Tokyo: University of Tokyo Press.

Auden, W. H. and Kronenberger, L. (1962) *The Faber Book of Aphorisms*, London: Faber.

Bachor, D. and Anderson, J. (1994) 'Elementary teachers' assessment practices as observed in the province of British Columbia, Canada', *Assessment in Education* 1(1): 63.

Ball, C. (1992) 'Ladders, and links: prerequisites for the discussion of an international framework of qualifications', in New Zealand Qualifications Authority (ed.) *Qualifications for the 21st Century: Conference Papers*, Wellington: New Zealand.

Bandura, A. (1977) *Social Learning Theory*, Englewood Cliffs NJ: Prentice-Hall.

Barthes, R. (1973) *Mythologies*, London: Cape.

Beloe, R. (1960) *Secondary School Examinations other than G.C.E.*, report of a Committee appointed by Secondary School Examinations Council, London: HMSO.

Berlak, A. and Berlak, H. (1992) *Toward a new Science of Educational Testing and Assessment*, Albany: New York State University Press.

Black, P. (1993) Conference Paper – Association of Assessment Inspectors and Advisers, reported in *Times Educational Supplement* 1 October.

Bourdieu, P. (1988) *Homo Academicus*, translated by Peter Collier, Cambridge: Polity Press.

Bray, W. P. (1979) NAFSA Newsletter, May: 178.

Brean, M. (1991) 'A plea to Buddha for exam success', *Times Educational Supplement* 15 January.

Broadfoot, P. (1979) 'Communication in the classroom: a study of the role of assessment in motivation', *Educational Review* 31(1).

Burt, C. (1933) *How the Mind Works*, London: George Allen and Unwin.

Chervel, A. (1874) *Dictionnaire Historique des Institutions moeurs et coûtunes de la France*, Paris: Librairie Hachette.

Christie, A. (1968) *Chinese Mythology*, Feltham: Paul Hamlyn.

Clark, L. (1994) 'Targets and target-related assessments: Hong Kong's Curriculum and Assessment Project', in Mauritius Examinations Syndicate, *School-based and External Assessments*, proceedings of the 1993 IAEA Conference, Mauritius.

Clodd, cited under 'myth' in the *Shorter Oxford English Dictionary*.

Collins, R. (1979) *The Credential Society*, New York: Academic Press.

Corbett, R. and Wilson, B. (1988) 'Raising the stakes in state-wide mandatory minimum competency testing', *The Politics of Education Association Yearbook* (special issue of *Journal of Education Policy*) 3(5).

Crooks, T. J. (1988) 'The impact of classroom evaluation practices on students', *Review of Educational Research* 58(4): 438–81.

Dore, R. (1976) *Diploma Disease*, London: Unwin Educational Books.

Durkheim, E. (1947) *The Evolution of Educational Thought: Lectures on the Formation and Development of Secondary Education in France*, London: Routledge and Kegan Paul.

Eckstein, M. and Noah, H. J. (1993) *Secondary School Examinations: International Perspectives on Policies and Practice*, New Haven and London: Yale University Press.

Foden, F. (1989) *The Examiner. James Booth and the Origin of Common Examinations*, Leeds School of Continuing Education.

Frey, J. (1992) 'History and future of qualifications', paper given at 'Qualifications for the 21st Century Conference', New Zealand Qualifications Association.

Habermas, J. (1968) 'Technology and science as ideology' (for Herbert Marcuse on his seventieth birthday later published in *Towards a Rational Society*), London: Heinemann.

Hartog, Sir P. and Rhodes, E. C. (1935) *An Examination of Examinations*, London: Macmillan.

Heynemann, S. (1993) Keynote address to World Congress of Comparative Education Societies, Prague.

HMI (1992) *Assessment Recording and Reporting: A Report by HM Inspectorate on the Second Year*, London: HMSO.

Holmes, E. (1911) *What is and What Might Be*, London: Constable.

Hoskin, K. W. and MacVe, R. H. (1988) 'The genesis of accounting: the West Point connections', *Accounting Organizations and Society* 13(1): 37–73.

Ingenkamp, K. (1977) *Educational Assessment*, Slough: NFER.

Johnson, P. (1991) 'Rethinking assessment', *Language Matters*, CLPE, no.2.

Kamin, L. A. (1974) *The Science and Politics of IQ*, New York: Wiley.

Klenowski, V. (1995) 'Student self-evaluation processes in student-centred teaching and learning contexts of Australia and England', *Assessment in Education* 2(2).

Kula, W. (1986) *Measures and Men*, translated by R. Szreter, Princeton NJ: Princeton University Press.

Lave, J. and Wenger, E. (1991) *Situated Learning: Legitimate Peripheral Participation*, Cambridge: Cambridge University Press.

Lawson, J. and Silver, H. (1973) *A Social History of Education in England*, London: Methuen.

Lee-Smith, M. (1991) *The Role of Testing in Elementary School*, SCE Technical Report 321 Arizona State University, Los Angeles: UCLA Centre for the Study of Evaluation.

McMeniman, M. (1989) 'Motivation to learn', in P. Langford (ed.) *Educational Psychology: An Australian Perspective*, London: Longman.

Madaus, G. (1992) 'A technological and historical consideration of equity issues associated with proposals to change the nation's testing policy', paper prepared for the symposium on equity and educational testing and assessment, BERA Washington D.C.

Madaus, G. F. (1993) 'A national testing system: manna from above? An historical/technological perspective', *Educational Assessment* 1(i): 9–26.

Madaus, G. and Kellaghan, T. (1991) 'Student examination systems in the EC: lessons for the United States', Contractor report submitted to the Office of Technology Assessment, US Congress.

Merrett, J. and Merrett, F. (1992) 'Classroom management for project work: an application of correspondence training', *Educational Studies* 18(1): 3–10.

Merton, R. K. (1964) Foreword in E. Jacques (ed.) *The Technological Society*, New York: Vintage.

Mislevy, R. J., Yamamoto, K. and Anacker, S. *et al.* (1991) 'Towards a test theory for assessing student understanding, *Research Report*, Princeton NJ: ETS.

Mortimore, P., Sammons, P., Stoll, L., Lewis, D. and Ecob, R. (1988) *School Matters: The Junior Years*, Wells: Open Books.

Nuttall, D. L. (1987) 'The validity of assessments', *European Journal of Psychology of Education* II(2): 109–18.

Pirsig, R. M. (1976) *Zen and the Art of Motorcycle Maintenance*, London: Corgi.

Pollard, A., Broadfoot, P., Croll, P., Osborne, M. and Abbott, D. (1994) *Changing English Primary Schools? The Impact of the Education Reform Act at Key Stage One*, London: Cassell.

Salvia, J. and Hughes, C. (1989) *Curriculum-based Assessment. Testing What is Taught*, London: Macmillan.

Shephard, L., Flexer, R. J., Hiebert, E. H., Marion, S. F., Mayfield, V. and Weston, T. J. (1994) 'Effects of introducing classroom performance assessments on student learning', paper presented at the annual meeting of the American Educational Research Association, New Orleans.

Stiggins, R. (1993) 'Two disciplines of educational assessment', *Measurement and Evaluation in Guidance and Counselling* 26: 93–104.

Sutton, R. (1991) *Assessment: A Framework for Teachers*, Windsor: NFER/Nelson.

de Tocqueville, A. cited in *Oxford Dictionary of Quotations*.

Tomlinson, J. (1992) *Retrospect on Ruskin: Prospect on the 1990s*, Mimeo: University of Warwick.

Williams, P. (1974) 'The growth and scope of the school psychological service', in M. Chazan, T. Moore, P. Williams and J. Wright, *The Practice of Educational Psychology*, London: Longman.

Index

Abbs, P. 133
abstraction, rule 113, 114–18
Academic Achievers 147–51, 156, 166
academic goals: and school effectiveness
77, 80, 81, 83, 85
academic work: associated with
effeminacy 147, 148–9
accountability: and assessment 220; and
managerialism 47–50, 53
achievement: and school effectiveness
85; and school improvement
strategies 98, 103; valid 174
affective responses 176, 182
African-Caribbeans: cultures of
masculinity 158, 169–70
Aggleton, P. 150, 153, 154, 157, 167
aims: in National Curriculum 1–9
Alexander, R.J. 25–8, 57–8, 61, 71
alienation, pupil 184
analogies: role in assessment 189–90
Angus, L. 74
Apple, M.W. 40
apprentice learners 125
Aronson, E. 123–4
arts: associated with effeminacy 148–9;
in proposed National Curriculum 5
Asians: cultures of masculinity 158,
169–70
assessment: evolution of 208–12;
formal group 194–202; integration
with learning 173–93; myth of
measurement 203–30; in National
Curriculum 4, 8
Assessment of Performance Unit (APU)
175–6, 182, 184–5, 187, 189–90,
192
attainment: in secondary schools
effectiveness study 75

attitudes, pupil: and school improvement
strategies 98
authority: and cultures of masculinity
145, 152, 153–4, 161; linked to
grammar 11–12

Ball, C. 206–7
Ball, S.J. 38, 39, 54
Barthes, R. 206
behaviour, pupil: and school improve-
ment strategies 98
bilingualism 13–15
Black, P. 217
Black, Paul 4
black people: cultures of masculinity
158, 169–70; unemployment 158
Bolton, Eric 4
book production project 129–30, 133
breakthroughs in learning 127–43
Bruner, J. 177
Burt, C. 214
Butler, Samuel 222

chaos theory
cheating 203–4
Chervel, A. 210
China: examinations 208–9
choice: professional 53; in proposed
National Curriculum 7–8
citizenship: and language 13–15; in
National Curriculum 3, 4
Clark, L. 221
class, social: and cultures of masculinity
148, 150, 155–60, 161–5; and
English language 13, 15–17; and
school effectiveness 73–89
classical mode of knowledge 218
closures, school 90; symbolic 100